Learn
JavaScript™

Check the Web for Updates:

To check for updates or corrections relevant to this book and/or CD-ROM visit our updates page on the Web at **http://www.prima-tech.com/updates**.

Send Us Your Comments:

To comment on this book or any other PRIMA TECH title, visit our reader response page on the Web at **http://www.prima-tech.com/comments**.

How to Order:

For information on quantity discounts, contact the publisher: Prima Publishing, P.O. Box 1260BK, Rocklin, CA 95677-1260; (916) 787-7000. On your letterhead, include information concerning the intended use of the books and the number of books you want to purchase.

Learn
JavaScript™

Sunrise Midday Sunset

In a Weekend ®

Evening Sunrise Sunset

Jerry Lee Ford, Jr.

PRIMA TECH

A DIVISION OF PRIMA PUBLISHING

A Division of Prima Publishing

Prima Publishing and colophon are registered trademarks of Prima Communications, Inc. PRIMA TECH and In a Weekend are trademarks of Prima Communications, Inc., Roseville, California 95661.

Publisher: Stacy L. Hiquet

Managing Editor: Sandy Doell

Acquisitions Editor: Lynette Quinn

Development Editor: Melba Hopper

Project Editor: Kelly Talbot

Technical Reviewer: Jason Wyatt

Copy Editor: Alice Martina Smith

Interior Layout: Shawn Morningstar

Cover Design: Prima Design Team

Proofreader: Linda Seifert

Indexer: Sharon Hilgenberg

Microsoft, Windows, Internet Explorer, Notepad, VBScript, ActiveX, JScript, and FrontPage are trademarks or registered trademarks of Microsoft Corporation. Netscape, Netscape Navigator, JavaScript, Visual JavaScript, Visual JavaScript Pro, and LiveAudio are trademarks or registered trademarks of Netscape Communications Corporation. Opera is a trademark or registered trademark of Opera Software AS. Java and Sun Microsystems are trademarks or registered trademarks of Sun Microsystems, Inc. Adobe and Adobe Acrobat are trademarks or registered trademarks of Adobe Systems, Inc.

Important: Prima Publishing cannot provide software support. Please contact the appropriate software manufacturer's technical support line or Web site for assistance.

Prima Publishing and the author have attempted throughout this book to distinguish proprietary trademarks from descriptive terms by following the capitalization style used by the manufacturer.

Information contained in this book has been obtained by Prima Publishing from sources believed to be reliable. However, because of the possibility of human or mechanical error by our sources, Prima Publishing, or others, the Publisher does not guarantee the accuracy, adequacy, or completeness of any information and is not responsible for any errors or omissions or the results obtained from use of such information. Readers should be particularly aware of the fact that the Internet is an ever-changing entity. Some facts may have changed since this book went to press.

ISBN: 0-7615-3332-x

Library of Congress Catalog Card Number: 00-109623

Printed in the United States of America

01 02 03 04 HH 10 9 8 7 6 5 4 3 2 1

For my mother and father.
Thanks for always being there.

CONTENTS AT A GLANCE

CONTENTS

SATURDAY EVENING
Doing Really Cool Things with Your Web Pages 171

SUNDAY AFTERNOON
Advanced JavaScript Programming 273

SUNDAY EVENING
Putting It All Together 319

ABOUT THE AUTHOR

Jerry Lee Ford, Jr. is an author, educator, and IT professional with over 13 years experience in information technology. Jerry is an MCSE and has earned a Masters in Business Administrations from Virginia Commonwealth University in Richmond, Virginia. Jerry also serves as an adjunct instructor at John Tyler Community College where he teaches networking courses in the Information Services Technology Department. Jerry lives in Richmond, Virginia with his wife, Mary, and their sons, William and Alexander.

ACKNOWLEDGMENTS

There are many people to whom I owe thanks for their work on this book. I especially want to thank Lynette Quinn for her work as acquisitions editor, Kelly Talbot for doing such a good job as the book's project editor, and Melba Hopper for her editorial contributions. I also want to acknowledge the book's copy editor, Alice Martina Smith, its technical editor, Jason Wyatt, and its formatter, Randall Clark. Special thanks also goes to Arlie Hartman for the great job done on the book's CD-ROM and to everyone else at Prima Tech for all their hard work.

Introduction

Congratulations on your decision to learn JavaScript. JavaScript is a powerful scripting language that, when combined with HTML, allows you to create exciting and powerful Web pages. You can use these Web pages to run a small business or to share information with family and friends over the Internet.

What you are probably asking yourself is, "Can I really learn JavaScript in a single weekend?" The answer is "yes!" I am not promising you that you will become a programming guru in just a few days, but if you will dedicate a full weekend to this book and follow along with its examples, you will be able to write your own JavaScripts and make dramatic improvements to your Web pages.

But what if you have only limited HTML experience or have not worked with HTML in a while? Not to worry. This book provides you with all the information and examples you need to get up and running in a single weekend.

What This Book Is About

This book is about learning how to write JavaScripts and creating exciting Web sites. This book is designed to present you with everything you need to know from the ground up. Only very basic experience with HTML is assumed. The book provides the rest for you. This includes a thorough HTML review in Appendix E, which is included on the book's CD, and a quick HTML refresher of working with forms and frames in Chapter 5. By the time the weekend is over, you will have learned how to do the following:

✪ Integrate JavaScripts into your Web pages

- Take control of the browser status line
- Display pop-up alert, prompt, and confirmation dialog boxes so that you can interact with your visitors
- Create graphic effects
- Detect the types of browsers your visitors are using and customize your Web pages accordingly
- Create banners, clocks, and other animation effects
- Detect keyboard and mouse events and react accordingly
- Manage frames using JavaScript
- Validate forms and email the contents of those forms to yourself
- Write JavaScripts that collect and save visitor information using cookie technology
- Leverage the power of plug-ins
- Debug your JavaScripts

Who Should Read This Book?

This book is for anyone who needs or wants to start creating exciting Web pages using the JavaScript programming language. You do have to be comfortable navigating the World Wide Web and working with Internet browsers such as Netscape Navigator or Microsoft Internet Explorer. You also need a basic understanding of computer terminology and concepts.

It would not hurt for you to already have a basic understanding of HTML. Hopefully, you already have your own Web site or have practiced creating Web pages on your own computer. If you feel that your HTML skills are a little weak, you might want to brush up on them by referring to Prima Tech's Learn HTML In a Weekend. However, the book you are holding now provides a review of HTML basics that covers the HTML programming knowledge you will require.

It is also helpful but not required that you know another programming language such as Basic, Perl, or C. Although knowledge of another computer programming language is not a prerequisite for success, having that background will make your learning experience this weekend a little easier and less stressful. Do not worry if you lack this experience; everybody has to start somewhere, and JavaScript is a perfect language to start with.

What You Need to Begin

The great thing about JavaScripts is how easy they are to write. You also do not have to spend a lot of money for programming tools before you can begin developing JavaScripts. In fact, all you really need are the following items:

- **Your computer.** Just about any computer will work because you don't need a lot of horsepower to develop and test JavaScripts.

- **Internet access.** Whether it is from work or home, you must be able to access the Internet so that you can upload your Web pages to your Web site.

- **An Internet Web browser.** Several Internet browsers support JavaScript, including Microsoft Internet Explorer, Netscape Navigator, and Opera. You need at least one of these browsers to test your JavaScripts; you should have copies of all of them to make sure that your JavaScripts work correctly with each browser.

- **A Web server.** This is the computer connected to the Internet on which you will store your Web pages when you are ready to share them with the world. If you do not already have your own Web site, the odds are that your local Internet service provider can set you up with access to one of their Web servers.

- **A text editor.** You can use any basic text editor to write and save your JavaScripts. You even can use the Windows Notepad application. Included on this book's CD-ROM is a trial copy of Allaire's HomeSite 4.5.1 editor. You can use this powerful, full-featured editor to create both your HTML code and your JavaScripts. You can even take advantage of the HomeSite JavaScript Wizard and allow it to create some basic scripts for you.

- **A graphics editor.** This tool is optional; it is required if you plan to add any graphic images to your Web pages. For example, you might want to design your own banner pages or Web site logo.

How This Book Is Organized

This book is written so that you can complete it in seven sessions over the course of a single weekend. Of course, you can read it anytime you want. The first three sessions focus on building up a strong JavaScript foundation. By Saturday evening your hard work will begin to pay off, and you'll be ready to write your own scripts. The basic outline of the book is shown here:

- **Friday Evening: "Introducing JavaScript."** This session provides prerequisite background information for working with JavaScript. It overviews the kinds of enhancements you can make to Web pages using this language. Background information includes a brief history of JavaScript and a comparison of it to other languages. The session ends by showing you how to write your first JavaScript.

- **Saturday Morning: "Learning the Basics of JavaScript Coding."** This session provides you with a programming foundation. It discusses scripting and JavaScript syntax before starting a series of lessons that outline the basic programming constructs that comprise the JavaScript language. You will learn how to work with variables, literals, functions, expressions, operators, and statements. The session ends with a discussion on arrays.

- **Saturday Afternoon: "Mastering Object-Oriented Programming with JavaScript."** This session covers object-oriented programming and outlines the JavaScript object model. It introduces the concept of objects, their properties, and the methods you can use with them. A host of commonly used objects are introduced. The session concludes with a discussion on JavaScript events and how to handle them with event handlers.

- **Saturday Evening: "Doing Really Cool Things with Your Web Pages."** In this session, things start getting really exciting. You'll learn how to write JavaScripts that manipulate the browser status line, create scrolling messages, and open pop-up dialog boxes. The session concludes with a discussion on the differences between Netscape Navigator and Internet Explorer and how to work with both browsers using JavaScript.

- **Sunday Morning: "Enhancing Web Pages with Frames and Forms."** This session continues to show you how to take control of your Web pages by using JavaScript to create and control frames and forms. The examples show you how to validate forms and to allow the user to submit form data in an email message.

- **Sunday Afternoon: "Advanced JavaScript Programming."** This session finishes the main instruction on JavaScript by showing you how to work with plug-ins, create basic animation effects, and bake cookies using JavaScript. It concludes with a detailed discussion on debugging JavaScripts, including tips for preventing errors and using tools that aid in problem determination.

- **Sunday Evening: "Putting It All Together."** This session helps tie together everything you have learned. It demonstrates the creation of an online bookstore that combines HTML and JavaScript into an effective Web site.

- **What's on the CD.** This presents a brief listing of the software included on the book's CD as well as where to find all the scripts that are demonstrated throughout the book.
- **Glossary.** This element presents a list of terms used throughout this book.

Conventions Used in This Book

This book uses a number of conventions to help make it easier for you to use.

NOTE *Notes* provide additional helpful or interesting information.

TIP *Tips* often suggest techniques and shortcuts to make your life easier.

CAUTION *Cautions* warn you of situations where errors or unforseen problems might arise.

Introducing JavaScript

- ✪ What is JavaScript?
- ✪ A brief overview of HTML
- ✪ Integrating JavaScript with HTML
- ✪ Understanding browser compatibility issues

Good evening! Tonight you begin your first step on your journey to learning how to use JavaScript on your Web pages. This evening introduces you to JavaScript and covers a little of its history while pointing out many of its benefits. You will also get an HTML refresher that is designed to make sure that you have the prerequisite knowledge of HTML required to complete this book. Of course, if you are current on your HTML skills, you may just want to skim over this section and move on to the later sections.

The remainder of the evening is dedicated to explaining how JavaScript is integrated in HTML and how its functionality is dependent on the Internet browser.

What Is JavaScript?

JavaScript is a computer language specially designed to work with Internet browsers. It lets you create small programs called *scripts* and embed them inside HTML pages to provide interactive content on your Web pages.

JavaScript is an interpreted language. This means that the script is not compiled before it is executed (as is typical of most programming languages such as C++). Each JavaScript statement in the script is processed as the browser reads it. This makes writing and testing JavaScript very intuitive and easy. You simply write a few lines of code inside an HTML page, save the page, and open the page in your Web browser to test how it looks.

JavaScript is an object-based scripting language. This means that it views everything as an *object*. The browser is an object. A window is an object. A button in a window is an object. Every object has *properties*, and you can use JavaScript to manipulate these properties. For example, you can change the background color of a window or the size of a graphic image. In addition to properties, objects have *methods*. Methods are the actions that objects can perform. For example, windows can be opened and closed, and buttons can be clicked. With JavaScript, you write scripts that work with objects by manipulating their properties and executing methods against them.

JavaScript supports event-driven programming. An *event* is an action that occurs when the user does something such as click a button or move the pointer over a graphic image. JavaScript allows you to write scripts that are triggered by events. Did you ever wonder how buttons dynamically change colors on some Web sites when you move the mouse over them? It's simply a JavaScript technique known as a *rollover*. The event—the mouse moving over the button (object)—triggers an *event handler* called onMouseover() that then runs your JavaScript. In this example, the script simply replaces the button with another one that uses a different color.

Don't worry if this all sounds a bit complex. I am just providing you with an overview of what JavaScript is and what it can do. You will revisit objects, properties, methods, and events in more detail on Saturday morning. The main point here is that you can write scripts that interact directly with the user. For example, you can create a Web page that contains a form that collects the user's name, address, phone number, and so on; the form then sends this information to you in an e-mail message after the user clicks a button. You can use JavaScript to check that the user filled in every field on the form and to notify the user to try again if something is missing. After the user properly fills in and submits the form, you can have the JavaScript display a thank-you message.

What Can You Do with JavaScript?

I have already talked a little about the kinds of things you can do with JavaScript. There are plenty more possibilities where they came from. For example, JavaScripts can do any of the following:

- ⚙ Detect the browsers and plug-ins being used by people visiting your Web site
- ⚙ Redirect people using older browsers to non-JavaScript HTML pages
- ⚙ Display pop-up messages so that you can send alerts or collect information from users
- ⚙ Validate forms and package their contents in an e-mail message

- Give you control of the status bar and create scrolling messages
- Perform simple animations such as rollovers
- Give you greater control over HTML frames
- Allow you to create dynamic Web content based on user input
- Perform calculations based on user input
- Open new windows
- Create rotating banners using JPEG files
- Create clocks and calendars
- Automatically time-stamp your Web documents

However, JavaScript cannot do two things. The first thing JavaScript cannot do is run outside of the browser. This "limitation" helps make JavaScript more secure because users do not have to worry about somebody writing a JavaScript that might erase their hard drive or read their address book and extract private information. The second thing JavaScript cannot do is access databases or other information on the Web server where the HTML pages that contain the JavaScript reside. To develop a Web application that provides database access, for example, you would have to team JavaScript up with another language such as Java, where JavaScript is running on the client and Java is performing the back-end processing.

 NOTE Actually, a server-side version of JavaScript is available. This version allows JavaScript to access server resources such as databases that professional Web programmers can use to provide Web-enabled database applications. However, a discussion about server-side JavaScript is beyond the scope of this book. From this point on, when I refer to JavaScript, I will be talking about client-side scripting.

A Little History

Years ago, the programmers at Netscape recognized that HTML alone was not robust enough to support interactive Web programming. So they developed a scripting language called LiveScript, which gave the Web page developer greater control over the browser.

Later, Sun Microsystems came along and developed a new programming language named Java. Java quickly became a hot item and received an enormous amount of media and industry attention. Netscape added support for Java in Netscape Navigator 2. At the same time, Netscape decided to rename LiveScript to JavaScript, which earned the scripting language a little more attention thanks to its name. That's about all the two languages have in common. Neither is related to the other, although both are supported by modern Internet browsers as a way of delivering interactive Web content.

JavaScript has continued to mature over the years with each new version of Netscape Navigator. As the language has evolved, so have browsers and their support for JavaScript as shown in Table 1.1.

You may have noticed that the table does not show an entry for Navigator 5. This is because Navigator 5 was never very stable and as such was never released. So even though the JavaScript 1.4 specification has been around for a while, modern browsers still support only version 1.3. However, at press time, Netscape has made the first beta version of Netscape Navigator 6 downloadable for free trial use.

TABLE 1.1 HISTORICAL VIEW OF INTERNET BROWSER SUPPORT FOR JAVASCRIPT

JavaScript Version	Netscape Version	Internet Explorer Version
1.0	Navigator 2.0	Internet Explorer 3
1.1	Navigator 3.0	Internet Explorer 4
1.2	Navigator 4.0–4.05	Internet Explorer 4 & 5
1.3	Navigator 4.06 & above	
1.4	Navigator 6*	

* Navigator 6 is not officially released yet but can be downloaded at http://www.netscape.com.

Comparing JavaScript to CGI, Perl, Java, VBScript, and ActiveX

JavaScript is not the only option available for Web pages. Other languages offer varying levels of capabilities as outlined in the following sections.

CGI and Perl

Common Gateway Interface (CGI) is not a computer language. It is a specification about how programs run on Web servers. CGI statements are embedded into other programs (languages), most commonly into Perl.

As is JavaScript, Perl is an interpreted language. Unlike JavaScript, Perl runs on the server and not in the browser client. Therefore, CGI-based Perl programs have read and write access on the server and can read from databases and save form contents in those databases.

For example, when a user clicks a link or submits a form, the browser sends the request to the Web server where the Perl/CGI program executes. The program accesses a local database as it executes and returns dynamic HTML pages to the client, where they are displayed in the user's browser.

Java

Java is a complete language; beyond the name similarity, Java has no direct relationship to JavaScript. Java is an object-oriented language that evolved out of the C and C++ programming languages. Unlike JavaScripts, Java programs are not interpreted on the fly and must be compiled before they can be executed.

Java was developed by Sun Microsystems. Its original purpose was to provide support for consumer electronic devices. However, its popularity quickly grew beyond this niche market.

Java is a full-featured programming language capable of running standalone applications. However, on the Internet, small Java programs, known as Java *applets*, can be downloaded from Web servers to client computers. Links to Java applets are embedded in HTML pages using the <APPLET> tag.

Because of security reasons, applets are confined to a specific area of a browser window and cannot affect anything outside that area. This means that applets cannot manipulate other parts of the browser like JavaScript can. Java applets are not stored on the local computer. Instead, the browser discards applets when they are no longer needed. Every time you visit a site that employs Java applets, the applets must be downloaded again along with the Web page that references them before they can execute within the browser. JavaScripts are not stored on the visitor's computer either. Instead, a script is downloaded as part of the Web page that contains the script each time the page's URL is loaded by the visitor's browser.

VBScript

VBScript (Visual Basic Scripting Edition) is one of Microsoft's alternatives to JavaScript. VBScript is an interpreted scripting language that provides the same functionality as JavaScript.

VBScripts are embedded inside HTML in the same way that JavaScripts are embedded. The main advantage of the VBScript language is that it is easy for Visual Basic programmers to learn. The main disadvantage of VBScript is that it is supported only by Internet Explorer. However, if you are developing content solely for Internet Explorer browsers, which might be the case on a corporate intranet, you will find VBScript just as powerful, versatile, and easy to work with as JavaScript.

 NOTE Although this book focuses how JavaScript can be written to execute inside of the visitor's Internet browser (that is, as client-side processing), I think that I need to mention that JavaScript, VBScript, and JScript support server-side script development as well, including the ability to connect to databases and create robust applications.

JScript

JScript is another Microsoft alternative to JavaScript. In fact, JScript is really just Microsoft's own version of JavaScript. JScript provides roughly the equivalent functionality as JavaScript and, like VBScript, is less popular than JavaScript. Also like VBScript, JScript is handicapped because it runs only on Internet Explorer browsers.

ActiveX

ActiveX is a Microsoft specification that allows regular Windows programs to run inside a browser. These programs or controls can be written in different languages including Visual C++ and Visual Basic.

ActiveX provides an alternative to using Java applets in Internet Explorer. Like Java applets, ActiveX controls are downloaded from the Web server. However, unlike Java applets, ActiveX controls can be permanently installed on the computer and used over and over again. A major drawback to ActiveX is that it is supported only by Internet Explorer version 4 and above.

NOTE Although the focus of this section is on the capabilities of client-side ActiveX controls, I think that I still need to mention that there are also ActiveX components that can be run on the Server that can return information to the browser in much the same manner as is performed by Perl and CGI.

ActiveX is much harder to learn than JavaScript and is also known for having weak security. This is because ActiveX programs can "reach outside" the browser and potentially do things such as access local disk drives. In an effort to improve ActiveX security, Microsoft has added support for *digital signatures*. This security feature gives you the opportunity to accept or reject an ActiveX control; however, digital signatures cannot help after you have accepted a control that someone created to delete your hard drive.

A WORD ABOUT VISUAL JAVASCRIPT

Netscape has developed a new *RAD* (*Rapid Application Development*) tool for creating JavaScripts. It comes in two flavors: Visual JavaScript and Visual JavaScript Pro.

These tools are designed for professional developers who need to create large cross-platform applications that include integrated database access. The tools include a WYSIWYG HTML editor that allows you to create JavaScript applications visually by dragging and dropping prebuilt HTML, Java, and JavaScript components. You can download Visual JavaScript from `http://www.netscape.com`.

A Brief Overview of HTML

Because you are interested in JavaScript, you probably already have at least a basic familiarity with HTML. Just in case, I am going to provide a quick review of HTML and some of its more common programming statements. Specifically, I am going to review the HTML statements used throughout this book. If you want to learn even more about HTML than is provided in this section, take a look at Prima Tech's *Learn HTML in a Weekend* by Steve Callihan. It's a perfect primer for this book.

HTML (*HyperText Markup Language*) is a programming language that allows you to create static Web pages. Basically, you can use HTML to provide noninteractive transfers of information in the form of text and graphics. HTML allows you to specify how a Web page is logically (not physically) designed by placing descriptive *tags* into the body of the text. The browser uses these tags to determine how to format and present the data. Of course, not all browsers are the same; the way Netscape Navigator interprets your instructions and the way Internet Explorer does may not be the same. If you use HTML, you should install copies of multiple browsers on your computer and view your HTML pages in each of the browsers to make sure that things look the way you want them to.

Examining HTML Structure

HTML pages are saved with a `.html` or `.htm` extension and contain HTML statements. HTML documents are identified by the starting and ending `<HTML>` `</HTML>` tags. The first tag appears at the top of the page and indicates that this is an HTML page. The last tag appears at the bottom of the document and identifies the end of the page.

There are two types of HTML tags: paired and single. The `<HTML>` and `</HTML>` tags just mentioned are an example of *paired tags*. You use these tags to mark sections of Web pages to tell browsers how to format the sections. The first tag identifies the HTML element being used and the section of text where it should start being applied. The second tag tells the browser where the element ends; the closing tag always starts with a slash (/) in front of the tag name. The *single tag* allows you to perform an action that affects a single element in the Web page as opposed to a section. For example, the single `<HR>` tag tells the browser to insert a horizontal line in the document.

HTML tags are not case sensitive. This means that `<HTML>`, `<Html>`, and `<html>` are the same thing.

NOTE As a matter of convention, I am going to display all HTML statements in uppercase letters in this book. This convention will make it easier to distinguish HTML tags from JavaScript statements later on.

Some tags allow you to pass *arguments* inside the tag that further define the tag. Here is the general format of these tags:

```
<TAGNAME ARGUMENT="xxxxxxx"> </TAGNAME>
```

In this syntax, *TAGNAME* identifies the HTML tag. *ARGUMENT* identifies the parameter being passed, and `</TAGNAME>` ends the tag. Arguments can be passed only in the first tag, never in the second tag. For example, the following line of HTML code instructs the browser to use a yellow background when displaying the HTML page:

```
<BODY BACKGROUND="Yellow"> </BODY>
```

Had `BACKGROUND="Yellow"` been omitted from the `<BODY>` tag, the browser would have displayed the HTML page with a default background (usually white).

Now that you have seen how HTML documents are identified (with the `<HTML>` and `</HTML>` tags) and understand the basics of HTML syntax, it's time to look at how the rest of an HTML document is structured.

HTML documents are divided into two main sections, the *head* and *body*, as shown in the following example:

```
<HTML>
  <HEAD>
    <TITLE>Script 1.1 - My First HTML Page</TITLE>
  </HEAD>
  <BODY>
    Hello World!
  </BODY>
</HTML>
```

The head section of the HTML page is marked off using the `<HEAD>` and `</HEAD>` tags. The head of the page always comes before the `<BODY>` tag and contains information that is not displayed within the browser. A limited number of HTML tags are supported within the head section. One of these is the `<TITLE></TITLE>` tags, *which are required*. The `<TITLE>` tags allow you to provide a description of the HTML page and its reason for existing. As you will learn on Saturday, you can also put JavaScript code in the head section.

 NOTE Although I have stated that the `<TITLE></TITLE>` tags are required, you might be thinking to yourself that you have seen HTML pages that did not include them and that displayed perfectly in your Web browser. This is because, while required, most browsers are forgiving enough to let it slide when these tags are left out. So although you can get away with not including them, it's considered a poor programming practice.

The body section of the HTML page is marked off using the `<BODY>` and `</BODY>` tags. The body section of the page contains the visible portion of your HTML page. In the preceding example, the body contains the text *Hello World*. Figure 1.1 shows the results of opening this HTML page in Netscape Navigator.

Notice that the information contained in the `<TITLE>` tags is displayed in the browser's title bar. Of course, you always have the option of including the `<TITLE></TITLE>` tags without adding any text in between them. In this case Netscape browsers will display the word "Netscape" in the title bar, while Internet Explorer browser will display the URL of the script followed by the words "Microsoft Internet Explorer" in the title bar, which you may not find all that attractive.

The TITLE

Text from the
BODY section

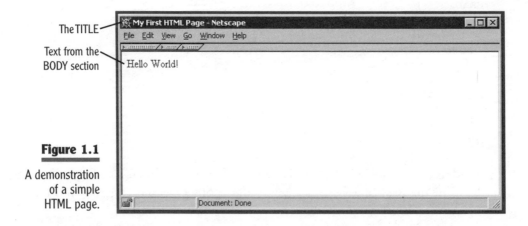

Figure 1.1

A demonstration
of a simple
HTML page.

The <BODY> tags also accept arguments that allow you to add a little style to your Web page. Consider this example:

```
<BODY BACKGROUND="tulips.gif">
```

This tag includes the BACKGROUND argument and displays the specified GIF file as the Web page's background. If the background image is too small to fill the screen, the browser automatically tiles the image to fill the screen.

Here are a few more examples of arguments you can use with the <BODY> tag.

- ✿ <BODY BGCOLOR="GREEN">. Displays a green background color.
- ✿ <BODY TEXT="WHITE">. Displays regular text in white.
- ✿ <BODY LINK="YELLOW">. Displays links in yellow.

TIP ■
Two important points that I want to stress are that your Web pages can only have one set of <BODY></BODY> tags and that all arguments must be included in that set of tags. For example, the following tag includes four different arguments:

```
<BODY BACKGROUND="tulips.gif" BGCOLOR="GREEN" TEXT="WHITE"
LINK="YELLOW"></BODY>.
```

■ ■

Common HTML Tags

As is any computer language, HTML code is comprised of a number of programming *statements*. These statements are written in the form of tags. A review of the most commonly used HTML tags and some of their attributes follows. Although this review is hardly comprehensive, it ensures that you have the HTML knowledge necessary to begin JavaScript programming.

Regular Text

Any text typed into the body section of an HTML page that is not commented out or that is not part of an HTML tag statement will appear in the browser.

NOTE A comment is text that documents the code that makes up the Web page but is not displayed when the page is loaded. I will talk more about comments a little later in the evening.

Addresses

Although they can be used anywhere, `<ADDRESS>` tags are typically used to display author, address, or signature information at the bottom of a document. Most browsers take the text enclosed in the `<ADDRESS>` tags and format it in italic.

Syntax:

```
<ADDRESS>
  Address information...
</ADDRESS>
```

Example:

This example shows you a stylistic way to publish your address. Figure 1.2 shows how this example looks in the Navigator browser.

```
<HTML>
  <HEAD>
    <TITLE>Script 1.2 - Example of using the Address tag</TITLE>
  </HEAD>
  <BODY>
    <ADDRESS>
      Jerry Lee Ford, Jr.<BR>
      President of the Inner IV<BR>
      900 Mary Washington Street<BR>
      Fredericksburg, Virginia 23233
    </ADDRESS>
  </BODY>
</HTML>
```

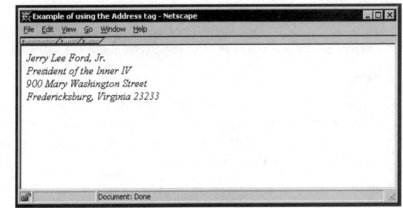

Jerry Lee Ford, Jr.
President of the Inner IV
900 Mary Washington Street
Fredericksburg, Virginia 23233

Document: Done

Figure 1.2

Using
<ADDRESS> tags
to publish address
information.

Anchors

Anchor tags are the glue that connects HTML pages together. They provide the links between pages. An *anchor* is text or a graphic that identifies the origin or destination of a link.

Syntax:

```
<A attribute="value"> description </A>
```

Attributes:

HREF   Specifies a destination URL to load.

NAME   Specifies a link to a target within the same HTML page.

TARGET   An optional attribute that specifies the name of the frame where the refer-
              enced document should be loaded.

Examples:

When the user clicks it, the following link transports the user to Netscape's Web site:

```
<A HREF="http://www.netscape.com"> Click here to visit Netscape </A>
```

When the user clicks it, this next link displays the `picture.jpg` file:

```
<A HREF="picture.jpg"> Click Here to see the Picture</A>
```

The following example establishes a destination link named "INTRO" that can be referenced by another link. This use of a named anchor allows the calling link to send the user to this exact point in the HTML page. (Normally, HTML pages open at the top.)

```
<A NAME="intro"> <H3>Introduction</H3> </A>
```

The following two examples show how the preceding named anchor can be referenced. The first example references the anchor from within the same document; the second example references the anchor from another HTML page. Note the use of the # sign to indicate that the reference is to an anchor.

```
<A HREF="#intro"> Introduction Section </A>
```

```
<A HREF="pagename#intro"> Introduction Section </A>
```

Blockquotes

Blockquote tags allow you to define a lengthy quotation that browsers usually display with left and right indentations and pad with white space on the top and bottom.

Syntax:

```
<BLOCKQUOTE>

  quote...

</BLOCKQUOTE>
```

Example:

The following example quotes a few lines from Shakespeare's *Hamlet.* Figure 1.3 shows how this example looks in the Navigator browser.

```
<HTML>

  <HEAD>

    <TITLE>Script 1.3 - Example of using the Blockquote tags</TITLE>

  </HEAD>

  <BODY>

    A quote from Hamlet, Act II, Scene II:

    <BLOCKQUOTE>
```

```
     "What a piece of work is man. How noble in reason. How infinite
     in faculty.  In form and moving how express and admirable. In
     action how like an Angel. In apprehension how like a God. The
     beauty of the world. The paragon of animals."

   </BLOCKQUOTE>

   *****************************************************************

   </BODY>

</HTML>
```

Center

The <CENTER> tags allow you to center your text. You can put as much or as little text as you want between the tags.

Syntax:

```
<CENTER>

   text...

</CENTER>
```

Example:

The following example demonstrates the use of the <CENTER> tags. Figure 1.4 shows how this example looks in the Navigator browser.

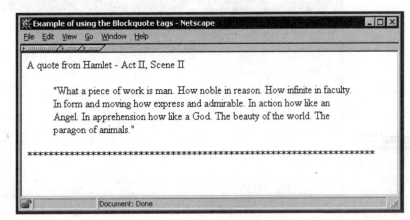

Figure 1.3

Using <BLOCKQUOTE> tags to indent a block of text.

```
<HTML>

  <HEAD>

    <TITLE>Script 1.4 - Example of Centering Text</TITLE>

  </HEAD>

  <BODY>

    <P><CENTER><B>This text is centered!</B></CENTER></P>

    <P>But this text is not centered!</P>

  </BODY>

</HTML>
```

Character Emphasis

A number of HTML tags allow you to describe the logical or physical emphasis of text.
Rather than review each individual tag, the following example demonstrates the more
popular character-emphasis tags.

Syntax:

```
<TAG>

  text...

<TAG>
```

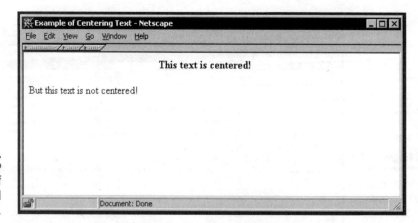

Figure 1.4

An example of
centered and
noncentered text.

Example:

The following example demonstrates the use of an assortment of tags. Figure 1.5 shows how this example looks in the Navigator browser.

```
<HTML>
  <HEAD>
    <TITLE>Script 1.5 - Character Emphasis</TITLE>
  </HEAD>
  <BODY>
    <P>
    Logical emphasis: <BR>
    <CODE>This is an example of code</CODE><BR>
    <EM>This is an example of emphasis</EM><BR>
    <STRONG>This is an example of strong</STRONG><BR>
    <CITE>This is an example of cite</CITE><BR>
    </P>
    <P>
    Physical emphasis:<BR>
    <B>This is an example of bold</B><BR>
    <I>This is an example of italics</I><BR>
    <U>This is an example of underline</U><BR>
    <STRIKE>This is an example of strike</STRIKE><BR>
    <FONT SIZE="-2">This is an example of font -2</FONT><BR>
    <FONT SIZE="4">This is an example of font 4</FONT>
    </P>
  </BODY>
</HTML>
```

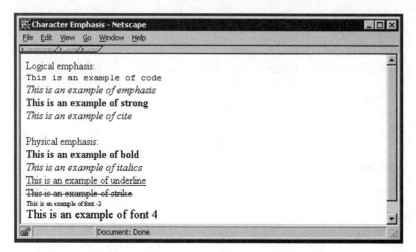

Figure 1.5

Changing the appearance of text.

By default, normal text appears as plain unformatted text. HTML provides two means for formatting text: logical and physical. *Logical* formatting defines how you want portions of text to be emphasized within a page. However, this leaves it up to the browser to ultimately determine just how the text will appear. For example, most browsers will display text formatted with the `<EM></EM>` tags as italic.

Physical formatting provides complete control over how the text will appear in any Web browser. Formatting text with the `<I></I>` tags will guarantee that the selected text will appear in italic format. In the end, it is up to your own preference as to whether you work with logical or physical formatting styles, or even a combination of the two styles.

Comments

Comments allow you to place some documentation into your HTML page that explains how and why you wrote the page the way you did. Comments make it easier for someone else to follow in your programming footsteps. The information placed inside the comment is not displayed in the browser window.

Syntax:

```
<!--

text...

-->
```

Example:

The following example contains two comments, demonstrating that comments can be located on a line by themselves or at the end of a line just after an HTML statement. Figure 1.6 shows how this example looks in the Navigator browser.

```
<HTML>
  <HEAD>
    <TITLE>Script 1.6 - Example of HTML Comments</TITLE>
  </HEAD>
  <BODY>
    <!--This is a comment -->
    Comments do not appear in the browser window.
    <!--This is a comment also-->
  </BODY>
</HTML>
```

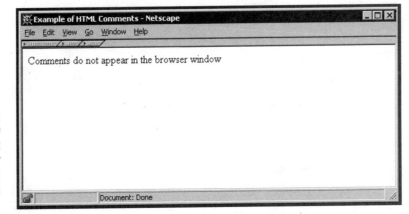

Figure 1.6

Comments do not appear in your HTML page when viewed in a browser.

Divisions

The division tag allows you to group elements within the body section of the HTML page and treat them as a single block. The <DIV> tag forces a line break after the block. You can then format all the text within the block using the ALIGN attribute.

Syntax:

```
<DIV>
  block of text...
</DIV>
```

Attributes:

ALIGN="value"   The ALIGN attribute supports the following values:

LEFT   Aligns the text on the left side of the Web page.

CENTER   Centers the text in the middle of the line.

RIGHT   Aligns the text on the right side of the Web page.

JUSTIFY   Aligns text along both the right and left margins.

Example:

This example uses two pairs of division tags to block off and format two portions of the HTML page differently. Figure 1.7 shows how this example looks in the Navigator browser.

```
<HTML>
  <HEAD>
    <TITLE>Script 1.7 - Division Tags</TITLE>
  </HEAD>
  <BODY>
    <DIV ALIGN="CENTER">
      <H4>An example of the using the division tag</H4>
      You can use the division tag to format portions of the page
      using a common set of attributes. For
      example everything in this section is centered.
    </DIV>
    <DIV ALIGN="LEFT">
      <H4>A second example of using the division tag</H4>
```

```
        As you can see this section is formatted differently. Instead

        of being center justified, everything is left justified.

     </DIV>

   </BODY>

</HTML>
```

NOTE In the previous example, I formatted all text neatly on separate lines in order to make the code easier to read. However, when you load this example, you will see that the browser automatically concatenates all text together except where it has been directed not to do so by an HTML tag such as the `<BR>` or `<P></P>` tags.

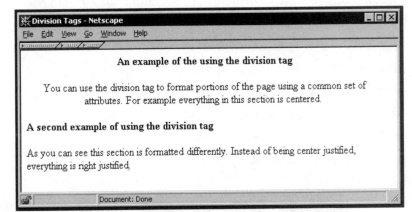

Figure 1.7

An example of formatting entire sections on an HTML page using division tags.

Headings

HTML provides for six levels of headings using the `<Hx>` tag, where H denotes a heading and x represents a heading level of 1 through 6 with 1 being the largest and 6 being the smallest. You may use the headings in any order you see fit, but you typically use a higher-level heading to establish a topic and smaller-level headings as subtopics.

Syntax:

`<Hx> Heading </Hx>`

Where x is a number from 1 to 6.

Attributes:

ALIGN="*value*" The ALIGN attribute allows you to tell the browser how you want the header to be aligned. Unless you include this argument, all headers are left aligned by default. The following alignment options are available:

LEFT Aligns the header on the left side of the Web page.

CENTER Centers the header in the middle of the line.

RIGHT Aligns the header on the right side of the Web page.

JUSTIFY Aligns text along both the right and left margins.

Examples:

The following statements demonstrate the entire range of HTML headers. Figure 1.8 shows how this example looks in the Navigator browser.

```
<H1> This is a H1 heading </H1>
<H2> This is a H2 heading </H2>
<H3> This is a H3 heading </H3>
<H4> This is a H4 heading </H4>
<H5> This is a H5 heading </H5>
<H6> This is a H6 heading </H6>
```

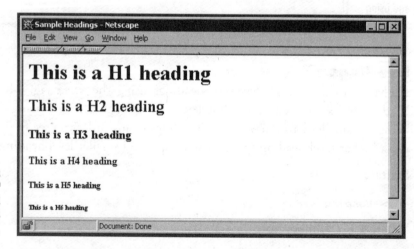

Figure 1.8

Examples of the six levels of headings supported by HTML.

NOTE The exact size and font of each heading is dependent on the browser. The only way to be sure how your heading looks is to load your Web pages using different Web browsers.

The following example demonstrates the use of the ALIGN attribute to control header location. Figure 1.9 shows how this example looks in the Navigator browser.

```
<HTML>
  <HEAD>
    <TITLE>Script 1.8 - Headings Example Page</TITLE>
  </HEAD>
  <BODY>
    <H4 ALIGN="LEFT"> This H4 header is left aligned. </H4>
    <H4 ALIGN="CENTER"> This H4 header is center aligned. </H4>
    <H4 ALIGN="RIGHT"> This H4 header is RIGHT aligned. </H4>
    <H4 ALIGN="JUSTIFY"> This rather long and wordy H4 header has been
    increased in size to demonstrate left and right justification
    </H4>
  </BODY>
</HTML>
```

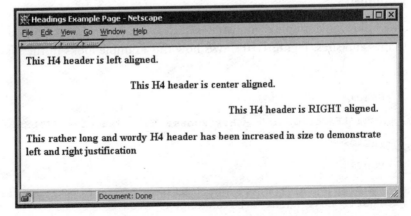

Figure 1.9

Examples of header alignment.

Horizontal Rule

The horizontal rule tag provides a simple way of separating portions of your Web page. Note that this HTML element does not have an ending tag. You can also change the size, width, and justification of the horizontal rule.

Syntax:

```
<HR attributes="">
```

Attributes:

SIZE	The height of the horizontal rule as measured in pixels or based on a percentage of the current browser window size.
WIDTH	The width of the horizontal rule as measured in pixels or based on a percentage of the current browser window size.
ALIGN="value"	The ALIGN attribute allows you to tell the browser how you want the horizontal rule to be aligned. Unless you include this argument, all horizontal rules are left aligned by default. The following alignment options are available:
LEFT	Aligns the horizontal rule on the left side of the Web page.
CENTER	Centers the horizontal rule in the middle of the line.
RIGHT	Aligns the horizontal rule on the right side of the Web page.
JUSTIFY	Aligns the horizontal rule along both the right and left margins.

Example:

The following example demonstrates how to create various horizontal rules of different shapes and sizes. Figure 1.10 shows how this example looks in the Navigator browser.

```
<HTML>
  <HEAD>
    <TITLE>Script 1.9 - Horizontal Rule Example</TITLE>
  </HEAD>
  <BODY>
    A simple way to separate portions of your web page is with the
    Horizontal Rules Line as shown below.
```

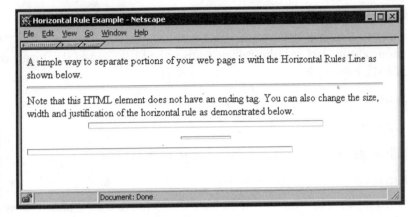

Figure 1.10

Using horizontal
rules to separate
portions of an
HTML page.

```
<HR>
```

Note that this HTML element does not have an ending tag. You can
also change the size, width and justification of the horizontal
rule as demonstrated below.

```
<HR SIZE="8" WIDTH="66%">

<HR SIZE="3" WIDTH="75">

<HR SIZE="8" WIDTH="400" ALIGN="left">

</BODY>

</HTML>
```

Take a Break

Well, this is a good time to take a quick break and stretch your legs. When you come
back, you'll finish the HTML review and learn a little more about JavaScript and
JavaScript syntax. Then, you'll write and test your first JavaScript and learn how to
begin building your own library of JavaScripts.

More HTML

If you are ready to get started again, let's return to our HTML review. After this, I will
review a few JavaScript basics and then show you how to write your first script.

Images

The images tag allows you to place graphics directly into your HTML documents. It has no closing tag. It is typically used to embed JPEG and GIF images directly into your HTML pages.

Syntax:

```
<IMG SRC="url">
```

Where SRC="*url*" specifies the location of the graphic.

Attributes:

ALIGN="*value*" The ALIGN attribute allows you to tell the browser how you want the image to be aligned. The following alignment options are available:

BOTTOM	Aligns the image at the bottom of the current line position.
MIDDLE	Centers the image in the middle of the current line position.
TOP	Aligns the image at the top of the current line position.
ALT	An alternate text message that non-image supporting browsers will display in place of the graphic.
HEIGHT	The height of the image in pixels or as a percentage of the actual object size.
WIDTH	The width of the image in pixels or as a percentage of the actual object size.
BORDER	The thickness in pixels of the border to be placed around the image. A value of 0 means no border.

Example:

The following example demonstrates how to display an image with and without accompanying attributes. Figure 1.11 shows how this example looks in the Navigator browser.

```
<HTML>
  <HEAD>
    <TITLE>Script 1.10 - IMG Tag Example</TITLE>
  </HEAD>
  <BODY>
```

```
<IMG SRC="ms.jpg"> Example without additional arguments

<P>

<IMG SRC="ms.jpg" ALT="If you upgrade your browser you will be able
    to see a really nice image here!" ALIGN="MIDDLE" HEIGHT="70"
    WIDTH="70" BORDER="5">
    Example with ALT, ALIGN, HEIGHT, WIDTH and BORDER arguments

  </P>

 </BODY>

</HTML>
```

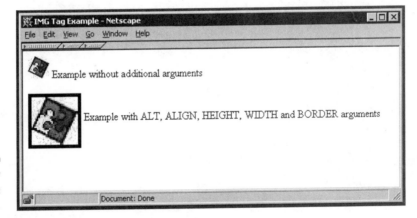

Figure 1.11

Examples of how to manipulate inline images.

Line Breaks

The line break tag allows you to tell the browser where to end a line and begin a new one. This tag allows you to specify a specific location where you want to force a line break.

> **NOTE** Although it is considered poor programming practice, you may often see where others have chosen to use multiple line breaks to insert blank lines. The `<P>` tag, presented later in this chapter, provides the preferred way of inserting blank lines.

Syntax:

```
<BR>
```

Example:

The following example uses line break tags to prevent the browser from arbitrarily wrapping the text. Figure 1.12 shows how this example looks in the Navigator browser.

```
<HTML>
  <HEAD>
    <TITLE>Script 1.11 - Line Break Example</TITLE>
  </HEAD>
  <BODY>
  Do not use the line break tag in place of the paragraph tag.<BR>
  It is only intended as a means for creating breaks at the end
  of a line.<BR>
  While many browsers will allow you to use multiple line breaks in
  place of paragraph tags, it is considered poor programming
  to do so.<BR>
    <BR>
    <BR>
    Plus, as this example shows, it is not very pretty to look at.
  </BODY>
</HTML>
```

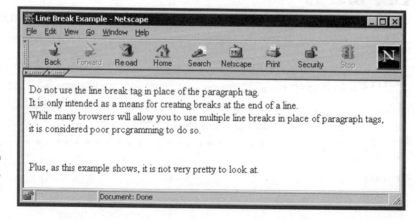

Figure 1.12

Using line breaks to control when new lines begin.

Lists

There are two types of lists supported in HTML: glossary lists and regular lists. A *glossary list* contains a term followed by a definition. A *regular list* can be either ordered or unordered; these lists are simply lists of words, sentences, or paragraphs preceded by a special character or number.

Syntax:

Glossary Lists:

```
<DL>
   <DT>Term</DT>
   <DD>Definition </DD>
</DL>
```

The `<DL>` and `</DL>` tags combined with the `<DT>` `</DT>` and `<DD>` `</DD>` tags allow you to build glossary lists.

`<DL>` `</DL>`   Marks the beginning and end of the definition list.

`<DT>` `</DT>`   Identifies the definition term.

`<DD>` `</DD>`   Identifies the definition, which is treated as a paragraph.

Regular Lists:

Unordered List	Ordered List
`<UL>`	`<OL>`
`<LI>First list element </LI>`	`<LI>First list element </LI>`
`<LI>Second list element </LI>`	`<LI>Second list element </LI>`
`<LI>. </LI>`	`<LI>. </LI>`
`<LI>. </LI>`	`<LI>. </LI>`
`<LI>Last list element </LI></UL>`	`<LI> Last list element </LI></OL>`

Unordered lists are enclosed within `<UL></UL>` tags and contain one or more pairs of `<LI></LI>` tags that identify each entry in the list. Likewise, ordered lists are enclosed within `<OL></OL>` tags.

Examples:

This example shows you how to build a glossary list. Figure 1.13 shows how this example looks in the Navigator browser.

```
<HTML>

  <HEAD>

    <TITLE>Script 1.12 - Glossary List Example</TITLE>

  </HEAD>

  <BODY>

    <H4>Glossary</H4>

    <DL>

      <DT>HTML</DT>

      <DD>Hypertext Markup language - A simple language that allows
      you to develop content for display on the World Wide Web using
      browsers like Netscape Communicator and Internet Explorer. </DD>

      JavaScript</DT>

      <DD>A scripting language developed by Netscape that integrates
      with HTML and allows you to create interactive web pages </DD>

      <DT>VBScript</DT>

      <DD>A scripting language developed by Microsoft that provides
      roughly equivalent capabilities to JavaScript. </DD>

    </DL>

  </BODY>

</HTML>
```

This next example shows you how to build regular unordered and ordered lists. Figure 1.14 shows how this example looks in the Navigator browser.

```
<HTML>

  <HEAD>

    <TITLE>Script 1.13 - Regular List Examples</TITLE>

  </HEAD>
```

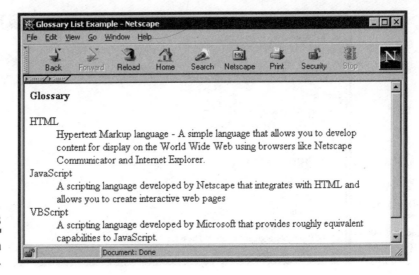

Figure 1.13

Example of a glossary list.

```
<BODY>

   Ingredients:

   <UL>

      <LI>Eggs</LI>

      <LI>Milk</LI>

      <LI>Sugar</LI>

      <LI>Secret Ingredient</LI>

   </UL>

   Instructions:

   <OL>

      <LI>Pre-heat the oven to 350 degrees</LI>

      <LI>Mix the ingredients</LI>

      <LI>Place into a greased pan and heat for 30 minutes</LI>

   </OL>

   </BODY>

</HTML>
```

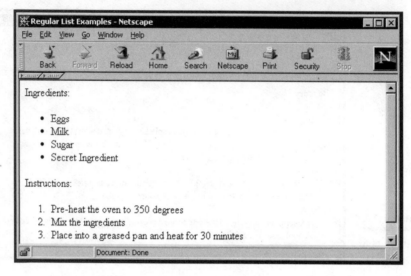

Figure 1.14

Examples of unordered and ordered lists.

Paragraphs

Paragraph tags are used to delineate the beginning and end of paragraphs. Actually, the ending `</P>` tag is optional because, if you have back-to-back paragraphs, the browser automatically starts a new paragraph the next time it sees a `<P>` tag, even if there was no preceding `</P>` tag. However, if you plan on using the ALIGN attribute, discussed below, you need to remember to always include the `</P>` tag to ensure that the attribute affects only the portion of text that you intend.

Syntax:

```
<P>

paragraph text...

</P>
```

Attributes:

ALIGN="*value*"   The paragraph tag accepts the ALIGN argument so that you can tell the browser how you want to align the paragraph. By default, all paragraphs are left aligned. The following alignment options are available:

    LEFT   Aligns the paragraph on the left side of the Web page.

CENTER	Centers the lines of text in the paragraph in the middle of the page.
RIGHT	Aligns the paragraph on the right side of the Web page.
JUSTIFY	Aligns the text along both the right and left margins.

Example:

The following example and Figure 1.15 show you how the browser formats text that has been organized as paragraphs.

```
<HTML>
  <HEAD>
    <TITLE>Script 1.14 - Example of using the Paragraph tag</TITLE>
  </HEAD>
  <BODY>
    <P>This is the first of two short paragraphs which demonstrate the
      use of the paragraph tag.  This tag provides an effective
      means of formatting large papers for display on web sites.</P>
    <P>Of course, as I already stated the second part of the tag is
      optional</P>
  </BODY>
</HTML>
```

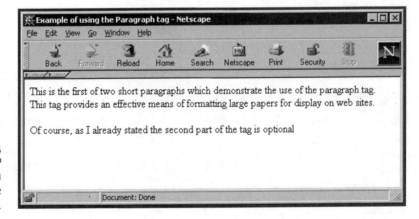

Figure 1.15

Using paragraph tags to organize your Web page.

Preformatted Text

Controlling the exact layout of text is very difficult to do in an HTML page. One way around this limitation is to use preformatted text. Preformatted text is text that is displayed in its original format. The browser displays this text in a monospaced format exactly as you type it in the HTML file. This allows you to include text in a specific format without worrying about the browser changing its appearance by removing blank spaces and line feeds.

Syntax:

```
<PRE>
   preformatted text...
</PRE>
```

Example:

The following example shows how you might format a portion of a report. Figure 1.16 shows how this example looks in the Navigator browser.

```
<HTML>
   <HEAD>
      <TITLE>Script 1.15 - Preformatted Text Example</TITLE>
   </HEAD>
   <BODY>
      <PRE>
         Accounts        Jan        Feb        MAR        Apr
         _____        ___        ___        ___        ___

         Company X       $1,000     $  120     $  100     $1,120
         Company Y       $1,200     $1,080     $   50     $     0
         Company Z       $2,000     $    0     $4,400     $2,000

         _____        ___        ___        ___        ___

         Total           $4,200     $1,200     $4,550     $3,120
      </PRE>
   </BODY>
</HTML>
```

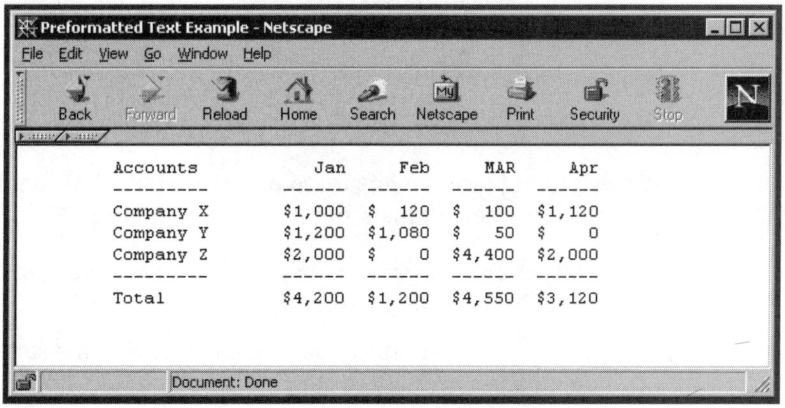

Figure 1.16

Embedding
preformatted text
into HTML pages.

```
┌─────────────────────────────────────────────────────────────────────────┐
│ ░ Preformatted Text Example - Netscape                          _ □ ×     │
│ File  Edit  View  Go  Window  Help                                        │
│   ↙       ↘       ➌      ⌂       ➋       My       ➎      ☞       ⚙    N   │
│  Back   Forward  Reload  Home   Search  Netscape  Print  Security  Stop    │
│ ▶░░░░/▶░░░                                                                 │
│                                                                           │
│       Accounts        Jan      Feb      MAR      Apr                       │
│       ---------      ------   ------   ------   ------                     │
│       Company X      $1,000   $  120   $  100   $1,120                     │
│       Company Y      $1,200   $1,080   $   50   $    0                     │
│       Company Z      $2,000   $    0   $4,400   $2,000                     │
│       ---------      ------   ------   ------   ------                     │
│       Total          $4,200   $1,200   $4,550   $3,120                     │
│                                                                           │
│ ░           Document: Done                                                │
└─────────────────────────────────────────────────────────────────────────┘
```

Scripts

Scripts such as JavaScript, VBScript, and JScript are embedded in HTML pages using the <SCRIPT> </SCRIPT> tag set. The text inside the script tags does not appear in the browser window—except for older browsers that do not understand JavaScript. Don't worry, I will tell you how to handle the problem of older browsers tomorrow morning. As you know, the script statements that appear between the <SCRIPT> and </SCRIPT> tags is the topic of discussion for the rest of the weekend.

Syntax:

<SCRIPT LANGUAGE="" TYPE="" SRC=""> </SCRIPT>

Attributes:

LANGUAGE   Allows you to specify the type of script language that is embedded between the tags. For example:

LANGUAGE="JavaScript"

LANGUAGE="VBScript"

LANGUAGE="JScript"

TYPE   An optional attribute that allows you to specify the script's MIME (Multipart Internet Mail extension) type. This attribute specifies the format of the data in the script. If included this attribute must specify that the document contains plain text and is formatted as a specific type of script. If the LANGUAGE attribute specifies JavaScript and the TYPE attribute is omitted, TYPE="Text/JavaScript" is assumed.

```
TYPE="Text/JavaScript"

TYPE="Text/VBScript"

TYPE="Text/JScript"
```

SRC   Allows you to place a reference to an external file that contains the script instead of embedding the script directly within the HTML page. For example:

SRC=`"http://www.myserver.com/tests.js"` runs a JavaScript located at the named URL.

SRC=`"test2.js"` runs a JavaScript located in the same location as the HTML page.

NOTE You can place more than one `<SCRIPT>` tag set on a single HTML page; each occurrence of the tag set can specify a different scripting language.

Example:

```
<SCRIPT LANGUAGE="JavaScript" TYPE=" Text/JavaScript">

  JavaScript statements...

</SCRIPT>
```

Tables

Table tags let you create tables so that you can display related information in column-and-row format.

Syntax:

```
<TABLE>

  <TR> <TH> </TH> </TR>

  <TR> <TD> </TD> </TR>

</TABLE>
```

Where TR defines a row in the table, TH defines a heading, and TD defines a table data entry.

Attributes:

BORDER	Adds a border to the table. A value of 0 means no border as measured in pixels.
CELLSPACING	Adds space between cells as measured in pixels.
CELLPADDING	Adds space within a cell as measured in pixels.
WIDTH	Determines the width of the table as measured in pixels or as a percentage of the browser window.
HEIGHT	Determines the height of the table as measured in pixels.
ALIGN	Controls the alignment of text within individual cells.
BGCOLOR	Controls the background color of individual cells.

Example:

The following example builds a simple table that is three columns wide and three rows deep. The table has been set to be 75 percent of the width of the browser window with a border thickness of 3 and a little extra cell padding just for good looks. Figure 1.17 shows how this example looks in the Navigator browser.

```
<HTML>
  <HEAD>
    <TITLE>Script 1.16 - Examining Tables</TITLE>
  </HEAD>
  <BODY>
    <TABLE BORDER="3" WIDTH="75%" cellpadding="10">
    <CAPTION ALIGN="CENTER">Operating System Comparison</CAPTION>
    <TR> <TH>Windows 95 </TH><TH>Windows 98 </TH><TH>Windows 2000
    </TH></TR>
    <TR> <TD>FAT</TD> <TD>FAT,FAT32</TD> <TD>FAT,FAT32,NTFS</TD> </TR>
    <TR> <TD>Not secure</TD> <TD>Not secure</TD> <TD>Secure</TD> </TR>
    </TABLE>
  </BODY>
</HTML>
```

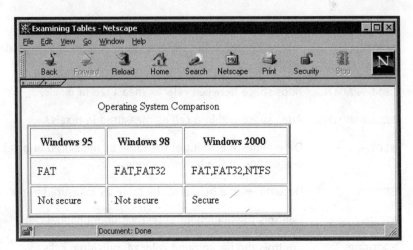

Figure 1.17

Adding a table to an HTML page.

 You may have noticed that I added caption tags in the previous example. This tag set is not part of the table. I used the `<CAPTION>` `</CAPTION>` tag set to give the table a polished look.

Integrating JavaScript with HTML

As you already know, a JavaScript is a program that you embed in an HTML document by placing it within `<SCRIPT>` and `</SCRIPT>` tags. You were introduced to these script tags in the HTML review earlier in the session. However, I want to take another look at these tags with a specific focus on how they work in JavaScript.

Understanding the Script Tags

Script tags were introduced with HTML 3.2. They can be placed within either the head or body section of an HTML page. Figure 1.18 outlines how the script tag set looks when embedded in an HTML page.

JavaScript begins after the `<SCRIPT>` tag and ends before the `</SCRIPT>` tag. Several arguments can be included within the first tag. The LANGUAGE attribute specifies the version of JavaScript you want to use. Here are your available options:

```
LANGUAGE="JavaScript"
```

```
LANGUAGE="JavaScript1.1"

LANGUAGE="JavaScript1.2"

LANGUAGE="JavaScript1.3"

LANGUAGE="JavaScript1.4"
```

Figure 1.18

Syntax of the script
tag set when used
with JavaScript.

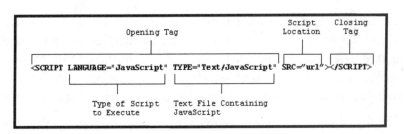

NOTE   Different versions of the Netscape Navigator and Internet Explorer browsers support different versions of JavaScript (as shown in Table 1.1, earlier in this session). With so many
different versions of JavaScript and browsers, things can get very confusing. You may
want to write your JavaScripts so that they conform to the lowest common denominator
(that is, so that your scripts don't use features in versions of JavaScript newer than the
oldest version visitors to your site are likely to have). Another option is to write your
JavaScripts to accommodate different browser versions. I will talk more about the latter
option on Saturday.

When working with JavaScript, the TYPE attribute will always be Text/JavaScript.
The SRC attribute allows you to place your JavaScript code in an external file with a .js
extension and to reference that file instead of embedding the script within the body of
the HTML page. Referencing an external script makes it a little more difficult for users
to view your JavaScript source code. It also makes it possible to share the same
JavaScript among multiple HTML pages.

Writing Your First JavaScript: "Hello World"

So far, we have gone over a lot, including a little background about JavaScript, a brief
comparison of the competing scripting languages, and an overview of HTML. Now it's

time to create your first JavaScript. It's going to be a very basic example, so don't get your hopes up too high. By tomorrow night, you'll be writing much more sophisticated scripts.

In this example, you will create the classic "Hello World" program that every programming book since the beginning of time has used as its introductory example. After all, who I am defy such an honored tradition?

But before you get started, I want to say a quick word about HTML and JavaScript editors. There are plenty of them available, and their features and capabilities vary as much as their prices. I have included several editors on the CD-ROM that accompanies this book. It really does not matter which editor you ultimately decide to use. In fact, for the code you see in this book, I used the Notepad program that comes with Windows 2000.

The first thing I did before approaching any of the coding examples in this book was to create an HTML template that I could use over and over again. Every time I worked on a new script, I used Notepad to open my template, typed in my JavaScript statements, and chose File, Save As from the Notepad menu to save my script with a new file name. If you are using a full-featured HTML editor, it may automatically provide a starting template for you whenever you create a new page. If not, you may want to build and use a template like I did. My template is shown here:

```
<HTML>

  <HEAD>

    <TITLE>Script 1.17 - Insert Descriptive Title Here</TITLE>

  </HEAD>

  <BODY>

  </BODY>

</HTML>
```

As you can see, my template contains <HEAD> </HEAD>, <TITLE> </TITLE>, and <BODY> </BODY> tag sets all wrapped inside the starting and ending <HTML> </HTML> tag set. If you want to do so, create your own template now. When you are done, add the following lines inside the body section:

```
<SCRIPT LANGUAGE="JAVASCRIPT" TYPE="TEXT/JAVASCRIPT">

  document.write("Hello World")

</SCRIPT>
```

These three statements are your first JavaScript program. You should recognize the first and last lines as script tags that tell your browser to execute the enclosed JavaScript statements. This script has just one statement. This statement tells the browser to write the message "Hello World" on the current document, which is the window in which the HTML page opened.

When you have added the three lines of JavaScript to your template, it should like this:

```
<HTML>

  <HEAD>

    <TITLE>Script 1.18 - Sample HTML Page</TITLE>

  </HEAD>

  <BODY>

    <SCRIPT LANGUAGE="JAVASCRIPT" TYPE="TEXT/JAVASCRIPT">

      document.write("Hello World")

    </SCRIPT>

  </BODY>

</HTML>
```

Testing Your First Script

Now that you have typed in your first script, you have to save it. I called my script `HelloWorld.html`. The HTML extension identifies the page as an HTML page. Your computer uses the information in the file's extension to associate the file with a particular application. A `.html` extension tells the operating system to open its default browser and pass the Web page file to it. Alternatively, you can use the `.htm` extension, which is also recognized as an extension for HTML pages.

If you are using a full-featured HTML editor, the editor may allow you to test your script with the click of a button. Because Notepad has no such automatic HTML testing feature, I simply started up a browser and used it to open the `HelloWorld.html` file. The browser opened my page and ran the script.

Depending on the browsers installed on your computer, the process of testing your script is slightly different as outlined in the following procedures.

Testing with Netscape Navigator:

1. Start Netscape Navigator.
2. In the menu bar, click on File and then click on Open Page.
3. In the dialog box that opens, type the location of your HTML page and click on Open. Alternatively, click on the Choose File button to navigate to the HTML page in your file system and then click on Open. Netscape Navigator opens the page as shown in Figure 1.19.

Testing with Internet Explorer:

1. Start Internet Explorer.
2. In the menu bar, click on File and then click on Open Page.
3. In the dialog box that opens, type the location of your HTML page and click on OK. Alternatively, click on the Browse button to navigate to the HTML page in your file system and then click on OK. Internet Explorer opens the page as shown in Figure 1.20.

TIP ■
Because of differences between Netscape Navigator and Internet Explorer (the two browsers visitors to my Web site will most likely be using), I always test my scripts twice, once with each browser.
■ ■

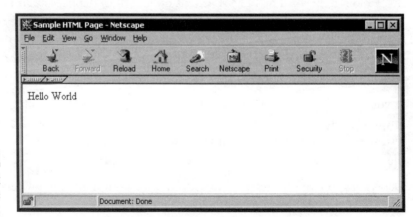

Figure 1.19

Testing your script with Netscape Navigator.

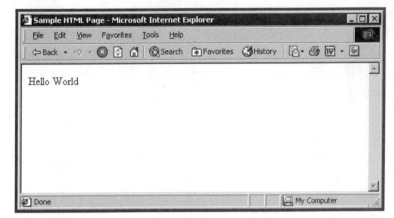

Figure 1.20

Testing your script with Internet Explorer.

After loading your script and seeing it work the way that you intended in both Netscape Navigator and Internet Explorer, you know that you probably have a good script. However, the current versions of both of these browsers do a really good job of hiding errors when they occur. I will show you how to look for and fix these errors on Sunday afternoon. For now, assume that if you saw what you expected when you loaded your Web page that everything is okay.

Recognizing Case Sensitivity in JavaScript

Case sensitivity is an important issue in JavaScript programming. JavaScript is case sensitive (unlike HTML, which doesn't care how you capitalize tags). This means that you must type JavaScript elements exactly as they appear in this book for them to work. In JavaScript, the words `document` and `Document` are recognized as two different things. So pay special attention when typing in your scripts. For example, if I had accidentally typed a capital `D` in the `document.write()` statement used in the preceding example, my script would have displayed an error and not the *Hello World* message I intended.

Four Ways to Integrate JavaScript into HTML Pages

As you know, there are two places you can put your JavaScripts in an HTML page: in either the head or body section. In addition, I have told you that you can either embed JavaScript directly into the HTML page or reference it in a `.js` file. One more way you can integrate JavaScript into an HTML page is as a component in an HTML tag. Examples of each of these four options follow.

Placing JavaScript in the Body Section of the HTML Page

In this example, the JavaScript is embedded with the script tags somewhere in the body section of the HTML page. Scripts embedded in the body section are executed as part of the HTML document when the page loads. This allows the script to begin executing as the page loads.

```
<BODY>

  <SCRIPT LANGUAGE="JAVASCRIPT" TYPE="TEXT/JAVASCRIPT">

    document.write("This JavaScript is located in the body section")

  </SCRIPT>

</BODY>
```

Placing JavaScript in the Head Section of the HTML Page

In this example, the JavaScript is embedded with the script tags at the top of the HTML page within the <HEAD> </HEAD> tags. Scripts embedded in the head section are not automatically executed when the page loads but can be executed when called by other scripts in the page. It is typical to move all functions and most variables to the head section because this ensures that they will be defined before being referenced by scripts located in the body section of the page.

Variables are containers for storing information, and *functions* are groups of JavaScript statements that you can call to perform a specific task. I'll talk more about the benefits of using functions and variables tomorrow.

```
<HEAD>

  <TITLE>Sample HTML Page</TITLE>

  <SCRIPT LANGUAGE="JAVASCRIPT" TYPE="TEXT/JAVASCRIPT">

    alert("This JavaScript is located in the head section")

  </SCRIPT>

</HEAD>
```

Referencing JavaScript in an External .js File

In this example, the SRC attribute is set to reference an external file that contains the JavaScript statements.

```
<SCRIPT SRC="FileName.js" LANGUAGE="JAVASCRIPT" TYPE="TEXT/JAVASCRIPT">
</SCRIPT>
```

The .js file being referenced here is named `FileName.js` and might contain a line of JavaScript like the following example:

```
document.write("This is an external JavaScript.")
```

> **NOTE**
> The `.js` file can appear in either the head or body section of the HTML page. There is no limit to the number of statements that can be placed in the `.js` file. If you find that your HTML pages and JavaScripts are rather large, placing the JavaScript in an external `.js` file may make them both easier to read and maintain.

> **NOTE**
> External JavaScript files can contain only JavaScript statements. They cannot contain HTML tags.

Placing JavaScript in an HTML Tag

JavaScript can also be placed with the HTML tags as shown in the following example. In this case, the JavaScript `onLoad=document.write("xxxx")` statement has been added to the HTML `<BODY>` tag. This particular JavaScript statement tells the browser to write the enclosed text when the browser first loads the HTML page.

Placing small JavaScript statements inside HTML tags provides an easy way to execute small pieces of JavaScript code. Functionally, the result is no different than embedding actual JavaScripts into the Web page. Of course, this option is really only beneficial when executing small JavaScript statements and is impractical for larger JavaScript statements or situations that require multiple lines of code.

```
<BODY onLoad=document.write("This JavaScript is located inside the
BODY tag")> </BODY>
```

> **NOTE**
> You may have noticed the spelling of `onLoad`. The *L* in the middle of the word is capitalized and rest of the word is in lowercase letters. This type of notation is known as *Camel-Back notation*. This is a perfect example of JavaScript's case sensitivity. If you change the capitalization of this word in any way, you'll get an error when you run your JavaScript.

Locating This Book's Source Code on the CD-ROM

The best way to learn JavaScript is to write your own scripts. One way to begin your own script-writing career is to look at somebody else's JavaScripts and modify them to see what happens. To make things as easy as possible, I made all the example scripts in the book available to you on the accompanying CD-ROM.

Building Your Own Collection of JavaScript Scripts

In addition to the scripts from this book, you can find literally thousands of free JavaScripts on the World Wide Web, which you can download and play with. Following are some of my favorite sites, which you can use as a starting point to begin building your own JavaScript library. In fact, you may even want to submit your own JavaScripts to these sites so that you can share your work with everybody else.

- JavaScript.com at `http://www.javascript.com` (shown in Figure 1.21). This Web site provides an assortment of free scripts that you can cut and paste into your Web pages, access to free news, and tons of information on other Web technologies such as DHTML.

- JavaScript World at `http://www.jsworld.com` (shown in Figure 1.22). This Web site provides a wealth of information about JavaScript, including free scripts and JavaScript tutorials. It also provides an abundance of information about HTML and DHTML.

- The JavaScript Source at `http://javascript.internet.com` (shown in Figure 1.23). This Web site provides tons of free cut and paste JavaScript examples, access to free newsletters, and an excellent JavaScript tutorial.

- JavaScript City at `http://www.javascriptcity.com` (shown in Figure 1.24). This Web site provides free cut and paste JavaScripts as well as JavaScript tutorials and a JavaScript discussion forum.

Understanding Browser Compatibility

Browser compatibility is a major issue for any Web scripting language, including JavaScript. It is an issue because Microsoft and Netscape have different opinions about how things should be done and do not cooperate with one another. The result is that both companies have continued to develop browsers that often behave differently when asked to do the same things.

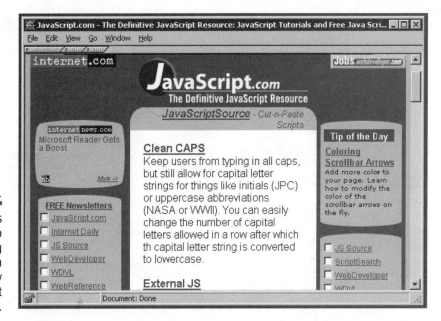

Figure 1.21

JavaScript.com is a searchable Web site featuring information on virtually every aspect of JavaScript programming.

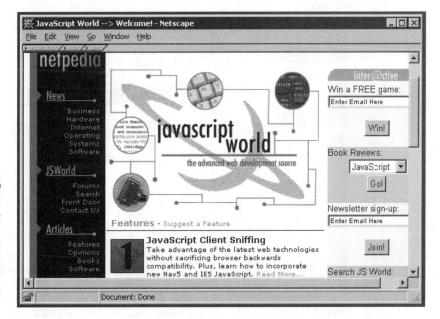

Figure 1.22

JavaScript World provides free scripts, articles, and technical information covering an assortment of Web technologies.

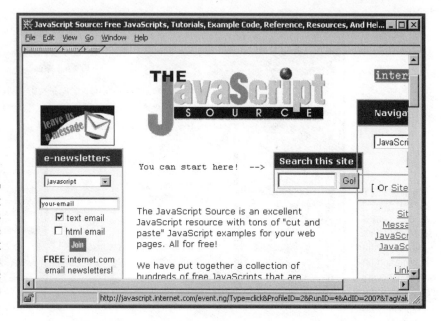

Figure 1.23

The JavaScript Source provides hundreds of free JavaScripts just waiting for you to cut and paste into your own Web pages.

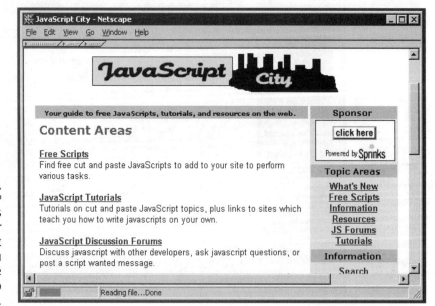

Figure 1.24

JavaScript City is another source for free JavaScript code that you view online before adding it to your own pages.

One key difference between Internet Explorer and Netscape Navigator is their object models. Earlier this evening, I introduced the idea of object-based programming and told you that JavaScript has its own object model. This means that within JavaScript is a defined collection of objects, all of which have certain properties and can be affected by certain methods. JavaScript can also interact with objects defined by the browser within which it runs. The problem is that Netscape Navigator and Internet Explorer have different object models, so some objects that exist in the Netscape browser do not exist in the Internet Explorer browser. A JavaScript written to access a Navigator object will be out of luck when it is run in an Internet Explorer browser.

Another browser issue has to do with the version of JavaScript the browser can support (refer back to Table 1.1). JavaScript support was introduced with the Netscape 2 browser. But that version of the browser supports only JavaScript version 1.0. Microsoft began to provide JavaScript support in Internet Explorer 3. The problem is that there are still a lot of people out there running older versions of both browsers; trying to write JavaScript code that accommodates them all is very difficult.

As you can surmise, not all browsers are created equal. In fact, things are made more difficult because Microsoft and Netscape are not the only companies that make browsers. Other browsers available on the market provide varying degrees of JavaScript support. For example, the Lynx browser, shown in Figure 1.25, is a simple text-based browser that does not support graphics or JavaScript.

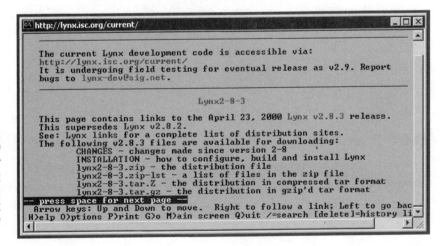

Figure 1.25

The Lynx browser is lightning fast when interacting with Web sites that support text-only browsers.

Obviously, one option you have when writing your JavaScripts is to ignore all non-JavaScript browsers and code for just the Netscape Navigator and Internet Explorer browsers. You might also choose to write scripts that support only the last version or two of both browsers. Writing code to this "limited" browser audience will still satisfy about 98 percent of your potential visitors. However, if you want to attract as many people as possible to your Web site, you may want to consider finding ways to accommodate the other browsers. We'll look at different options for dealing with this problem tomorrow.

LOCATING OLDER BROWSERS

Testing your JavaScripts with multiple browsers is simply a matter of downloading and installing the browsers and then using them one at a time to see how they handle your script. But if you also want to test how older versions of those browsers work, you may need another computer. As I was writing this book, I was able to download versions as old as Netscape 3 and Internet Explorer 3 from popular shareware sites such has www.tucows.com **and** www.download.com.

One other Internet browser you might want to be on the lookout for is called Opera, pictured in Figure 1.26. It is currently available for trial download at www.opera.com. The Opera browser is less than half the size of its Netscape and Internet Explorer competitors, yet it provides support for all the features you'd expect, including JavaScript 1.3. Best of all, Opera loads Web pages fast. There is just one catch: Opera is not free. But more and more people are starting to pay attention to it, and you may want to get a copy for testing.

What's Next?

Okay, that's enough for tonight. Time to get some sleep and let all the material we covered tonight soak in. We'll start off first thing tomorrow morning by learning about the basic building blocks of JavaScript programming.

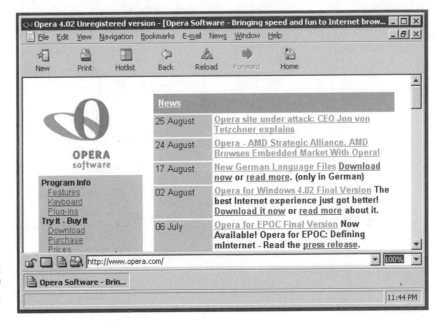

Figure 1.26

The Opera
Internet browser.

Learning the Basics of JavaScript Coding

- A few words about scripting
- Working with values
- JavaScript statements
- Streamlining your JavaScripts with functions
- Using arrays

Good morning! I hope you had a good night's sleep and that you are rested and ready to go. There is a lot for you to do today.

Yesterday, I focused on providing you with the background that you need to understand and work with JavaScript. You should now feel comfortable enough with HTML to focus on JavaScript. If you are worried that you are still a little rusty with HTML, you can always return to Friday Evening's material to brush up on HTML syntax.

If you have not already done so, now is a good time to pull together all the tools you plan to work with. While you can certainly use Window's Notepad application to write all your scripts, you might also want to look at some more advanced HTML/JavaScript editors. You might also want to download copies of Internet browsers such as Netscape, Internet Explorer, and Opera. I have provided an assortment of such tools on the accompanying CD-ROM. You might also want to check out the various shareware sites such as `www.shareware.com`, `www.download.com`, and `www.tucows.com` on the Internet for other alternatives.

Assuming that you have everything you need, let's review what I have planned for this morning and then jump right in. You will start out the morning by learning the basic programming constructs available to you in JavaScript. *Programming constructs* allow you to do such things as storing information for later use, comparing values, and developing logical routines to handle different circumstances. You'll also learn to create code that lets you streamline your script using techniques such as looping, calling functions, and building arrays.

A Few Words about Scripting

Perhaps you are wondering what the difference is between *scripting* and *programming*. Well, the answer is nothing. They are the same thing. Many people like to think of scripts as small units of program code that perform a specific useful function and of programs as larger, more robust code. As you will soon learn, JavaScript can be used to write code that fulfills both of those definitions.

One possible way to differentiate a script from a program is to define scripts as interpreted programs that are processed one line at a time and to define programs as collections of code that must be compiled before they can execute. *Compiling* is the process of converting a program's instructions into machine language so that the computer can process them. Because JavaScript is an *interpreted language*, it needs something to interpret the code as it executes. This is the job of the Internet browser. The browser also provides JavaScript with a programming environment complete with an *object model* that allows access to windows, history information, and so on.

I know that I keep mentioning objects and object models; I will continue to do so throughout the morning before I finally provide detailed coverage this afternoon. Learning a new programming language is not always easy and is made only more difficult by the fact that just about every new concept depends on your knowing another one. Unfortunately, I can only teach you one concept at a time. So hang in there!

Getting Comfortable with JavaScript Syntax

JavaScript is case sensitive. This means that you must be careful to use correct spelling and capitalization when typing. For example, in a few minutes you are going to learn how to work with variables in JavaScript. If you create a variable in the beginning of your script with the name `total_value`, you must use this exact spelling throughout your script. Change a single element of spelling, and you will get an error because JavaScript will think that you are referencing a different variable.

Something else you will learn more about this weekend is JavaScript's *event handlers*. These are special built-in routines you can use to write code that reacts to user actions such as a mouse click. There are a dozen event handlers, and they all use CamelBack notation. For example, the `onClick()` event is presented in all lowercase letters except for the letter *C*. You must remember to type keywords such as this using the correct capitalization.

TIP

If you are like me, you will never be able to remember the correct spelling of every JavaScript language element. That means you'll be checking Appendixes A and B on the CD a lot. Appendix A provides a list of JavaScript objects, methods, and properties; Appendix B provides a list of JavaScript events. If you are ever in doubt about how to spell any of these types of elements, check these appendixes first. This will save you a lot of time and frustration. You might also want to visit www.netscape.org.

JavaScript is a very easygoing language in that it does not impose a strict set of rules about how you should format your scripts. You can have JavaScript statements begin on one line and end on the next, or you can place multiple statements on a single line by typing a semicolon (;) at the end of each statement. The ; explicitly tells JavaScript where a statement ends. However, packing more than one statement on a single line of code can get ugly if you do it too much.

TIP

Although the ; is not required for any JavaScript statement, it's a good idea to get into the habit of ending all your statements with one. It makes your script easier for the next person to read and work with.

Hiding JavaScript Statements

HTML comments begin with the characters <!-- and end with -->. The browser knows not to display anything in between these sets of characters. You also know that the HTML <SCRIPT> tag is used to embed JavaScript into HTML pages. Both JavaScript and non-JavaScript browsers know not to display the <SCRIPT> tags.

However, non-JavaScript browsers do not know what to make of the statements within the <SCRIPT> tags, so they will display the actual lines of the script. I am sure that this is not what you want your visitors to see. To get around this unsightly mess, enclose all the JavaScript statements after the beginning <SCRIPT> tag and before the ending </SCRIPT> tag within HTML comments as demonstrated in the following example:

```
<HTML>
    <HEAD>    <TITLE>Script 2.1 -Example of Comment Statements</TITLE>
```

```
</HEAD>
<BODY>
  <SCRIPT LANGUAGE="JavaScript" TYPE="Text/JavaScript">
  <!-- Start hiding JavaScript statements
    document.write("Non-JavaScript browsers will not see this
    message.");
  // End hiding JavaScript statements -->
  </SCRIPT>
</BODY>
</HTML>
```

Because browsers are smart enough to not process any HTML that they do not understand, the starting and ending <SCRIPT> tags are ignored by non-JavaScript browsers. At the same time non-JavaScript browsers view everything between the HTML comment tags as one big comment and ignore it, thus hiding all JavaScript statements and preventing any errors.

JavaScript-enabled browsers, on the other hand, recognize the starting and ending <SCRIPT> tags and process them accordingly. These browsers also recognize the opening HTML comment tag and the line beginning with the // as a JavaScript comment and ignore them as well.

As long as you model your scripts after this example, you'll trick old browsers into thinking that your JavaScript statements are just HTML comments, without affecting what JavaScript-aware browsers see.

USE THE <NOSCRIPT> TAG TO TALK TO NON-JAVASCRIPT BROWSERS

Although more than 95 percent of the browsers being used today support JavaScript, there are still many that do not. In addition, both the Netscape and Internet Explorer browsers allow users to turn off JavaScript support. What can you do to make your JavaScript-enhanced pages available to those visitors who want to view them while still making basic information available to visitors who do not have JavaScript-enabled browsers?

One option you can explore is to create both JavaScript and non-JavaScript versions of your HTML pages and to display the appropriate set of pages based on an inspection of the user's browser. I will talk more about this option later today.

A simpler solution is to display an HTML page that provides two links with an instruction to your visitor to click on one link if the browser supports JavaScript and to click on the other if it does not. However, you may be taking a big risk by assuming that all your visitors even know what JavaScript is, and more, that their browser supports it.

A really simple alternative is to use the <NOSCRIPT> tags. Every browser, even those with JavaScript support disabled, will recognize this HTML tag. Its purpose is to display a message for browsers that do not process your JavaScript. JavaScript-enabled browsers will ignore everything within the <NOSCRIPT> tags.

The following example demonstrates how to set up a page that can provide information to browsers regardless of their level of JavaScript support.

```
<HTML>
  <HEAD>
    <TITLE>Script 2.2 - The NOSCRIPT tag</TITLE>
  </HEAD>
  <BODY>
    <SCRIPT LANGUAGE="JavaScript" TYPE="Text/JavaScript">
    <!--Start hiding JavaScript statements
      document.write("Non-JavaScript browsers will not see
      this message but JavaScript-enabled browsers will.");
    // End hiding JavaScript statements -->
    </SCRIPT>
    <NOSCRIPT>
      JavaScript-enabled browsers will not see this message but
      JavaScript handicapped browsers will see it.
    </NOSCRIPT>
  </BODY>
</HTML>
```

Working with Values

JavaScript stores information in *values*. For example, if you were to create a form for your users to fill out, each entry in the form would contain a separate value.

In JavaScript, you can store values in variables and then use the variables throughout your script. A variable's value can change depending on the logic of your script.

Table 2.1 shows the list of the types of values supported by JavaScript.

Declaring Variables

To use a variable in your script, that variable must first be declared. JavaScript gives you two ways of doing this. The first option is to use the `var` keyword as demonstrated in the following example:

```
var first_name = "Bob";
```

This example creates a variable named `first_name` and assigns it the value of `Bob`. Your script would probably contain other variables that also contain last names, phone numbers, and so on.

You can also declare a variable by simply referencing it for the first time as shown in the following example:

```
first_name = "Bob";
```

TABLE 2.1 JAVASCRIPT VALUES	
Value	Description
Boolean	A value that indicates a condition of either true or false
Null	An empty value
Numbers	A numeric value such as 99 or 3.142
Strings	A string of text such as "Welcome" or "Click here to visit ptpmagazine.com"

In this example, JavaScript assigns the value of Bob to a variable named first_name (if the variable exists), thereby changing its value. If the referenced variable does not yet exist, JavaScript will create it and assign to it the new value.

Whether you choose to use the var keyword when creating variables is really just a matter of personal preference. The main benefits of using var are that it can make your scripts easier to read and it lets you declare variables for later use in your scripts without assigning them any starting values.

Creating Variables

I have to go over a few more things relating to variables that I want to mention before we move on. These important aspects of variables include the rules that govern the naming of variables and how to define variable *scope*.

Rules for Variable Names

Keep the following rules in mind when creating variables:

○ Variable names can consist only of uppercase and lowercase letters, the under-score character, and the numbers 0 through 9.

○ JavaScript is case sensitive. If you declare a variable with the name total_count, you must refer to it using the exact same case throughout your script. The variable Total_Count is, to JavaScript, a different variable.

○ Variable names cannot contain spaces.

○ You cannot use any *reserved words* as variable names. Refer to Appendix C on the CD-ROM for a list of JavaScript reserved words.

The following list is not a set of rules but is a set of guidelines you may want to follow when working with JavaScript variables:

○ JavaScript is considered to be a loosely typed language because it does not force you to define variables before using them. However, using the var keyword makes your code easier to understand later.

○ You should create variable names that describe their contents. For example, last_name is a much better variable name than ln. Variable names of only a few characters may be easier to type and may seem quite obvious when you are writing your scripts, but they may not be so obvious to you a year later or to someone else who is trying to read your script.

Defining a Variable's Scope

You can create variables that can be used throughout the HTML page or that can be used only within the constraints of a small section of code known as a *function*. Defining the space in which the variable is effective is known as defining the variable's *scope*. A variable can be either *local* or *global* in scope.

Local Variables

A *local variable* is one that is explicitly declared using the var statement inside a function. A *function* is a collection of JavaScript statements that can be called by another JavaScript statement to perform a specific action.

For example, the following code shows a function called ShowNotice() that displays a message every time it is called. The function contains a local variable named message, which has been set to "Are you sure you want to quit?". Because this variable is local in scope, it cannot be referenced by any other JavaScript statement in the page.

```
function ShowNotice()

{

  var message = "Are you sure you want to quit?";

  window.alert(message);

}
```

You'll learn more about functions in just a few minutes.

 NOTE The window.alert(message) statement in the preceding example is one of three popup dialog boxes that JavaScript can display. I will go over how to use these dialog boxes in greater detail this evening.

Global Variables

A *global variable* is any variable defined outside of a function. Such a variable is global because any JavaScript statement in the page can refer to it. You can create a global variable in several ways:

✪ Creating the variable by referencing it inside a function without first declaring it with the var keyword.

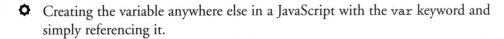

⚙ Creating the variable anywhere else in a JavaScript with the var keyword and simply referencing it.

The following example demonstrates the differences between local and global variable scope. Three variables are created with a global scope. The first is gl_var_msg1 in the head section of the page. The second and third variables are gl_var_msg2 and gl_var_msg3 in the body section of the page. The gl_var_msg2 variable is global in scope even though it is located within a function because it was not created using the var keyword. The lc_var_msg1 variable is local in scope because it is in a function and was created with the var keyword.

```
<HTML>
  <HEAD>
    <TITLE>Script 2.3 - A demonstration of variable scope</TITLE>
    <SCRIPT LANGUAGE="JavaScript" TYPE="Text/JavaScript">
    <!-- Start hiding JavaScript statements
      gl_var_msg1 = "Global variables created in the HEAD section can be
        referenced anywhere in this page.";
      function CreateVariables()
      {
      var lc_var_msg1 = "Local variables created inside a function
      cannot be referenced anywhere else.";
      gl_var_msg2 = "Global variables created inside functions in the HEAD
        section can be referenced anywhere in this page.";
      }
    // End hiding JavaScript statements -->
    </SCRIPT>
  </HEAD>
  <BODY>
    <SCRIPT LANGUAGE="JavaScript" TYPE="Text/JavaScript">
    <!-- Start hiding JavaScript statements
      CreateVariables();
```

```
    gl_var_msg3 = "Global variables created in the BODY section can be
        referenced anywhere in this page.";
    document.write(gl_var_msg1 + "<BR>");
    document.write(gl_var_msg2 + "<BR>");
    document.write(gl_var_msg3 + "<BR>");
    document.write(lc_var_msg + "<BR>");
  // End hiding JavaScript statements -->
  </SCRIPT>
 </BODY>
</HTML>
```

NOTE You may have noticed that I embedded the `<BR>` tag inside the `document.write()` statement. Doing so provides me with one way of controlling line breaks with my JavaScript. To make it work, I placed the `<BR>` tag in parentheses and concatenated it with the rest of the text in the `document.write()` statement using the **+** operator.

TIP You may also have noticed that the JavaScript in the head section contains a function named `CreateVariables()`. This line and the statements following it—all the statements between the left and right braces { }—are part of a function. This function does not execute until it is called by the `CreateVariables()` statement in the body section of the page. Don't worry if this seems a bit confusing; I'll explain functions at the end of the morning. You might want to bookmark this example to come back and look at again after reading the material on functions.

Figure 2.1 shows what happens when the preceding script executes. The four `document.write()` statements attempt to display the value of each variable. However, because `lc_var_msg1` is not global in scope, it is not displayed.

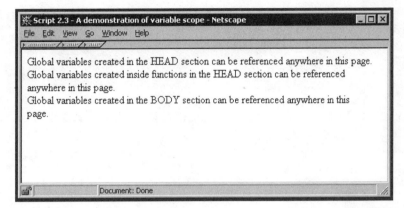

Figure 2.1

Only global variables—or those local in scope to the `document.write()` statements—will appear when the page is displayed.

Inside the figure window:

Script 2.3 - A demonstration of variable scope - Netscape

File   Edit   View   Go   Window   Help

Global variables created in the HEAD section can be referenced anywhere in this page.
Global variables created inside functions in the HEAD section can be referenced anywhere in this page.
Global variables created in the BODY section can be referenced anywhere in this page.

Document: Done

Manipulating Variables

You can alter the value of a variable by simply assigning it a new value as follows:

```
variable_name = 100;
```

JavaScript also provides a number of other operators you can use to affect the value of variables. These are outlined in Table 2.2.

I'll bet you are wondering what's going on with the last four operators in Table 2.2. I will take a quick moment to explain them a little further.

Both x++ and ++x operators increment the value of x by 1. The difference between them is when the update occurs. I can best demonstrate this difference with an example. Suppose that I have a script with two variables, `total_count` and `no_units_sold`. Suppose that `no_units_sold` is equal to 10 and that I add the following line of code somewhere further down in my script:

```
no_units_sold = 10;
total_count = ++no_units_sold;
```

What happens here is that first `no_units_sold` would be incremented by 1 to a value of 11. Then `total_count` would be set to 11.

Now suppose that I rewrote the assignment statement to be the following:

```
total_count = no_units_sold++;
```

TABLE 2.2 JavaScript Operators		
Operator	**Description**	**Example**
x + y	Adds the value of x to the value of y	`total = 2 + 1`
x - y	Subtracts the value of y from x	`total = 2 - 1`
x * y	Multiplies the value of x and y	`total = x * 2`
x / y	Divides the value of x by the value of y	`total = x / 2`
-x	Reverses the sign of x	`count = -count`
x++	Post-increment (Returns x, then increments x by one)	`x = y++`
++x	Pre-increment (Increments x by one, then returns x)	`x = ++y`
x--	Post-decrement (Returns x, then decrements x by one)	`x = y--`
--x	Pre-decrement (Decrements x by one, then returns x)	`x = --y`

What happens here is totally different than in the preceding example. This time, `total_count` is first set to the value of `no_units_sold`, which is 10. Then the value of `no_units_sold` is incremented by 1 to 11.

The `--x` and `x--` operators work the same way, only they decrease the value of the variables by 1.

Assigning Values

As I have already alluded to, you assign values to variables using an *assignment operator*. For example, the following statement assigns a value of 44 to a variable named `total_count`:

```
total_count = 44
```

In this example, the assignment operator is the old-fashioned equal sign. JavaScript provides many ways to assign values to a variable, as outlined in Table 2.3.

TABLE 2.3 ASSIGNMENT OPERATORS (ASSUME THAT Y = 5)

Operator	Description	Examples	Result
=	Sets a variable value equal to some value	x = y + 1	6
+=	Shorthand for writing x = x + y	x += y	11
-=	Shorthand for writing x = x - y	x -= y	6
*=	Shorthand for writing x = x * y	x *= y	30
/=	Shorthand for writing x = x / y	x /= y	6

The following example demonstrates the use of each of these operators. In this example, the script establishes two variables, x and y, and assigns a value of 10 to x and 5 to y. The next statements then test the five examples listed in Table 2.3 to make sure that they are accurate. The first two of these statements set x = y + 1 and then use the document.write() statement to display the results. The remaining statements duplicate this methodology changing only the mathematical formula each time. Figure 2.2 shows the results of running this script.

```
<HTML>
  <HEAD>
    <TITLE>Script 2.4 - A demonstration of JavaScript operators</TITLE>
  </HEAD>
  <BODY>
    <SCRIPT LANGUAGE="JavaScript" TYPE="Text/JavaScript">
    <!-- Start hiding JavaScript statements
      x = 10;
      y = 5;
      x= y + 1;
      document.write("x = y + 1 ...Result = " + x);
```

```
        x += y;

        document.write("<BR>x += y ...Result = " + x);

        x -= y;

        document.write("<BR>x -= y ...Result = " + x);

        x *= y;

        document.write("<BR>x *= y ...Result = " + x);

        x /= y;

        document.write("<BR>x /= y ...Result = " + x);

    // End hiding JavaScript statements -->

    </SCRIPT>

  </BODY>

</HTML>
```

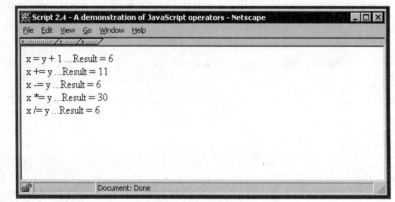

Figure 2.2

A demonstration of the use of JavaScript operators.

Comparing Values

One of the things you will find yourself doing in your scripts is comparing the values of variables. For example, you might take one action if a variable has a value less than 10 and a different action when the variable is greater than 10. Table 2.4 provides a list of JavaScript comparison operators you can use in your JavaScripts.

The following example demonstrates the use of the greater-than operator. In this example, the two variables x and y are initialized with values of 12 and 5 respectively. Next, the script tests to see whether x is greater than 10. This condition is true, so the

TABLE 2.4 JAVASCRIPT COMPARISON OPERATORS

Operator	Description	Example	Result
==	Equal to	x == y	True if both x and y are the same
!==	Not equal to	x !== y	True if x and y are not the same
>	Greater than	x > y	True if x is greater than y
<	Less than	x < y	True if x is less than y
>	Greater than or equal to	x >= y	True if x is greater than or equal to y
<	Less than or equal to	x <= y	True if x is less than or equal to y
!x	False	!x	True if x is false
&&	Both true	x && y	True if x and y are both true
||	Either true	x || y	True if either x or y is true

script writes a message to the browser window. Then the script tests the value of y to see whether it is greater than 10. This test is false, so no action is taken.

```
<HTML>
  <HEAD>
    <TITLE>Script 2.5 - Example of a Value Comparison</TITLE>
  </HEAD>
<BODY>
    <SCRIPT LANGUAGE="JavaScript" TYPE="Text/JavaScript">
    <!-- Start hiding JavaScript statements
      x = 12;
      y = 5;
      if (x > 10)
```

```
        {
           document.write("x is greater than 10!");
        }
        if (y > 10)
        {
           document.write("y is greater than 10!");
        }
     // End hiding JavaScript statements -->
     </SCRIPT>
   </BODY>
</HTML>
```

Writing Text with Strings

We have spent a lot of time already this morning learning about how to work with JavaScript values. One object in particular, the string, you will find yourself using over and over again in your JavaScripts. I thought I'd spend a little time going over the String object now, even though the lesson on JavaScript objects isn't until this afternoon. Consider this a sneak preview.

A string object is made up of a collection of text characters. You create a string with the new keyword as shown in the following example:

```
MyString = new String("This is an example of a text string.");
```

This statement creates a string called MyString and assigns text to it. The new keyword is used to create JavaScript objects. However, you are not required to use it. You can also create a string object by simply referring to it as in the following example:

```
MyString = "This is an example of a text string.";
```

You can change a string value by simply assigning it a new value. The following example changes the value of the MyString string:

```
MyString = "This is a second example of a text string.";
```

Because a string is a JavaScript object, it has properties. In the case of the string object, there is just one property, its length. You can refer to an object's property by typing the name of the object, followed by a period and the name of the property. In the case of the `MyString` object's length property, you'd use `MyString.length`. The `length` property contains the number of characters in the string. The following example demonstrates how to display the value of this property, which is 40.

```
document.write("The length of MyString is " + MyString.length);
```

String Methods

Although the `String` object has only one property, it has many methods. A *method* is an action that can be taken against the object. For example, you can use the `String` object's `bold()` method to display the string in bold as shown in this example:

```
document.write(MyString.bold());
```

When referencing an object's methods, the correct syntax to use is the name of the object, a period, the name of the method, and the left and right parenthesis. In this example, the parenthesis did not contain anything. Some methods allow you to pass *arguments* to the method to further define its actions.

You can display the string in all uppercase characters using the `toUppercase()` method:

```
document.write(MyString.toUpperCase());
```

Similarly, there is a `toLowerCase()` method. Other methods allow you to affect the string's font color and font size or to display it in italic, blinking, or strikethrough text. A particularly useful method is `substring()`. This method allows you to extract a portion of a string's text.

For example, you might create a string that contains people's names and addresses. You could reserve the first 15 character positions of the string for the person's name, the next 20 characters for his or her street address, and the last 17 characters for the city, state, and ZIP code information. Following are three examples of such strings:

```
Cust1Info = "Bobby B Jones   9995 Park Place Ct   Richmond VA 23232   ";

Cust2Info = "Sue K Miller    1112 Rockford Lane   Richmond VA 23232   ";

Cust3Info = "Bobby B Jones   9995 Richland Drive Richmond VA 23223   ";
```

Using the `substring()` method, you can extract just the name portion of any string as shown in the following example:

```
<HTML>
  <HEAD>
    <TITLE>Script 2.6 - Substring Method Example</TITLE>
  </HEAD>
  <BODY>
    <SCRIPT LANGUAGE="JavaScript" TYPE="Text/JavaScript">
    <!-- Start hiding JavaScript statements
     Cust1Info = "Bobby B Jones  9995 Park Place Ct  Richmond VA
     23232";
     Cust2Info = "Sue K Miller    1112 Rockford Lane  Richmond VA
     23232";
     Cust3Info = "Bobby B Jones  9995 Richland Drive Richmond VA
     23223";
     document.write(Cust1Info.substring(0,14),"<BR>");
     document.write(Cust2Info.substring(0,14),"<BR>");
     document.write(Cust3Info.substring(0,14),"<BR>");
    // End hiding JavaScript statements -->
    </SCRIPT>
  </BODY>
</HTML>
```

As you can see, the `document.write(Cust1Info.substring(0,14),"<BR>");` statement copies the contents of the first 15 characters in the string, starting with character 0 and ending with character 14, and writes those characters to the browser window. The script then repeats this logic for the remaining string objects. Figure 2.3 shows the result of loading this page.

 NOTE For a complete list of string methods, refer to the CD's Appendix A, "A Brief JavaScript Object Reference."

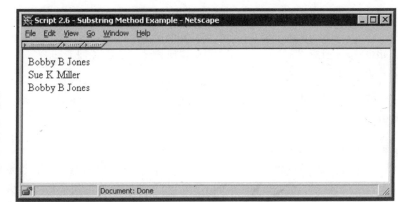

Figure 2.3

A demonstration of how to extract portions of a string using the `substring()` method.

Concatenation

You can do many cool things with strings. For example, you can concatenate two or more of them together using the + operator as shown in the following example:

```
<HTML>

  <HEAD>

    <TITLE>Script 2.7 - Example of String Concatenation</TITLE>

  </HEAD>

  <BODY>

    <SCRIPT LANGUAGE="JavaScript" TYPE="Text/JavaScript">

    <!-- Start hiding JavaScript statements

       String1 = "Once upon a time, ";

       String2 = "there was a little house on a hill.";

       String3 = String1 + String2;

       document.write(String3);

    // End hiding JavaScript statements -->

    </SCRIPT>

  </BODY>

</HTML>
```

The script first establishes two strings, String1 and String2, and assigns them some text. Then, it concatenates these two strings to create a new object named String3. Finally, the script displays the results in the browser window.

Notice that an extra space was added to the end of the String1 object so that when it was concatenated with String2, the resulting String3 would read better as shown in Figure 2.4.

NOTE In many computer languages the programmer must specify the type of data that a variable will contain. This is known as the variable's *data type*. JavaScript supports a range of data types, including numeric, Boolean, and string values. One nice thing about JavaScript is that it does not require you to specify a data type. In fact, it does not even allow it. Based on the context within which a value is created, JavaScript knows what type of value it is. For example, JavaScript knows the difference between a string and a number. If you use the + sign with two numeric variables, JavaScript automatically adds them. If you use the + sign with two strings, JavaScript automatically concatenates them. If you use the + sign with a numeric value and a string, JavaScript first converts the numeric value to a string and then concatenates the strings together.

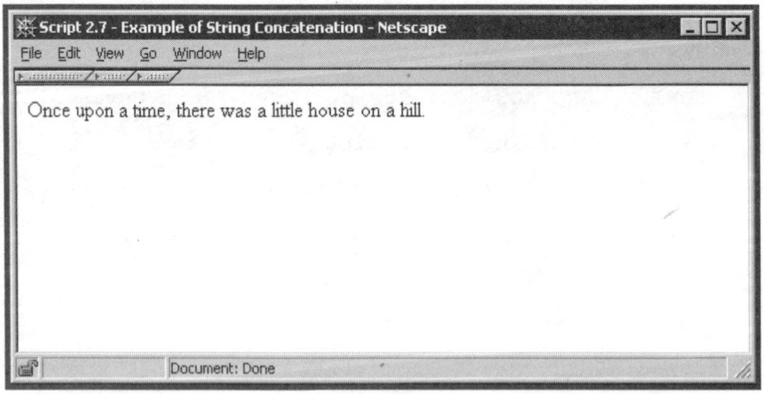

Figure 2.4

This example demonstrates how JavaScript concatenation allows you to seamlessly combine String objects.

```
Script 2.7 - Example of String Concatenation - Netscape
File   Edit   View   Go   Window   Help

Once upon a time, there was a little house on a hill.

                                                     Document: Done
```

The Math Object

Having introduced you to the String object, it seems only proper that I talk about the Math object as well. This object is automatically created in every JavaScript, so you do not have to create an instance of it as you do with `String` objects. You can simply refer to the `Math` object when you need to. Like other objects, the `Math` object has properties and methods associated with it.

The `Math` object's properties contain mathematical constants. For example, the `Math` property `PI` stores the value of pi. The `Math` object's methods contain built-in mathematical functions. For example, there are methods that round numbers up and down, that generate random numbers, and that return the absolute value of a number.

The following example demonstrates how to use several of the `Math` object's properties and methods:

```
<HTML>
  <HEAD>
    <TITLE>Script 2.8 - Example of working with the Math object</TITLE>
  </HEAD>
  <BODY>
    <SCRIPT LANGUAGE="JavaScript" TYPE="Text/JavaScript">
    <!-- Start hiding JavaScript statements
      //Generate a random number between 0 and 1
      document.write("<B>Random number between 0 - 1 = </B>",
            Math.random(), "<BR>");
      //Generate a random number between 0 and 10
      document.write("<B>Random number between 1 - 10 = </B>",
            Math.random() * 10, "<BR>");
      //Rounding a number to the nearest whole number
      document.write("<B>Rounding 6.777 = </B>", Math.round(6.777),
      "<BR>");
      //Getting the value of PI
      document.write("<B>Value of PI = </B>", Math.PI, "<BR>");
      //Getting the absolute value of a number
      document.write("<B>Absolute value of -55 = </B>",
      Math.abs(-55));
```

```
    // End hiding JavaScript statements -->

    </SCRIPT>

  </BODY>

</HTML>
```

NOTE

You may have noticed that I slipped in the `<B>` and `</B>` HTML tags into my JavaScripts to add bold formatting to my text. The key when using HTML tags is to keep them within the quotation marks. I could just as easily have inserted any of the other HTML tags within my script using the same technique.

The first three `document.write()` statements include executions of the `Math` object's `random()` and `round()` methods. The fourth `document.write()` statement does not use a `Math` method. Instead, it accesses the `Math PI` property as evidenced by the lack of parenthesis. The last of the `document.write()` statements demonstrates the `Math abs()` method, which returns the absolute value of any given number. Figure 2.5 shows the results of loading this page.

NOTE

For a complete listing of `Math` properties and methods, refer to Appendix A, "A Brief JavaScript Object Reference."

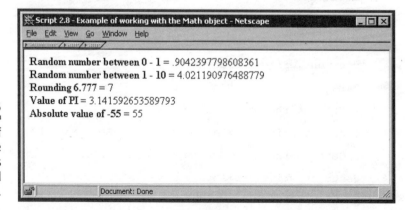

Figure 2.5

An example of how to access the `Math` object's properties and methods.

Take a Break

Okay, let's take a break. We have covered quite a bit of material since breakfast. Why don't you give yourself a few minutes to let it sink in. When you return, you will wrap up the morning by reviewing examples of the programming statements that make up the JavaScript language. A solid understanding of these statements will allow you to begin writing more powerful scripts.

JavaScript Statements

JavaScripts consist of a series of statements. These *statements* are the programming instructions, or logic, that you write to tell the browser what you want to do. JavaScript statements can be organized into the following categories:

- Conditional statements
- Comments
- Variable declaration and assignment statements
- Looping statements
- Object manipulation statements

Using Conditional Statements to Alter Script Flow

Conditional statements allow you to test for various conditions and take action based on the results of the test. Specifically, conditional statements execute when the tested condition proves to be true. Conditional statements include the `if`, `if...else`, and `switch` statements.

The if Statement

The `if` statement checks whether a logical condition is `true`; if it is, it then executes one or more statements. The basic syntax of the `if` statements is shown here:

```
if (condition)
   statement
```

For example, the following pair of statements shows a simple `if` statement. The first line sets up a conditional test. If the test proves `true` (for example, if the `counter` variable is currently less than 10), the statement immediately following is executed. In this example, the current value of the variable counter is then incremented by 1.

```
if (counter < 10)
  counter++;
```

There will be times when executing a single statement is just not enough. In this case, you can write your if statement using the following format:

```
if (counter > 10) {
 counter++;
 window.alert("This is a test");
}
```

The preceding example shows an if statement where the condition is followed immediately by the { sign and terminated with the } sign. In between the braces can be any number of JavaScript statements.

The following sample script uses the two types of if statements you just looked at plus a third variation:

```
<HTML>
  <HEAD>
    <TITLE>Script 2.9 - Demonstration of if statements</TITLE>
  </HEAD>
  <BODY>
    <SCRIPT LANGUAGE="JavaScript" TYPE="Text/JavaScript">
    <!-- Start hiding JavaScript statements
      account_status = open;  //assume all accounts are open by default
      //Prompt the user for a account name
      account_name = window.prompt("Enter your account name:");
      //Test whether the supplied account name equals Morganstern
      if (account_name == "Morganstern")
        document.write("The account number for this account is
        12321. <BR>");
      //Set account_status equal to warning if the account name
```

```
    //equals Davidson
    if (account_name == "Davidson") {
      document.write("The account number for this account is
      88844. <BR>");
      account_status = "warning";
    }
    //Display one of two messages based on the value of
    //account_status
    if (account_status != "warning") {
      document.write("You may accept new orders from this
      customer.");
    }
    else {
      document.write("Do not accept new orders for this account.");
    }
  // End hiding JavaScript statements -->
  </SCRIPT>
 </BODY>
</HTML>
```

This example starts by displaying a prompt dialog box asking the user to input the name of a business account using the window.prompt() method. Next, it executes three if statements, each of which compares the user's input against three separate criteria. Any conditional test that proves true results in some actions. As you can see, the if statement allows you to create different logical flows in your scripts based on user input.

The third if statement adds a new twist by adding an else statement. In the event that the if statement's conditional test proves true, the statements following the if statement are executed, and the else statement is skipped. But if the if statement proves false, the logic in the else statement is processed. The else statement allows you to provide alternative actions for any test.

Figures 2.6 and 2.7 show the logical flow of the script when the user inputs the account name of Morganstern.

Figure 2.6

The `window.` `prompt()` method allows you to create a dialog box that gathers user input interactively.

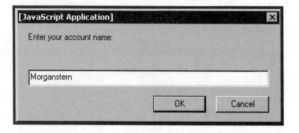

Figure 2.7

Here are the results of what happens when the user types in a valid business account name.

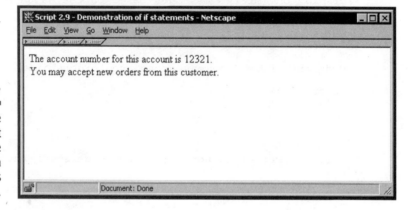

Before I move on, there is one final variation of the `if` statement I want to mention. This is the *nested* `if` *statement*. A nested `if` statement is a series of two or more `if` statements nested within one another. The following example shows a nested `if` that is two `if` statements deep. The second `if` statement is executed only if the first `if` statement proves `true`:

```
if (account_status != "warning") {

  if (account_number > 10000) {

    document.write("You may accept new orders from this customer.");

  }

  else {

    document.write("Invalid account number. Notify bank security.");

  }

}

else

  document.write("This Account has been marked with a warning!");

}
```

The switch Statement

The switch statement evaluates a series of conditional tests or cases and executes additional statements based on whether the case proves true. The syntax of the switch statement is shown here:

```
switch (expression) {
  case label:
    statements;
  break;

    .

    .

    .

  case label:
    statements;
  break;
  default:
   statements;
}
```

The switch statement compares the result of the expression against the label for each case. The statements for the first case that proves true are executed. If no case proves true, the statements associated with the default statement are executed if the optional default statement was included.

The break statement at the end of each case is optional. Its purpose is to tell JavaScript to exit the switch statement as soon as the statements in the first matching case are executed and to proceed with the next JavaScript statement following the switch statement. If you remove the optional break statements, the script will continue to examine each case and execute the statements of any case that matches the expression.

The following example shows a variation of the example used to explain the if statement. In this example, the user is prompted to type the name of a business account into a prompt dialog box. The expression in the switch statement is the variable that contains the account name provided by the user. Starting with the first case statement,

JavaScript compares the account_name to the case label; if the condition proves true (that is, if there is a match), the statements for that case are executed and the break at the end of the case tells JavaScript to jump to the first statement after the switch statement, which in this case happens to be an if statement. If none of the case statements proves true, the statement associated with the default statement executes, stating that the account name the user typed is not registered. Figures 2.8 and 2.9 show what this example looks like when it's executed.

```html
<HTML>
  <HEAD>
    <TITLE>Script 2.10 - Demonstration of the switch statement</TITLE>
  </HEAD>
  <BODY>
    <SCRIPT LANGUAGE="JavaScript" TYPE="Text/JavaScript">
    <!-- Start hiding JavaScript statements
      account_name = window.prompt("Enter your account name:");
      switch (account_name) {
        case "Morganstern":
          document.write("The account number for this account is
          12321.");
          account_status = "approved";
          break;
        case "Davidson":
          document.write("The account number for this account is
          88844.");
          account_status = "warning";
          break;
        default:
          document.write("The account is not registered in this
          system.");
          account_status = "error";
      }
```

```
    if (account_status == "warning") {

        document.write(account_status);

        window.alert("Contact the on-duty supervisor");

    }
// End hiding JavaScript statements -->

</SCRIPT>

</BODY>

</HTML>
```

Figure 2.8

The user is prompted to enter an account name; in this example, the user types **Paterson**.

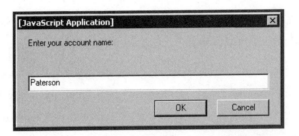

Figure 2.9

The script flags **Paterson** as an invalid account name.

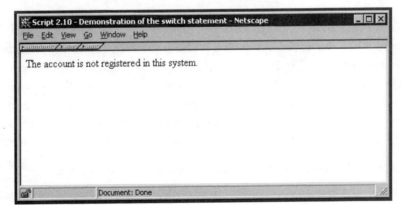

Adding Comments for Clarity

Comment statements have no effect on the logical performance of the script but make the script easier to understand when it is read. Comments have two very important roles in JavaScript. The first is to allow you to document your script by adding remarks that explain why you wrote the script the way you did. The second role is to hide JavaScript code from older non-JavaScript browsers.

You can place a comment in your JavaScripts in either of two ways. To place a single comment line within the body of your script, type `//` followed by your comment as shown here:

```
//This is a JavaScript comment
```

As the following example shows, you can also add a comment at the end of a JavaScript statement using this notation:

```
document.write("Hello World");   //Write a message to the current Window
```

Multiple-line comments are created by typing `/*` followed by the comment and then ending with `*/` as demonstrated here:

```
/* This is an example of a multiple line JavaScript comment.
Typically, you use comments to document sections of your
script in order to explain its logic. This make it easier
for other people to follow behind you. */
```

Comments are not always for other people; they are for you as well. You will be very happy that you added comments if you find that you have to modify scripts that you wrote years ago. For example, you might have a large script, several pages long, that allows customers to fill in a form and place orders for some type of product. If the tax rate changes, you'll have to find the portion of the script that does this calculation and change it. If you had added a comment that identifies the line of code where the tax calculation is performed, it sure would make it easier to modify the script:

```
//Compute the amount of tax to apply to the order
total_order = total_order + (total_order * .05);
```

The following script provides an example of how you might document your own JavaScripts:

```
<HTML>
  <HEAD>
    <TITLE>Script 2.11 - Comment Example</TITLE>
```

```
  </HEAD>
  <BODY>
    <SCRIPT LANGUAGE="JavaScript" TYPE="Text/JavaScript">
    <!-- Start hiding JavaScript statements
      total_order = 100;
      //Compute the amount of tax to apply to the order
      total_order = total_order + (total_order * .05);   //Tax rate = 5%
      /*The following statement simply demonstrates the use of
    the document statement to write a message on the current
    browser window.*/
      document.write(total_order);
    // End hiding JavaScript statements -->
    </SCRIPT>
  </BODY>
</HTML>
```

Declaring and Assigning Data to Variables

We already examined variable declaration and assignment statements at the beginning of this session. The var statement allows you to create new variables, but it is not required. Most assignments are performed using the equal sign (=), but you can use any of the assignment operators listed in Table 2.3.

Optimizing Code with Looping Logic

A *loop* is a series of statements that repeatedly execute, allowing you to perform iterative operations within your script. JavaScript statements that support looping logic include the for, while, do...while, label, break, and continue statements. The nice thing about loops is that they allow you to write just a few lines of code and to reuse them repeatedly, making your scripts easier to write and maintain.

The for Statement

The for statement executes until a condition becomes false and uses a variable to control the number of times the loop executes. The for loop is comprised of three parts: a starting expression, a test condition, and an increment statement. The syntax of the for statement is shown here:

```
for (expression; condition; increment) {

  statements

}
```

For example, the statement for (i=0; i<5;i++) establishes a for loop that has an initial count of 0, with the condition that the count is less than 5, and that the count will then increment by 1. All the statements within the starting and ending brackets are executed with each execution of the for loop.

The following example shows how the for loop can be used to loop five times. When the script begins to execute, the value of i is 0. Each time the loop executes, the value of i is incremented by 1 (in the i++ clause). Although this example displays just five lines of text that show the value of i as it grows, I think you can see that it can be easily modified to do just about anything—such as repeatedly prompting the user for input and iteratively processing that input.

```
<HTML>

  <HEAD>

    <TITLE>Script 2.12 - Demonstration of a for loop</TITLE>

  </HEAD>

  <BODY>

    <SCRIPT LANGUAGE="JavaScript" TYPE="Text/JavaScript">

    <!-- Start hiding JavaScript statements

      for (i=0; i<5; i++) {

        document.write("Watch as the variable grows with each

              execution: ",i,"<BR>");

      }

    // End hiding JavaScript statements -->

    </SCRIPT>

  </BODY>

</HTML>
```

Figure 2.10 shows the result of loading the previous example. If you run this script yourself, you should take note just how quickly JavaScript can execute the script.

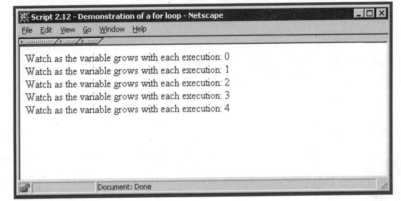

Figure 2.10

An example of using a `for` loop to perform iterative processes.

The while Statement

The `while` statement executes a loop as long as a condition is `true`. The syntax of the `while` statement is shown here:

```
while (condition) {

  statements

}
```

For example, you might write a `while` loop that looks like this:

```
while (counter > 0) {

  counter++;

  document.write("counter = ", counter , "<BR>");

}
```

In this example, the loop processes as long as the value of `counter` is greater than 0. As soon as `counter` becomes 0 or less, the loop terminates. To control the termination of the loop, I include the variable `counter` and decrement it each time through the loop. When working with `while` loops, be sure that you set them up so that they will properly break out of the loop; otherwise, they will run forever, leaving the user no option other than to close the page or perhaps even the browser.

Unlike the for loop in the preceding section, the while loop does not depend on updating a controlling variable to manage loop execution. This is because the while loop is designed to iterate for as long as the tested condition remains true.

The following example shows how you can use a while loop to count backward to 0. Figure 2.11 shows the results of loading the page.

```html
<HTML>
  <HEAD>
    <TITLE>Script 2.13 - Demonstration of the while statement</TITLE>
  </HEAD>
  <BODY>
    <SCRIPT LANGUAGE="JavaScript" TYPE="Text/JavaScript">
    <!-- Start hiding JavaScript statements
      counter = 10;
      document.write("<B>Watch me count backwards!</B><BR>");
      while (counter > 0) {
        counter--;
        document.write("counter = ", counter , "<BR>");
      }
    // End hiding JavaScript statements -->
    </SCRIPT>
  </BODY>
</HTML>
```

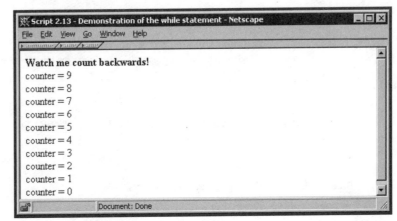

Figure 2.11

An example of looping backward using a `while` loop.

The do...while Statement

The `do...while` statement executes a loop until a condition becomes `false`. The syntax of the `do...while` statement is shown here:

```
do {
  statements
} while (condition)
```

The difference between the `do...while` loop and the `while` loop is that the `do...while` loop executes at least once. This is because the condition is checked at the *end* of the first execution instead at the beginning of it. However, you can use either style to achieve the same end as demonstrated in the next example.

For example, you might write a script that looks like the following. The results of running this script are exactly the same as those displayed in Figure 2.11.

```
<HTML>
  <HEAD>
    <TITLE>Script 2.14 - Demonstration of the do...while statement
    </TITLE>
  </HEAD>
<BODY>
    <SCRIPT LANGUAGE="JavaScript" TYPE="Text/JavaScript">
```

```
<!-- Start hiding JavaScript statements
  counter = 10;
  document.write("<B>Watch me count backwards!</B><BR>");
  do {
    counter--;
    document.write("counter = ", counter , "<BR>");
  }
  while (counter > 0)
// End hiding JavaScript statements -->
</SCRIPT>
</BODY>
</HTML>
```

. . . .

NOTE   You may have noticed my used of commas in the `document.write` statement in the preceding example. In this context commas are used to separate a list of arguments used in the `document.write` statement. For example, in `document.write("counter = ", counter , "<BR>");`, three arguments are passed. The first argument is a text message surrounded by double quotes, the second argument is a variable named `counter` whose value will be displayed when the statement is executed, and the final argument is an HTML line break tag.

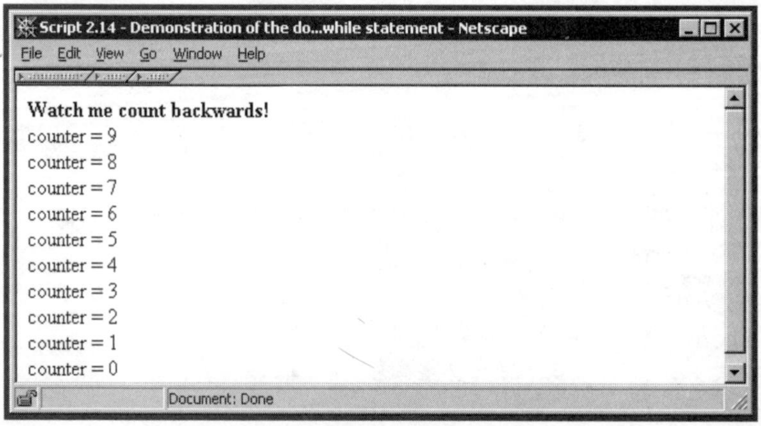

. . . .

Figure 2.12

An example of using a `do...while` loop.

The label Statement

The label statement lets you specify a reference point in your script. Typically, the label statement is associated with loops. A label statement can be referenced by the break and continue statements. The syntax of the label statement is shown here:

```
label:
  statements
```

In the following example, I have created a label called counter_loop. When the script executes the first time, the browser ignores the label statement. Within the while loop, I set up a test that checks to see whether the value of counter is equal to 5. If it is, the script executes the continue statement that tells the browser to skip the rest of the statements in the while statement and continue with the next execution of the loop.

```
<HTML>
  <HEAD>
    <TITLE>Script 2.15 - Demonstration of the label statement</TITLE>
  </HEAD>
  <BODY>
    <SCRIPT LANGUAGE="JavaScript" TYPE="Text/JavaScript">
    <!-- Start hiding JavaScript statements
      counter = 10;
      document.write("<B>Watch me count backwards!</B><BR>");
      counter_loop:
      while (counter > 0) {
        counter--;
        if (counter == 5 ) continue counter_loop;
        document.write("counter = ", counter , "<BR>");
      }
    // End hiding JavaScript statements -->
    </SCRIPT>
  </BODY>
</HTML>
```

When you load this script, you will see that the continue statement has the effect of skipping the writing of the fifth statement (see Figure 2.12).

The break Statement

The break statement lets you terminate a label, switch, or loop. The browser then begins processing the first statement following the label, switch, or loop statement that was broken out of.

The following example shows how the break statement can be used to terminate a while loop when a given condition is met. In this case, the break statement terminates the loop as soon as the value of counter equals 5. Because there are no other statements following the while loop, script execution stops when it meets the break statement. Figure 2.13 shows the results of loading this page.

```
<HTML>
  <HEAD>
    <TITLE>Script 2.16 - Demonstration of the break statement</TITLE>
  </HEAD>
  <BODY>
    <SCRIPT LANGUAGE="JavaScript" TYPE="Text/JavaScript">
    <!-- Start hiding JavaScript statements
      counter = 10;
      document.write("<B>Watch me count backwards!</B><BR>");
      counter_loop:
      while (counter > 0) {
        counter--;
        document.write("counter = ", counter , "<BR>");
        if (counter == 5 ) break;
      }
    // End hiding JavaScript statements -->
    </SCRIPT>
  </BODY>
</HTML>
```

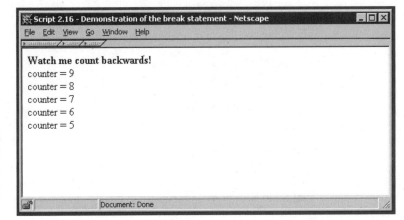

Figure 2.13

A demonstration of how the break statement can be used to terminate a loop at any time.

The continue Statement

The continue statement is similar to the break statement. However, instead of terminating the *execution* of the loop, it merely terminates the *current iteration* of the loop.

The following example demonstrates how the continue statement can be used to terminate a given iteration of a loop. In this example, the loop examines four different cases as part of a switch statement. The result is that the iteration of the loop when counter equals 8, 6, 4, or 2 is skipped, but processing of the loop does not terminate as would be the case when using break statements. Instead, the loop simply continues with the next iteration.

```
<HTML>
  <HEAD>
    <TITLE>Script 2.17 - Demonstration of the continue statement
    </TITLE>
  </HEAD>
  <BODY>
    <SCRIPT LANGUAGE="JavaScript" TYPE="Text/JavaScript">
    <!-- Start hiding JavaScript statements
      counter = 10;
      document.write("<B>Watch me count backwards!</B><BR>");
      counter_loop:
```

```
            while (counter > 0) {
              counter--;
              switch (counter) {
                case 8:
                  continue counter_loop;
                case 6:
                  continue counter_loop;
                case 4:
                  continue counter_loop;
                case 2:
                  continue counter_loop;
              }
              document.write("counter = ", counter , "<BR>");
            }
        // End hiding JavaScript statements -->
        </SCRIPT>
      </BODY>
    </HTML>
```

As Figure 2.14 shows, the continue statement, like the break statement, allows a great
deal of control over loop execution.

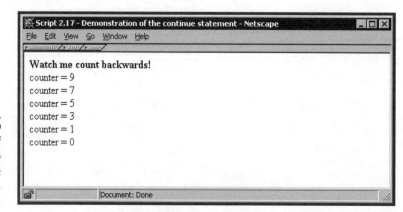

Figure 2.14

An example of
skipping a loop
iteration using the
continue
statement.

Manipulating Objects

JavaScript allows you to create scripts that work with objects. You can think of an object as being similar to variables except that it can contain multiple values known as its properties. Objects also can contain functions, which are collections of JavaScript statements that are designed to work with the object's data. Examples of objects include browser windows and form elements. Detailed information about objects is provided in this afternoon's session.

Object manipulation statements help you to work with properties that belong to a specified object. These statements include the `for...in` and `with` statements. The `for...in` statement allows you to access all the properties for a specified object while the `with` statement provides easy access to specific object properties and methods.

The for...in Statement

The `for...in` statement is used to iterate through all the properties belonging to a specified object. The syntax of the `for...in` statement is shown here:

```
for (variable in object) {

  statements

}
```

This statement works by creating a variable that is used to iterate through all of an object's properties. The following example shows how to loop through all the properties in the screen object. The screen object contains information about the user's screen including such things as screen height, width, and color depth.

```
<HTML>
  <HEAD>
    <TITLE>Script 2.18 - Demonstration of the for…in statement</TITLE>
  </HEAD>
  <BODY>
    <SCRIPT LANGUAGE="JavaScript" TYPE="Text/JavaScript">
    <!-- Start hiding JavaScript statements
      for (i in screen) {
```

```
              document.write(i,"<BR>");

        }
    // End hiding JavaScript statements -->
    </SCRIPT>
  </BODY>
</HTML>
```

Figure 2.15 shows the result of loading the preceding page. By modifying this example, you can easily view all the properties for any object. However, I'd recommend that you save yourself the trouble of modifying this example and reference Appendix A to get information about the various properties of any object.

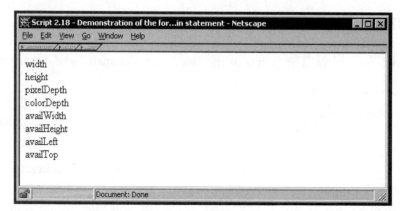

Figure 2.15

Using the for...in statement to loop through the screen object's properties.

The with Statement

The with statement is a convenient way of saving a few keystrokes when writing your JavaScripts. It allows you to set a default object for a group of statements. The syntax of the with statement is shown here:

```
with (object) {
   statements
}
```

The following example shows how you can use the with statement to set the document object as the default object and then apply all the statements contained within the opening and closing braces to that object. As you can see, by using this shortcut statement, I was able to type `write()` in place of `document.write()`. Although this did not save me much work in this example, it certainly would have if I needed to work a lot with a given object.

```html
<HTML>
  <HEAD>
    <TITLE>Script 2.19 - Demonstration of the with statement</TITLE>
  </HEAD>
  <BODY>
    <SCRIPT LANGUAGE="JavaScript" TYPE="Text/JavaScript">
    <!-- Start hiding JavaScript statements
      with (document) {
        write("The with statement saved me a few keystrokes. <BR>");
        write("Its use is purely discretionary!");
      }
    // End hiding JavaScript statements -->
    </SCRIPT>
  </BODY>
</HTML>
```

As Figure 2.16 shows, the results are the same as if I had written out the `document.write()` statement the long way.

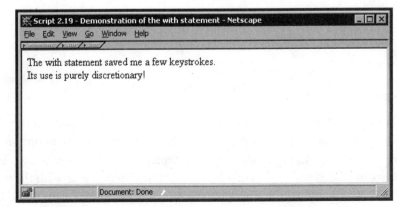

Figure 2.16

An example of taking advantage of the `with` statement to save keystrokes when writing JavaScripts.

Streamlining Your JavaScripts with Functions

A *function* is a collection of statements that perform a given task. Most functions are defined in the head section of the HTML page. Putting your functions in the head section is a good idea for two reasons: The first is that you'll always know where your functions are because they're in a common location. The second reason is that the head section always executes first, ensuring that functions are available when needed later in the script.

NOTE You may be wondering what the difference is between a function and a method. The answer is not much. Methods are simply functions that have been predefined. Methods are associated with specific objects, meaning that each object provides its own collection of methods that you can call from within your scripts.

TIP Make sure that you always place your functions in the head section of your Web pages. This helps to ensure that the browser will load them before your JavaScript statements that follow call them. If a JavaScript statement attempts to call a function before the browser has loaded it, an error will occur because the function is technically still undefined.

Defining a Function

The first step in working with a function is to define it. The syntax for a function is shown here:

```
function FunctionName (p1, p2,....pn) {

  statements

return

}
```

The `function` statement defines a new function with the name you specify. The function's name is followed by a pair of parentheses that may contain a list of optional arguments that the function can use as input. Commas separate multiple arguments. All function statements are placed within the curly braces { }. The function ends with the `return` statement, which allows optional information to be returned to the statement that called the function.

For example, the following few lines of code show a function named SayHello() that accepts a single argument, a person's name. It then uses the name argument to display a welcome message with the user's name. The return statement returns control of the script back to the JavaScript statement that called the function in the first place.

```
function SayHello(visitor_name) {
  window.alert("Hello and welcome, " + visitor_name);
return
}
```

Defining a function does not cause it to execute. For the function to do anything, it must be called by another JavaScript statement. The nice thing about functions is that you can call them over and over again as needed from any place in the page.

Calling Functions

Now that you know what a function is and how to define one, the question remains: How do you call it? The calling statement can take either of two forms. The first form calls the function but does not accept any returned results from the function. The following two function calls demonstrate this form of call. The first example calls a function named SayHello() without passing any arguments. The second example calls a function named SayGoodbye() and passes a single argument. When the function finishes executing, control is returned to the statement immediately following the function call.

```
SayHello();
SayGoodbye("Bob");
```

 NOTE It's up to you to make sure that the function is capable of handling the number of arguments that are passed to it.

Alternatively, you can make a call to a function in the form of an *expression*. This allows the function to return a value to the calling statement. For example, the following statement calls a function named GetUserName() and stores the result returned by the function in a String Object called UserName.

```
UserName = GetUserName();
```

The following example shows a function named SayHello() in the head section of the HTML page. It is executed by a SayHello() statement in the body section of the page and receives a single argument called name. The name argument is a variable established by the statement that precedes the function call. The function takes the name argument and uses it to display a dialog message to the user that includes the user's name. The script pauses until the user clicks on OK, at which time the function terminates and returns control to the statement that immediately follows the function call in the body section.

```html
<HTML>

  <HEAD>

    <TITLE>Script 2.20 - A simple function</TITLE>

    <SCRIPT LANGUAGE="JavaScript" TYPE="Text/JavaScript">

    <!-- Start hiding JavaScript statements

      function SayHello(visitor_name)

      {

        window.alert("Hello and welcome, " + visitor_name);

      }

    // End hiding JavaScript statements -->

    </SCRIPT>

  </HEAD>

  <BODY>

    <SCRIPT LANGUAGE="JavaScript" TYPE="Text/JavaScript">

    <!-- Start hiding JavaScript statements

      name = window.prompt("What is your name?","");

      SayHello(name);

    // End hiding JavaScript statements -->

    </SCRIPT>

  </BODY>

</HTML>
```

Figures 2.17 and 2.18 show how the script interacts with the user when it executes.

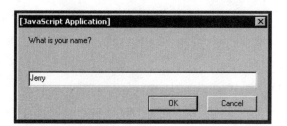

Figure 2.17

Prompting the
user to input his
or her name.

Figure 2.18

Using the user's
name as part of the
dialog message.

The following example shows how to write a function that returns a value back to the calling statement. This example is actually just a rewrite of the previous example and the results are the same. The only difference is that the function call does not supply an argument this time and instead receives back the name of the user from the function.

```
<HTML>

  <HEAD>

    <TITLE>Script 2.21 - Returning values from functions</TITLE>

    <SCRIPT LANGUAGE="JavaScript" TYPE="Text/JavaScript">

    <!-- Start hiding JavaScript statements

      function SayHello()

      {

        name = window.prompt("What is your name?","");

        return name;

      }

    // End hiding JavaScript statements -->

    </SCRIPT>

  </HEAD>

  <BODY>
```

```
<SCRIPT LANGUAGE="JavaScript" TYPE="Text/JavaScript">
<!-- Start hiding JavaScript statements
   result = SayHello();
   window.alert("Hello and welcome, " + result);
// End hiding JavaScript statements -->
</SCRIPT>
</BODY>
</HTML>
```

Using Arrays

An *array* is an indexed list of values that can be referred to as a unit. Arrays can contains any type of JavaScript value. Before you can use an array, you must first declare it. The following example shows how to create an array that will hold 10 strings that contain information about an automobile inventory.

```
Auto = new Array(10);
Auto[0] = 98 Ford Explorer;
Auto[1] = 97 Ford Explorer;
Auto[2] = 85 Plymouth Mustang;
Auto[3] = 96 Plymouth Voyager;
Auto[4] = 90 Honda Civic;
Auto[5] = 97 Honda Civic;
Auto[6] = 96 Plymouth Neon;
Auto[7] = 98 Plymouth Neon;
Auto[8] = 92 Ford Explorer Wagon;
Auto[9] = 95 Honda Civic Hatchback;
```

The first statement uses the new keyword to create an `Array` object named `Auto` that will contain 10 entries. The rest of the statements assign string values to the array. As you can see, the array's index starts with 0 and goes to 9.

Defining an Array

The following script uses the preceding array example to demonstrate how to display an array element by using the `document.write()` statement while referring to the array element's array name and index number.

```
<HTML>

  <HEAD>

  <TITLE>Script 2.22 - Sample Array</TITLE>

  </HEAD>

  <BODY>

    <SCRIPT LANGUAGE="JavaScript" TYPE="Text/JavaScript">

    <!-- Start hiding JavaScript statements

      Auto = new Array(10);

      Auto[0] = "98 Ford Explorer";

      Auto[1] = "97 Ford Explorer";

      Auto[2] = "85 Plymouth Mustang";

      Auto[3] = "96 Plymouth Voyager";

      Auto[4] = "90 Honda Civic";

      Auto[5] = "97 Honda Civic";

      Auto[6] = "96 Plymouth Neon";

      Auto[7] = "98 Plymouth Neon";

      Auto[8] = "92 Ford Explorer Wagon";

      Auto[9] = "95 Honda Civic Hatchback";

      document.write("The first element in the array is a <B>",

      Auto[0], "</B>");

    // End hiding JavaScript statements -->

    </SCRIPT>

  </BODY>

</HTML>
```

Figure 2.19 shows the results of loading the previous example. In this case, the first array element, `Auto[0]`, is displayed.

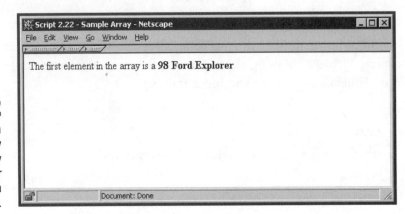

Figure 2.19

Array elements can be individually extracted by referencing their index number in the array.

Processing Arrays with for Loops

The next example shows the same Auto array. This time, rather than referencing a singe array element, we'll use a for loop to traverse the entire array and display its contents. The loop begins at the beginning of the array, Auto[0], and uses an increment of 1 to step through the elements of the array until it reaches the end. To determine the end of the array, the script creates a variable called array_length and sets its value equal to the array length property, which in this example is 10. Figure 2.20 demonstrates how the for loop was able to process every array element.

```
<HTML>

  <HEAD>

  <TITLE>Script 2.23 - Looping through an Array</TITLE>

  </HEAD>

  <BODY>

    <SCRIPT LANGUAGE="JavaScript" TYPE="Text/JavaScript">

    <!-- Start hiding JavaScript statements

      Auto = new Array(10);

      Auto[0] = "98 Ford Explorer";

      Auto[1] = "97 Ford Explorer";

      Auto[2] = "85 Plymouth Mustang";

      Auto[3] = "96 Plymouth Voyager";

      Auto[4] = "90 Honda Civic";
```

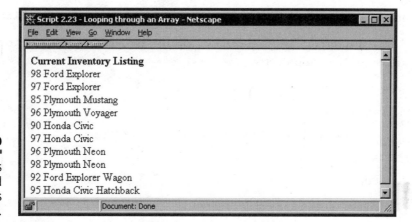

Figure 2.20

A `for` loop allows you to quickly read the entire contents of an array.

```
Auto[5] = "97 Honda Civic";

Auto[6] = "96 Plymouth Neon";

Auto[7] = "98 Plymouth Neon";

Auto[8] = "92 Ford Explorer Wagon";

Auto[9] = "95 Honda Civic Hatchback";

array_length = Auto.length;

document.write("<B>Current Inventory Listing</B><BR>");

for (var i = 0; i < array_length;i++) {

   document.write(Auto[i], "<BR>");

}
// End hiding JavaScript statements -->

</SCRIPT>

</BODY>

</HTML>
```

Using Arrays

You can also create dense arrays. A *dense array* is one that is populated at the time it is declared. This is a very efficient technique for creating small arrays. The following example shows you how to create a dense array named `animals` that consists of five entries. The array will have the following structure:

```
animals = new Array("mice", "dog", "cat", "hamster", "fish")
```

After creating the array, the script prints its contents using a `for` loop and the `animals.length` property.

```
<HTML>
  <HEAD>
    <TITLE>Script 2.24 - A Dense Array</TITLE>
  </HEAD>
  <BODY>
    <SCRIPT LANGUAGE="JavaScript" TYPE="Text/JavaScript">
    <!-- Start hiding JavaScript statements
      Animals = new Array("mice", "dog", "cat", "hamster", "fish");
      array_length = Animals.length;
      document.write("<B>List of animals in the Zoo</B><BR>");
      for (var i = 0; i < array_length;i++) {
        document.write(Animals[i], "<BR>");
      }
    // End hiding JavaScript statements -->
    </SCRIPT>
  </BODY>
</HTML>
```

Figure 2.21 shows the results of loading this example into your browser. Each array entry is listed beginning at index 0 and going through to the end of the array.

Sorting Arrays

Arrays have a `sort()` method you can use to sort their contents. The following example shows how to display a sorted list of the contents of an array. The script first defines a dense array with five entries. Next, it displays a heading, and it then uses the `sort()` method inside a `document.write()` statement to display the sorted list. Notice that I did not have to create a `for` loop to iteratively step through the array's index. The `sort()` method takes care of everything for me.

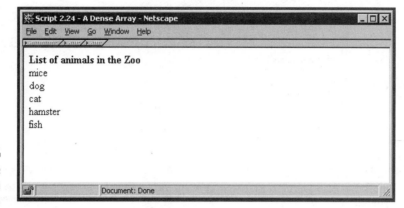

Figure 2.21

Displaying the
results of a
dense array.

```
<HTML>

  <HEAD>

  <TITLE>Script 2.25 - Sorting an Array</TITLE>

  </HEAD>

  <BODY>

    <SCRIPT LANGUAGE="JavaScript" TYPE="Text/JavaScript">

    <!-- Start hiding JavaScript statements

      Animals = new Array("mice", "dog", "cat", "hamster", "fish");

      document.write("<B>List of animals in the Zoo</B><BR>");

      document.write(Animals.sort());

    // End hiding JavaScript statements -->

    </SCRIPT>

  </BODY>

</HTML>
```

Figure 2.22 shows the results of loading the previous page into your browser. Note that
the result of the sort() method is a list displayed on a single line, with the elements
in the array separated by commas.

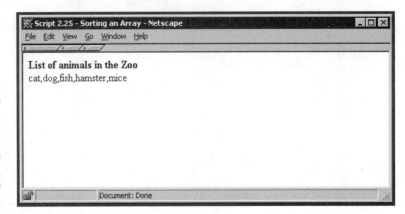

Figure 2.22

The array's
sort() method
provides an
efficient way of
sorting the
elements of
the array.

Building Dynamic Arrays

You can create scripts that allow users to create *dynamic arrays* and then populate them as the script executes. The following example prompts users to type their three favorite things and then creates an array to contain the list.

The script uses a for statement to control program execution. Each time the loop executes, it asks the user to type a response and assigns the response to the array by giving it the next available array index number (as designated by the current value of i).

```
<HTML>

  <HEAD>

    <TITLE>Script 2.26 - Building a dynamic Array</TITLE>

  </HEAD>

<BODY>

  <SCRIPT LANGUAGE="JavaScript" TYPE="Text/JavaScript">

  <!-- Start hiding JavaScript statements

    document.write("What are your 3 most favorite things? <BR>");

    Number_Array = new Array(3);

    for (var i = 0; i < 3;i++) {

      var your_number = prompt('I like: ', ' ');

      Number_Array[i] = your_number;
```

```
                document.write(Number_Array[i], "<BR>");

        }
    // End hiding JavaScript statements -->
    </SCRIPT>
  </BODY>
</HTML>
```

TIP

The preceding example shows you how to write a script that allows the user to populate its contents dynamically rather than requiring you to hardcode in its contents. Another way to make an array dynamic is by increasing its length during a script's execution. You can extend the size of an array by adding new array elements with an index number that is higher than the last index number in the array. For example, if I were to declare an array with an index of 50, I could later expand the array by adding a new array element with an index number of 99. This would cause JavaScript to increase the size of the array's index to 100.

Figure 2.23 shows the results of loading the previous example into your browser. As you can see, the heading is displayed followed by the contents of the new array.

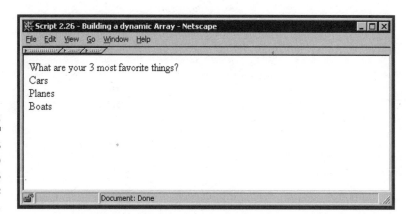

Figure 2.23

Dynamic arrays make it possible to show the contents of an array that the user just populated.

What's Next?

Oh my! I'd call this a full morning's work. Why don't you put this book down for a while, stretch your legs, and go get a bite to eat. Things are starting to get really good, and you need to keep your strength up. When you come back, we'll jump right in and start working with JavaScript objects, methods, and events. Before the afternoon ends, you will have a solid foundation for object-based programming.

Mastering Object-Based Programming with JavaScript

- ✿ Object-based programming
- ✿ The JavaScript object model
- ✿ Creating custom objects
- ✿ Handling events

Welcome back. Hopefully, you have had a good break and are ready for an afternoon full of learning. Yesterday evening, you were introduced to JavaScript and you reviewed the basics of HTML. This morning, you began delving into JavaScript programming by learning about the basic JavaScript programming components and statements. With this background now in place, it's time to talk in detail about object-based programming. First, though, I'll need to further explain the JavaScript *object model*.

The rest of the afternoon you will learn about built-in JavaScript objects and those objects provided by the Browser Object model. You'll end the afternoon by going over JavaScript events and how to add code to your scripts that responds to these events.

By the time you make it through the afternoon, you will have mastered all the basic building blocks of JavaScript programming. The rest of the book will build on what you have learned by showing you how to apply this knowledge to create JavaScripts that take advantage of objects and their methods and properties.

Object-Based Programming

JavaScript is known as an object-based programming language. It provides a subset of object-oriented programming features found in advanced languages such as C++ and Java.

JavaScript focuses on supporting Web-based content using object models. It exposes a default object model that provides a standard collection of objects. Additional objects that supplement JavaScript's internal object model are provided by the browser where the scripts execute.

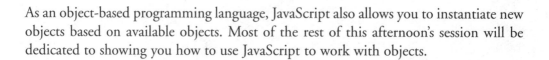

As an object-based programming language, JavaScript also allows you to instantiate new objects based on available objects. Most of the rest of this afternoon's session will be dedicated to showing you how to use JavaScript to work with objects.

OBJECT MODEL COMPATIBILITY

Objects are logically organized into a tree-like structure in which objects are linked in parent/child relationships. When you are designing Web pages using just HTML, you do not need to know or even understand the browser's object model. However, to effectively use JavaScript, you need a solid understanding of the object models provided by JavaScript and the browser.

All browsers that support JavaScript provide an object model. There are, however, inconsistencies between the browser's implementation of the object model. In other words, the Netscape Navigator and Internet Explorer object models are somewhat different. Not only are there a few fundamental differences between the object models provided by Netscape Navigator and Internet Explorer, but also both these browsers change their object models with each new version. So some objects that are available in the current version of Netscape Navigator are not available in earlier versions of Navigator. The same is true for Internet Explorer. The good news in all this confusion is that there are many more similarities than there are differences between the object models used by these browsers.

To make things even more challenging, both Netscape Navigator and Internet Explorer have introduced additional objects that only the particular browser supports. This means that there are objects in Navigator that only Netscape browsers recognize. The same is true for Internet Explorer. I am not going to try to cover every object that every browser version supports. To bring you up to speed in the fastest possible way, I will show you an object model that is common to all browsers that support JavaScript; then I'll show you additional objects supported by both Netscape 3 and 4 and Internet Explorer 4. Writing your JavaScript against this object model will allow you to target the widest possible range of users.

An Introduction to Objects

An *object* is a construct such as a browser window or form button that manages its own attributes, or properties, and that also provides methods that can be used to manipulate the object and its data.

 NOTE Not every object has both properties and methods—although most do. For a detailed list of available objects, see Appendix A, "A Brief JavaScript Object Reference."

Understanding Object Properties

Properties are attributes of an object that contain stored values. These values represent some quality of the object. For example, the `string` object's `length` property contains a value representing the length of the string. JavaScript properties are either JavaScript variables or other objects. For example, the `form` object is actually a property of the `document` object.

You can access an object's properties by typing the name of the object, a period, and then the name of the property as shown here:

```
object.property
```

For example, the following JavaScript can be used to display all the properties for a JavaScript object:

```
<HTML>
  <HEAD>
    <TITLE>Script 3.1 - Retrieving an Object's Properties</TITLE>
  </HEAD>
  <BODY>
    <SCRIPT LANGUAGE="JavaScript" TYPE="Text/JavaScript">
      function Customer(name, phone) {
        this.name = name;
        this.phone = phone;
      }
```

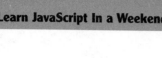

```
//Call the Customer function and pass a name and phone number
Customer1 = new Customer("Robert Robertson", 8043334444);
//Define a dense array called animals
animals = new Array("mice", "dog", "cat", "hamster", "fish");
//Prompt the user to enter a object
input = window.prompt("Type the name of a object to view its
properties","");
//Loop through the object and display Its properties
for (i in eval(input)) {
   document.write(i + " " + eval(input)[i] + "<BR>");
}
// End hiding JavaScript statements -->
</SCRIPT>
</BODY>
</HTML>
```

This script creates two objects. The first object is created when the following statement executes:

```
Customer1 = new Customer("Robert Robertson", 8043334444);
```

This statement calls a function named `Customer()` and passes it two arguments: a name and a phone number. The object that is created is named `Customer1` and is an instance of the object type `Customer`. The `Customer()` function uses the two arguments to create two properties for the object as shown here:

```
function Customer(name, phone) {
   this.name = name;
   this.phone = phone;
}
```

NOTE You may have noticed the use of the word `this` in both of these functions. The JavaScript keyword `this` provides you with an easy way to reference the current object.

These properties can be referenced from elsewhere in the script as `Customer1.name` and `Customer1.phone`. The second object created by this script is an instance of an array object named `Animals` that contains an indexed list of five elements as shown here:

```
Animals = new Array("mice", "dog", "cat", "hamster", "fish");
```

After establishing these two objects, the script displays a prompt asking the user to type the name of an object in order to view its properties. The script then establishes a `for` loop that iterates through every property in the specified object. The script uses the built-in JavaScript `eval()` function to evaluate the number of properties in the object. The `for` loop contains one statement that prints the index number of the property and its name as shown here:

```
input = window.prompt("Type the name of a object to view its
        properties","");
for (i in eval(input)) {
  document.write(i + " " + eval(input)[i] + "<BR>");
}
```

If you run this script, you will see a prompt similar to the one in Figure 3.1. If you type the name of an object that exists on the page (**Animals** or **Customer1**), the script displays a list of all that object's properties. Figure 3.2 shows what happens when the **Animals** object is specified.

 NOTE For this script to work, you must type a response to prompt the name of an object that has been defined on the page. In addition to the `Animals` and `Customer1` objects, there are several other objects that browsers automatically create when a Web page is opened. For example, the `window` and `document` objects are always present. You can run this script and type the names of either of these two objects to view their properties as well. However, if you type in the name of an object that it not present, you will get an error.

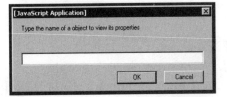

Figure 3.1

Specifying an object.

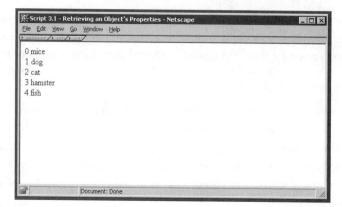

Figure 3.2

Viewing an object's
properties.

Working with Object Methods

A *method* is a function provided by an object for the purpose of working with the object. For example, the Date object supplies the methods getDay(), getHours(), getMinutes(), and getYear() that you can use to extract information from the object.

You can execute an object's methods in a similar manner to the way you access an object's properties. The syntax for executing a method is shown here:

```
objectname.method(p1, p2,...pn)
```

In this syntax, objectname is the name of the object whose method you want to execute, and method() is the name of the object's method. Some methods accept arguments that are passed in inside the parentheses and separated by commas. However, even if you are not passing any arguments, you must include the parentheses:

```
objectname.method()
```

An example of a method you have already used extensively is the write() method of the document object that is executed as follows:

```
document.write();
```

When you use this method, you pass the text you want to print within the parenthesis as an argument to the write() method.

Taking Advantage of Events

Events occur when something happens to an object inside the browser. For example, if a user moves the pointer over a link or types information into a text field, events occur.

JavaScript allows your scripts to recognize when events occur and to react to them. That's enough about events for now. I am eager to start talking about the JavaScript object model. I will return to the topic of events at the end of the chapter.

The JavaScript Object Model

One of the things that makes JavaScript so powerful and so flexible is its capability to work with objects. JavaScripts can work with objects from a variety of sources, which include:

- Built-in JavaScript objects
- Browser-based objects
- Objects you define within your JavaScripts

Working with Built-In Objects

JavaScript includes a collection of built-in objects. These objects are always available, and do not depend on you or the browser. These objects include the `Array`, `Boolean`, `Date`, `Function`, `Math`, `Number`, `Object`, and `String` objects.

> **NOTE** Notice that built-in JavaScript object names are always capitalized.

The Array Object

I touched on the `Array` object earlier this morning. To work with arrays, you must create an instance of an `Array` object.

An *array* is an indexed list of values that can be referred to as a unit. You can work with array elements by referencing their names and index numbers. An array has a `length` property that tells you how large the array is as well as an assortment of methods for manipulating its contents. These include methods to sort an array, to concatenate two arrays into a single array, to add or remove elements from the array, and to reverse the order of the array. The first entry in an array is assigned the index 0.

One thing I did not show you earlier is how to create multi-dimensional arrays; I showed you only single-dimension arrays. An example of a single-dimension array is a list of automobiles. For example, the following list contains three elements and is a single-dimension array:

- Ford
- Honda
- Jeep

A multiple-dimension array can be used to represent data stored in table format. For example, the following information could be stored in a two-dimensional array:

Ford	**Red**	**$4,000**
Honda	**Blue**	**$3,300**
Jeep	**Green**	**$6,950**

The example that follows shows you how to create a script that builds and displays the contents of a multi-dimensional array:

```
<HTML>
  <HEAD>
    <TITLE>Script 3.2 - Creating a Multi-Dimensional Array</TITLE>
  </HEAD>
  <BODY>
    <SCRIPT LANGUAGE="JavaScript" TYPE="Text/JavaScript">
    <!--Start hiding JavaScript statements
      //Part 1 - Prompt user for array size
      array_size = window.prompt("How many cars do you plan to list?","");
      MyArray = new Array(array_size);
      //Part 2 - Populate the array with user supplied information
      for (row=0; row < array_size; row++ ) {
        MyArray[row] = new Array(3);
        MyArray[row][0] = window.prompt("Type of car?","");
        MyArray[row][1] = window.prompt("Color of car?","");
        MyArray[row][2] = window.prompt("Sale price?","");
```

```
    }
    //Part 3 - Display the contents of the array
    for (row=0; row < array_size; row++ ) {
       for (column=0; column < 3; column++ ) {
          document.write(MyArray[row][column] + " ");
       }
       document.write("<BR>");
    }
    // End hiding JavaScript statements -->
    </SCRIPT>
  </BODY>
</HTML>
```

I've used comments to divide this script into three parts, each of which performs a specific activity. In Part 1, I defined a variable called `arraysize` that contains the number of cars the user wants to enter. I then created an array called `MyArray` using the value contained in `arraysize`. If you think of a multi-dimensional array as a table, then this step defines the table length as shown in Figure 3.3.

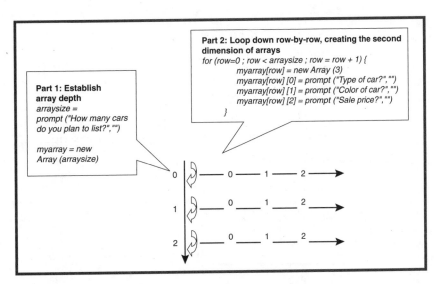

Figure 3.3

Building a two-dimensional table.

In Part 2, I added a `for` loop that creates the second dimension of the array. In this case, the `for` loop starts at 0, incrementing by 1 until it has executed for each element in the array. Again, if you look at the multi-dimensional array as a table, you can see that this step populates each column in the table as it iterates from top to bottom on a row-by-row basis. In each iteration, the user is asked to enter the type, color, and price of a car. In its first iteration, the script starts at row 0 (`MyArray[0]`) and populates each column in row 0 (`MyArray[0][0]`, `MyArray[0][1]`, `MyArray[0][2]`). On its next iteration, the value of `row` has been incremented by 1 to 1. Again, the script prompts the user for information about the car and populates the cells in the second row (`MyArray[1][0]`, `MyArray[1][1]`, `MyArray[1][2]`). The process repeats as many times as the user has cars to enter.

The end result is a multi-dimensional array that can be represented as a table. In the case of this example, the table is three rows and three columns deep and can be mapped out as shown in Figure 3.4. As Figure 3.4 shows, individual cells can be referenced.

In Part 3, the script prints out the contents of the multi-dimensional array using nested `for` loops. The first loop controls the row of the table that is processed. It starts at array element 0 and increments by 1 until the entire array has been processed. The second loop prints the contents of the multi-dimensional array by executing repeatedly for each row in the table, starting at column 0 and finishing with column 2.

```
for (row=0; row < array_size; row++) {

        for (column=0; column < 3; column = column + 1) {

          document.write(MyArray[row][column] + " ");

        }

        document.write("<BR>");

    }
```

Figure 3.5 shows the results I received when I tested the script.

Figure 3.4

A coordinate map of the two-dimensional table.

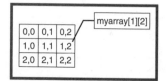

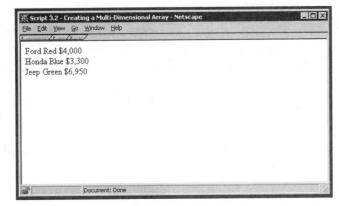

Figure 3.5

An example of a multi-dimensional array.

The Boolean Object

JavaScript lets you treat `boolean` values like objects. Use the following syntax to create new `Boolean` objects:

```
BooleanObject = new Boolean(value)
```

In this syntax, `value` must be either `true` or `false`. If you assign a `Boolean` object a value other than `true` or `false`, the value will be converted to a `boolean` value based on the following rule:

A value of `NaN`, `null`, `undefined`, `-0`, or `0` is converted to `false`; otherwise the value is converted to `true`.

Following is a list of sample `Boolean` objects:

```
TestObject1 = new Boolean();        //initial value is false

TestObject2 = new Boolean(-0);      //initial value is false

TestObject3 = new Boolean(false);   //initial value is false

TestObject4 = new Boolean(true);    //initial value is true

TestObject5 = new Boolean("Hello"); //initial value is true

TestObject6 = new Boolean("false"); //initial value is true

TestObject7 = new Boolean(false);   //initial value is false
```

 NOTE There is a distinction between `false` and `"false"` in the last two examples. This is because `"false"` is a string and `false` is a keyword.

By using `Boolean` objects instead of simple `boolean` values, you can take advantage of three `Boolean` object methods:

- `toSource()` Used internally by the browser to return a string that represents the `Boolean` object's source code.
- `toString()` Returns a string that represents the object.
- `valueOf()` Gets the object's value.

Each of these methods is demonstrated in the following example:

```
<HTML>
  <HEAD>
    <TITLE>Script 3.3 - Working with the Boolean Object</TITLE>
  </HEAD>
  <BODY>
    <SCRIPT LANGUAGE="JavaScript" TYPE="Text/JavaScript">
    <!--Start hiding JavaScript statements
      TestObject = new Boolean(false);
      //initial value is false
      document.write(TestObject.toString() + "<BR>");
      document.write(Test_Object.valueOf());
    // End hiding JavaScript statements -->
    </SCRIPT>
  </BODY>
</HTML>
```

The Date Object

JavaScript does not have a date value. Instead, you must use the `Date` object to work dates and times in your scripts. The `Date` object does not have any properties but provides a lot of methods.

JavaScript stores date information based on the number of millions of seconds that have passed since January 1, 1970.

You create instances of Date objects using the new operator as shown here:

```
Today = new Date();
document.write(Today);
```

This example creates a variable called today and sets it equal to the current date. The second line displays the results of the today variable. If you were to put these statements into a script and run it, you'd get a result similar to the following:

```
Thu Dec 10 12:21:29 GMT-0500 (Eastern Standard Time) 2000
```

As you can see, the default format for the Date object is the day of the week followed by the name of the current month, its numeric date, the current time, the offset from GMT time, time-zone information, and finally the current year.

If this is a bit more information than you want or need, you can use various Date methods to retrieve more specific information. The following example demonstrates some of the more commonly used Date methods:

```
Today = new Date();
the_Date = Today.getDate();
the_day = Today.getDay();
the_year = Today.getFullYear();
the_hour = Today.getHours();
the_minute = Today.getMinutes();
the_month = Today.getMonth();
the_second = Today.getSeconds();
the_time = Today.getTime();
the_localYear = Today.getYear();
```

The following example demonstrates how to use various Date methods. The result of each method is assigned to an array element in an array named MyDate, the total length of which is eight elements (MyDate[x] = "message = " + TodaysDate.datemethod()). After executing the Date object's methods and loading the array, the script executes a for loop to spin through the array and print its contents. The loop begins with array element 0 (i = 0) and increments by 1 (i = i + 1) with each iteration until it reaches the end of the array (that is, until i < array_length is no longer true). Figure 3.6 shows the results of executing this script.

```
<HTML>
  <HEAD>
    <TITLE>Script 3.4 - Using the Date Object</TITLE>
  </HEAD>
  <BODY>
    <SCRIPT LANGUAGE="JavaScript" TYPE="Text/JavaScript">
    <!-- Start hiding JavaScript statements
      TodaysDate = new Date();
      document.write("<B>Today's date is: </B>" + TodaysDate + "<P>");
      MyDate = new Array(8);
      MyDate[0] = "thedate = "   + TodaysDate.getDate();
      MyDate[1] = "theday = "    + TodaysDdate.getDay();
      MyDate[2] = "theyear = "   + TodaysDate.getFullYear();
      MyDate[3] = "thehour = "   + TodaysDate.getHours();
      MyDate[4] = "theminute = " + TodaysDate.getMinutes();
      MyDate[5] = "themonth = "  + TodaysDate.getMonth();
      MyDate[6] = "thesecond = " + TodaysDate.getSeconds();
      MyDate[7] = "thetime = "   + TodaysDate.getTime();
      array_length = MyDate.length;
      document.write("<B>Array of Date Method Examples</B><BR>");
      for (var i = 0; i < array_length; i++ ) {
        document.write(MyDate[i], "<BR>");
      }
    // End hiding JavaScript statements -->
    </SCRIPT>
  </BODY>
</HTML>
```

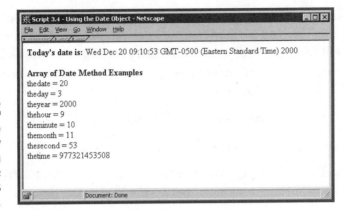

Figure 3.6

Using an array to store and display the results of data gathered using the `Date` object's methods.

NOTE

When working with the `Date` object's methods, you must use 0 to 59 when representing minutes and seconds, 0 to 23 to represent hours, 0 to 6 to represent days, 1 to 31 when working with dates, and 0 to 11 to represent months. In the example, the date given is Wednesday, December 20, 2000. Note, however, that the `getMonth()` method returns 11—not 12 for December as you'd expect. Remember that computer logic makes January month 0, February month 1, and so on.

The `Date` object also provides a set of methods for setting the value of `Date` objects, including:

- `setDate(12)`
- `setFullYear(2000)`
- `setHours(11)`
- `setMinutes(30)`
- `setMonth(4)`
- `setYear(2000)`

The Function Object

You have already learned that you can use functions to streamline your scripts. In just a little while, I will show you how you can write functions and use them as methods for custom objects.

JavaScript also allows you to create `Function` objects and provides you with access to `Function` properties and methods that are not available to normal functions. `Function` objects are easier to work with when your functions are composed of a single line of code. However, because of inefficiencies inherent in `Function` objects, you are better off sticking with declared functions.

You create `Function` objects using the following syntax:

```
FunctionName = new Function([p1,.......pn] body)
```

In this syntax, `p1` through `pn` are arguments that `Function` objects receive when called, and `body` is the JavaScript statement that is compiled as the function.

For example, the following code creates a `Function` object named `Warn`:

```
Warn = new Function("alert('HI!')");
```

You can call this function as follows:

```
Warn();
```

The preceding `Function` object is equivalent to the following declared function:

```
function Warn() {
  window.alert("Warning: You should not run this script!");
  return;
}
```

 NOTE Because the `Function` object is compiled, it is less efficient than using declared functions. Therefore, I recommend that you avoid using compiled functions and the `Function` object.

The following script demonstrates the use of the previous `Function` object examples. Figure 3.7 shows what happens if you load this page.

```
<HTML>
  <HEAD>
    <TITLE>Script 3.5 - Working with the Function Object</TITLE>
```

```
</HEAD>

<BODY>

   <SCRIPT LANGUAGE="JavaScript" TYPE="Text/JavaScript">

   <!--Start hiding JavaScript statements

     Warn = new Function("window.alert('Warning: You should not

     run this script!')");

     Warn();

   // End hiding JavaScript statements -->

   </SCRIPT>

</BODY>

</HTML>
```

Figure 3.7

Using the
Function object
in place of regular
functions.

The Math Object

The Math object provides mathematical constants in the form of properties; it provides mathematical functions in the form of methods. Earlier this morning, I demonstrated several Math properties and methods. Tables 3.1 and 3.2 provide a review of the Math object's properties and methods.

The Number Object

The Number object lets you treat numbers like objects and stores numerical constants as its properties. The values of these constants cannot be changed. You will most likely never need to know or work with the Number object, but just in case, Table 3.3 outlines its properties.

TABLE 3.1 SUMMARY OF MATH PROPERTIES

Property	Description
E	Euler's constant (2.718)
LN2	Natural logarithm of 2 (2.302)
LN10	Natural logarithm of 10 (.693)
LOG2E	Base 2 logarithm of e (.434)
LOG10	Base 10 logarithm of 10 (1.442)
PI	Ratio of the circumference of a circle to its diameter (3.141549)
SQRT1_2	Square root of _ (.707)
SQRT2	Square root of 2 (1.414)

TABLE 3.2 SUMMARY OF MATH METHODS

Method	Description
abs()	Returns the absolute value
cos(), sin(), tan()	Trigonometric functions
acos(), asin(), atan()	Inverse trigonometric functions
exp(), log()	Exponential and natural logarithms
ceil()	Returns the lowest integer greater than or equal to the argument
floor()	Returns the highest integer less than or equal to the argument
min(x,y)	Returns either x or y depending on which is lower

TABLE 3.2 SUMMARY OF MATH METHODS *(CONTINUED...)*

Method	Description
max(x,y)	Returns either x or y depending on which is higher
pow(x,y)	Returns the value of x^y
random()	Returns a random number between 0 and 1
round()	Rounds the argument to the nearest integer
sqrt()	Returns the square of the argument

TABLE 3.3 SUMMARY OF THE NUMBER OBJECT'S PROPERTIES

Property	Description
MAX_VALUE	Largest possible number
MIN-VALUE	Smallest possible number
NaN	Not a number
NEGATIVE_INFINITY	Positive infinity
POSITIVE_INFINITY	Negative infinity

You can define a Number object with the new keyword as shown here:

```
ANumber = new Number(99.99);
```

The Object Object

This object is the object on which all other objects are based. This means that all objects inherit this object's properties and methods.

You can create new `Object` objects by specifying an `Array`, `Boolean`, `Function`, `Number`, or `String` object in the `Object()` constructor as shown here:

```
MyNumberObject = new Object(99.99);

MyStringObject = new Object("Testing");
```

> **NOTE** A constructor is a function that each object provides that you can use to create instances of objects. For example, to create an instance of a `String` object named `MyString`, you would specify the following: `MyString = new String("Add your message text here.")`.

You'll probably never see anybody create objects in this manner. Instead, you'll see objects created using constructors specific to each object type, such as these constructors:

- `Array()`
- `Boolean()`
- `Function()`
- `Number()`
- `String()`

The String Object

The `String` object allows you to work with strings as objects. However, you should not need to use this object because JavaScript automatically converts simple strings into temporary `String` objects whenever you use a `String` object method or property on them.

The `String` object has just one property, `length`, which contains the number of characters that comprise the `String` object. However, the `String` object has a number of useful methods for manipulating the `String` object as outlined in Table 3.4.

The following example creates two `String` objects and then demonstrates the use of various `String` methods using these `String` objects and displaying their results with the `document.write()` method. Figure 3.8 shows the result of loading the page created in this example.

```
<HTML>

   <HEAD>
```

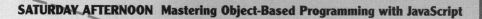

TABLE 3.4 SUMMARY OF STRING OBJECT METHODS

Method	Description
`charAt()`	Returns the character at the specified position in the string where the index of a String Object begins at zero
`concat()`	Combines two strings into one new string
`fromCharCode()`	Creates a string value based on the supplied code set
`indexOf()`	Returns the position of a specified substring
`lastIndexOf()`	Returns the last position of a specified substring
`splice()`	Creates a new string using a portion of the current string
`split()`	Organizes a string into an array
`substring()`	Returns the specified portion of a string
`toLowerCase()`	Returns the string in all lowercase characters
`toUppercase()`	Returns the string in all uppercase characters

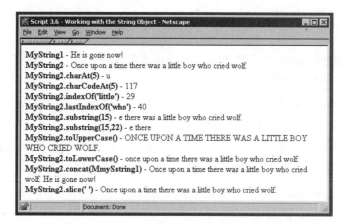

Figure 3.8

A demonstration of `String` object methods.

```
    <TITLE>Script 3.6 - Working with the String Object</TITLE>
</HEAD>

<BODY>
    <SCRIPT LANGUAGE="JavaScript" TYPE="Text/JavaScript">
    <!-- Start hiding JavaScript statements
      MyString1 = new String(" He is gone now!");
      MyString2 = new String("Once upon a time there was a little
      boy who cried wolf.");
      document.write("<B>MyString1 - </B>" + MyString1 + "<BR>");
      document.write("<B>MyString2 - </B>" + MyString2 + "<BR>");
      document.write("<B>MyString2.charAt(5) - </B>" +
      MyString2.charAt(5) + "<BR>");
      document.write("<B>MyString2.charCodeAt(5) - </B>" +
          MyString2.charCodeAt(5)  + "<BR>");
      document.write("<B>MyString2.indexOf('little') - </B>" +
          MyString2.indexOf("little")  + "<BR>");
      document.write("<B>MyString2.lastIndexOf('who') - </B>" +
     MyString2.lastIndexOf("who") + "<BR>");
      document.write("<B>MyString2.substring(15) - </B>" +
          MyString2.substring(15)  + "<BR>");
      document.write("<B>MyString2.substring(15,22) - </B>" +
          MyString2.substring(15,22)  + "<BR>");
      document.write("<B>MyString2.toUpperCase() - </B>" +
          MyString2.toUpperCase()  + "<BR>");
      document.write("<B>MyString2.toLowerCase() - </B>" +
          MyString2.toLowerCase()  +"<BR>");
      document.write("<B>MyString2.concat(MyString1) - </B>" +
          MyString2.concat(MyString1) + "<BR>");
      document.write("<B>MyString2.slice(' ') - </B>" +
     MyString2.slice(" ") + "<BR>");
```

```
    // End hiding JavaScript statements -->
    </SCRIPT>
  </BODY>
</HTML>
```

Take a Break

Now is as good a time as any to take a 10- or 15-minute break. When you return, I continue by showing you how to work with browser-based objects and how to create your own custom objects. Then you'll wrap up the afternoon by learning all about events and how JavaScript lets you trap and respond to them.

Working with Browser-Based Objects

You just reviewed the list of built-in JavaScript objects. Later, you will learn how to define your own custom objects. Right now, you're ready to look at objects that are provided by browsers.

When an HTML page loads in a browser such as Netscape Navigator or Internet Explorer, the browser builds a collection of objects based on the HTML tags it finds on the page. These objects are created in a top-down order as the page is scanned and loaded. As the browser builds the object references, it does so in a hierarchical fashion with all objects descending from the uppermost parent object, the window object. The object organizational hierarchy for a given browser is known as its *object model*.

 CAUTION Because the browser scans the page in a top-down fashion, you must be careful that your script does not reference an object until after that object has been established. For example, if your page includes an image object at the bottom of the page but the script at the top of the page references the image, you will get an error because the script executes before the image is established.

As both JavaScript and browsers have advanced over the years, so have their object models. Figure 3.9 presents an object model common to all versions of Netscape Navigator up to version 4.x and all versions of Internet Explorer up to version 5. This figure shows you what objects are common to both browsers. As you can see, all the objects in the clear boxes are supported by all the JavaScript-enabled browsers. If you work with only these objects in your JavaScript code, your script will be able to execute on the broadest possible range of browsers. Figure 3.9 also identifies objects that have been introduced in versions 3 and 4 of both Netscape Navigator and Internet Explorer. Referencing these objects in your scripts will provide you with a richer range of capabilities but could also mean losing the segment of your audience who have browsers of a less-recent version.

You have multiple alternatives: You can stick with the most broadly supported set of objects, or you can use objects supported by Netscape Navigator 3.x and Internet Explorer 4.x and accept a small loss of audience. Even if you decide to take full advantage of all available objects, you don't necessarily have to lose part of your audience. You can place logic in your scripts to check your visitors' browser types and version levels and then either ask visitors with older browsers to upgrade to the most recent version of their browser or add logic that redirects visitors to a page you've created that supports their particular browser's object model.

One point I want to mention is that Figure 3.9 includes only those objects common to all versions of Netscape Navigator and Internet Explorer through version 4 of each browser. Both browsers also provide objects that are supported only by that browser. In addition, Internet Explorer 5.x was recently released; it has additional objects that are not supported by earlier versions of Internet Explorer or by any Netscape browser. Although you can certainly write scripts that take advantage of these newer objects, using browser-specific objects means that your scripts will run only for the particular version of the browser with the object model you followed. This can significantly reduce your target audience.

The bottom line is that there is no simple answer. I simply want to point out what your options are so that you can decide for yourself what is best for you.

As Figure 3.9 shows, all objects are descendants of the window object. Many of the objects listed are present only if the browser detects an instance of them when it is loading the page. In other words, if you did not place an image on the page, there will be no image object. However, every JavaScript-enabled browser automatically provides a few objects:

○ The document object contains properties based on the current content of the document.

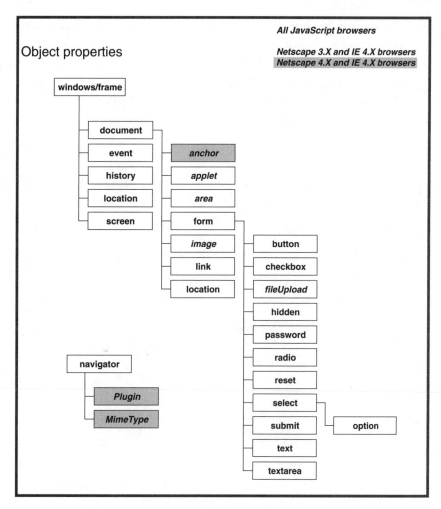

Figure 3.9

The browser object model.

- The `history` object contains properties that show the URLs the browser has previously visited.
- The `location` object contains properties that provide information about the current URL.
- The `navigator` object contains properties that can be used to identify the name and version of the browser as well as any plug-ins that might be installed.
- The `window` object contains properties that identify objects immediately below it in the hierarchy as well as properties that apply to the entire window.

This collection of objects provided by the browser is critical to any JavaScript; each of these five objects is described in the following sections. As you can tell from Figure 3.9, there are plenty of other objects, many of which you might want to include in your Web pages. You will learn more about these objects as you proceed through the remainder of the book. You can also refer to Appendix A on the CD, "A Brief JavaScript Object Reference," for additional information.

You can refer to most objects in your scripts by following the object model hierarchy, starting with the document object followed by a period and the name of the next child object. For example, if I had a page with a form named form1 that contained a button named button1, I could reference the button as follows:

```
document.form1.button1
```

I could examine one of the button's properties using the following syntax:

```
document.form1.button1.propertyname
```

The window Object

The window object is the ancestor of all other objects on the page. Multiple windows can be opened at the same time. The window object has dozens of objects and methods associated with it, many of which you have already worked with. For example, you've used the window.alert() method to display messages in the alert dialog box, window.prompt() to retrieve user input, and window.confirm() to seek user permission before taking action.

There are also methods for controlling navigation, such as window.back(), window.forward(), and window.home(), which are supported by the Netscape Navigator browser version 4 or later. Each of these window object methods is demonstrated in the following example:

```
<HTML>
  <HEAD>
    <TITLE>Script 3.7 - Working with the Window Object - 1</TITLE>
  </HEAD>
  <BODY>
    <FORM NAME="form1">
```

```
            <INPUT TYPE="button" VALUE="Back" onClick="window.back()">

            <INPUT TYPE="button" VALUE="Home" onClick="window.home()">

            <INPUT TYPE="button" VALUE="Forward" onClick="window.forward()">

        </FORM>

    </BODY>

</HTML>
```

The script defines a form that contains three buttons. Clicking on a button causes its onClick event to execute. In the case of the button labeled *Back*, the onClick event executes the window.back() method, causing the browser to load the previous Web page. Clicking on the *Forward* button causes the exact opposite action, while clicking on the *Home* button reloads the current page. Don't worry about the onClick event handler right now; you'll cover event handlers at the end of the afternoon. For now, just know that event handlers allow you to associate JavaScript statements and functions with user actions such as mouse clicks on objects.

Figure 3.10 shows what the browser looks like when you load the preceding example. Clicking on the *Home* button tells the browser to load the URL that the user has set up as the default home page. Clicking on the *Back* or *Forward* button produces the same effect as clicking on the browser's *Back* or *Forward* button.

The following script gives you another example of working with the window object's methods. In this example, the browser opens a second window as soon as the Web page loads using the window object's open() method. The window is named window1.

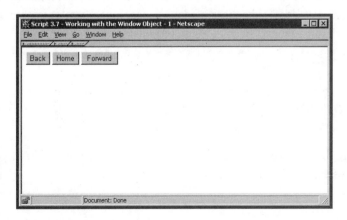

Figure 3.10

Building your own navigation buttons.

```
<HTML>
  <HEAD>
    <TITLE>Script 3.8 - Working with the Window Object - 2</TITLE>
  </HEAD>
  <BODY>
    <SCRIPT LANGUAGE="JavaScript" TYPE="Text/JavaScript">
    <!-- Start hiding JavaScript statements
      window1=window.open();
    // End hiding JavaScript statements -->
    </SCRIPT>
    <FORM NAME="form1">
      <INPUT TYPE="button" VALUE="Close the window"
      onClick="window1.close()">
      <INPUT TYPE="button" VALUE="Resize"
      onClick="window1.resizeTo(300,400)">
    </FORM>
  </BODY>
</HTML>
```

NOTE You have doubtless seen many Web sites in which multiple windows open when you click on links. Usually, the other windows appear in the form of smaller windows that try to sell you a product or point you to other links.

The script contains a form that defines two buttons, each of which contains an onClick event handler. If you click the first button, labeled *Close the window*, the window object's close() method is executed.

In order for the browser to know which window you want to close, you must specify the window's name—in this case, it's window1.

The second button in the form, *Resize*, executes the `window` object's `resizeTo()` method. This method tells the browser to change the size of the `window1` window object to a pixel size of 300 by 400.

Figure 3.11 demonstrates what you see when you first load this page. Two windows are opened. The first displays the form containing the script and the second window is opened as a result of the script's `window1=window.open()` statement.

The `window` object's `open()` method allows you a great deal of control over the appearance of the window. For example, you can control whether the window has certain features such as a menu bar, toolbar, scrollbar, and status bar, as well as whether the window can be resized. Figure 3.12 shows the location of these features on the browser window.

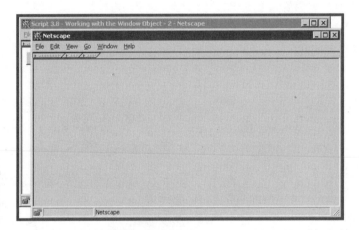

Figure 3.11

Opening
and controlling
browser windows.

Figure 3.12

Identifying major
browser features.

The example that follows demonstrates how to control each of these window features:

```
<HTML>
  <HEAD>
    <TITLE>Script 3.9 -Working with the Window Object - 3</TITLE>
  </HEAD>
  <BODY>
    <SCRIPT LANGUAGE="JavaScript" TYPE="Text/JavaScript">
    <!-- Start hiding JavaScript statements
      window.open("", "Window1", "menubar=no,toolbar=yes,scrollbar=yes,
      resizable=yes,status=yes,location=yes");
    // End hiding JavaScript statements -->
    </SCRIPT>
  </BODY>
</HTML>
```

By default, all the window features are enabled. To control them, you rewrite the statement containing the `open()` method as follows:

```
window.open("", "Window1", "menubar=no,toolbar=yes,scrollbar=yes,
resizable=yes,status=yes,location=yes");
```

When written this way, the `open()` method accepts three sets of parameters. The first parameter is the URL that should be opened in the new window. In the preceding example, I left this parameter blank, causing the browser to open an empty window. The second parameter is the name you are assigning to the window. You must assign a name to the window so that you can reference it from other parts of your script. The final parameter is comprised of one or more arguments separated by commas. Each argument identifies a window feature and assigns it a value of yes or no. A value assignment of yes tells the browser to include that option when creating the window. A value of no tells the browser to eliminate the specified feature. By default, all features are enabled. Therefore, I can get the same results by writing the statement to look like the following:

```
window.open("", "Window1, " menubar=no")
```

However, by writing the statement the way I did originally, it's easier to come back and change things later; I also think it makes things easier to understand. Figure 3.13 shows what the second window looks like when you load this example in your browser.

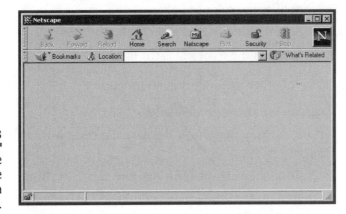

The document Object

The document object is the heart and soul of JavaScript. Each Web page can contain a single document object. You have already used it extensively to write output to the screen using the document.write() method.

The properties of the document object depend on the content of the page's HTML. For example, if a Web page contains images, the document properties for the page will contain an images[] array that lists every image on the page.

The document object has a host of properties you can use to control the appearance of the page and to gather information about its contents. For example, the document object stores property values for the following arrays:

- ✿ anchors[]: An array containing a list of all anchors in the document.
- ✿ applets[]: An array containing a list of all applets in the document.
- ✿ embeds[]: An array containing a list of all embedded object in the document.
- ✿ forms[]: An array containing a list of all forms in the document.
- ✿ images[]: An array containing a list of all images in the document.
- ✿ links[]: An array containing a list of all links in the document.
- ✿ plugins[]: An array containing a list of all plug-ins in the document.

Other `document` object properties allow you to affect appearance:

- ✿ `bgColor` Specifies the document background color.
- ✿ `fgColor` Specifies the color of document text.
- ✿ `linkColor` Specifies the color of links.
- ✿ `alinkColor` Specifies the color of active links.
- ✿ `vlinkColor` Specifies the color of visited links.

Here is a partial list of other useful document properties:

- ✿ `cookie` Lets you get and set cookie values.
- ✿ `lastModified` A string that shows the date and time at which the document was last changed.
- ✿ `referrer` A string showing the URL that the user came from.
- ✿ `title` A string containing the contents of the HTML `<TITLE>` tags.
- ✿ `URL` A string containing the document's URL.

The following example demonstrates the use of two document properties. The first statement in the script prints the title located in the HTML `<TITLE>` tags using the `document.title` property. The second statement displays the last modification date and time for the page using the `document.lastModified` property. Figure 3.14 shows the results of loading this example.

```
<HTML>
  <HEAD>
    <TITLE>Script 3.10 - Setting the Modification Date and Time</TITLE>
  </HEAD>
  <BODY>
    <SCRIPT LANGUAGE="JavaScript" TYPE="Text/JavaScript">
    <!-- Start hiding JavaScript statements
      document.write("<B>Document Title:</B> " + document.title +
      "<BR>");
      document.write("<B>Last Modified on:</B> " +
      document.lastModified);
    // End hiding JavaScript statements -->
```

```
</SCRIPT>

</BODY>

</HTML>
```

Figure 3.14

Displaying properties of the `document` object.

The form Object

This afternoon, I have used a few small forms, and I will dedicate a substantial portion of tomorrow morning to exploring them further. The information provided in this section should give you a good grounding in what a `form` object is and what you can do with it.

The `document` object's `forms[]` array maintains a list of every form on a page starting with `form[0]` and incrementing by 1 for each additional form. You can refer to individual forms using their `forms[]` array index number or by name.

For example, the following code creates a form called `form1` that contains a single button:

```
<FORM NAME="form1">

  <INPUT TYPE="button" NAME="backButton" VALUE="Back" onClick=
  "window.back()">

</FORM>
```

Assuming that this is the only form on the page, you can refer to it either as `document.forms[0]` or as `document.form1`. Forms can contain many elements such as

text boxes and buttons. To manage these form elements, each `form` object contains its own array named `elements[]`. The first element in the form is stored as `element[0]`, the second element is stored as `element[1]`, and so on.

The location Object

The `location` object is relatively simple. Its properties contain information about its own URL. For example, `location.href` specifies the URL of the page and `location.pathname` specifies just the path portion of the URL. If you make changes to the `location` object, the browser automatically attempts to load the URL again.

The `location` object has just two methods: The `reload()` method allows you to force a reload of the page, and `replace()` lets you specify a new URL to load. Because the `replace()` method writes a new entry to the history list on top of the current entry, this method prevents the user from using the browser's *Back* button to return to the previous page.

The following script shows how you can use the `location` object to force the browser to reload the current page or to load a new URL. First, the script defines a variable called `myurl` and sets it equal to the value of `location.href` (that is, to the URL of the current page). Then it defines a form with two buttons. The `onClick` event handler has been assigned to the first button. When the user clicks on this button, the `location.replace()` method instructs the browser to load http://www.netscape.com. When the user clicks on the second button, the `location.reload()` method instructs the browser to reload the current Web page. Figure 3.15 shows the results of loading this example.

```
<HTML>
  <HEAD>
    <TITLE>Script 3.11 - Working with the location object</TITLE>
  </HEAD>
  <BODY>
    <SCRIPT LANGUAGE="JavaScript" TYPE="Text/JavaScript">
    <!-- Start hiding JavaScript statements
      my_url= location.href;
      document.write("my_url = " + my_url + "<BR>");
```

```
      // End hiding JavaScript statements -->

      </SCRIPT>

      <FORM NAME="form1">

        <INPUT TYPE="button" VALUE="go to www.netscape.com"

          onClick="location.replace('http://www.netscape.com')">

        <INPUT TYPE="button" VALUE="Reload this page"

          onClick="location.reload()">

      </FORM>

    </BODY>

  </HTML>
```

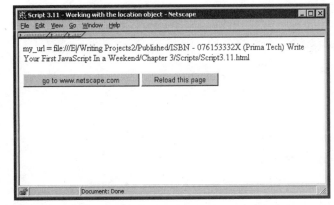

Figure 3.15

Using the
`location` object
to control browser
navigation and
page reload.

The history Object

The `history` object maintains a list of URLs that the browser has visited since it began its current session. One useful property of this object is the `length` property, which you can access using the following syntax:

```
history.length
```

The `history` object has three methods:

❂ The `back()` method loads the previously visited URL in the history list. This is the same as clicking on the browser's *Back* button.

○ The `forward()` method loads the next URL in the history list. This has the same affect as clicking on the browser's *Forward* button.

○ The `go()` method loads the specified URL in the history list. For example, `history.go(4)` loads the URL four entries ahead in the history list, `history.go(-4)` loads a URL four entries back in the history list, and `history.go(0)` reloads the current URL.

The following example demonstrates the use of the `history` object's `back()`, `go()`, and `forward()` methods. It defines a form with three buttons, each of which is assigned one of the methods. The `onClick` event handler is used to associate one of the methods with each button.

```
<HTML>
  <HEAD>
    <TITLE>Script 3.12 - Using History Object Methods
    for Navigation
    </TITLE>
  </HEAD>
  <BODY>
    <FORM NAME="form1">
      <INPUT TYPE="button" VALUE="Back"
        onClick="history.back()">
      <INPUT TYPE="button" VALUE="Reload"
        onClick="history.go(0)">
      <INPUT TYPE="button" VALUE="Forward"
        onClick="history.forward()">
    </FORM>
  </BODY>
</HTML>
```

Figure 3.16 shows the results of loading this example. Clicking on the three form buttons has the same effect as clicking on the *Back, Forward,* and *Reload* buttons on the browser's toolbar.

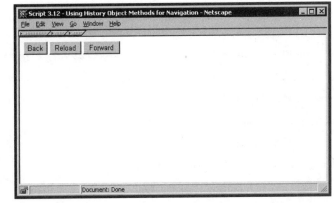

Figure 3.16

Adding navigation buttons to your Web pages.

The navigator Object

The `navigator` object is a top-level object like the `window` object. This means that the `navigator` object is not below any other object in the object hierarchy. It contains information about the browser that loaded the Web page. Both Netscape Navigator and Internet Explorer support this object, even though Internet Explorer's use of the object might seem a little funny. Some of the useful properties of the `navigator` object include the following:

- ✪ `navigator.appCodeName` Contains the code name of the browser.
- ✪ `navigator.appName` Contains the name of the browser.
- ✪ `navigator.appVersion` Contains the version number of the browser.

Your scripts can use the values of these properties to determine the browser (and its version number) that is loading the Web page. You can then use this information to direct the browser to a JavaScript you have written to work with that particular browser.

The following example shows you how to can create variables and assign them the values of `navigator` object properties. This script then prints the values of the variables. However, you could add additional logic to this script to interrogate the value of these variables and then direct the user's browser to a Web page you have designed to work with that particular browser.

```
<HTML>

  <HEAD>

    <TITLE>Script 3.13 - Displaying navigator object properties</TITLE>
```

```
</HEAD>
<BODY>
  <SCRIPT LANGUAGE="JavaScript" TYPE="Text/JavaScript">
  <!-- Start hiding JavaScript statements
    document.write("<B>navigator.appCodeName = </B>" +
    navigator.appCodeName + "<BR>");
    document.write("<B>navigator.appName = </B>" +
    navigator.appName + "<BR>");
    document.write("<B>navigator.appVersion = </B>" +
    navigator.appVersion + "<BR>");
  // End hiding JavaScript statements -->
  </SCRIPT>
</BODY>
</HTML>
```

Figure 3.17 shows the results that occurred when I loaded this script in my Netscape browser.

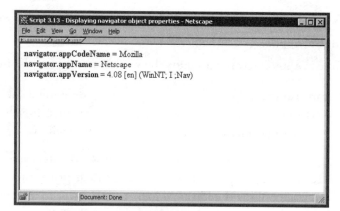

Figure 3.17

Viewing browser information.

Creating Custom Objects

In addition to core JavaScript object and browser-based objects, JavaScript provides you with the ability to build your own objects.

Three basic steps are required to create an instance of an object:

1. Define its structure.
2. Assign its properties.
3. Assign functions that will act as object methods.

There are two ways to create a new object. The first is to write a function that defines the format of the new object and then to use the new operator to instantiate a new object. For example, the following function defines a new object that contains two properties and one method:

```
function Customer(name, phone) {
        this.name = name;
        this.phone = phone;
        this.ShowAlert = ShowAlert;
    }
```

The first line defines a function that accepts two arguments. The next two lines use these arguments to establish property attributes. The last line assigns a method named ShowAlert. Notice that there is no associated argument with the defined method.

The ShowAlert method is itself just a function. As shown here, ShowAlert() displays an alert prompt that reveals the name and phone properties of a customer object:

```
function ShowAlert() {
        window.alert("Customer: " + this.name + " - Phone: " + this.phone);
    }
```

The following line of code can then be used to instantiate a new object using the customer() function:

```
Customer1 = new customer("Robert Robertson", 8043334444);
```

This statement creates a new object called Customer1 that has the following properties:

```
Customer1.name
Customer1.phone
```

You can call the function again and again to create other new objects.

The `Customer1` object also has a single method that can be invoked using the following statement:

```
Customer1.ShowAlert()
```

Now if you put this whole example together, you'll end up with the following script:

```html
<HTML>
  <HEAD>
    <TITLE>Script 3.14 - Creating a custom object</TITLE>
    <SCRIPT LANGUAGE="JavaScript" TYPE="Text/JavaScript">
    <!--Start hiding JavaScript statements
      function Customer(name, phone) {
        this.name = name;
        this.phone = phone;
        this.ShowAlert = ShowAlert;
      }
      function ShowAlert() {
        window.alert("Customer: " + this.name + " - Phone: " +
      this.phone);
      }
    // End hiding JavaScript statements -->
    </SCRIPT>
  </HEAD>
  <BODY>
    <SCRIPT LANGUAGE="JavaScript" TYPE="Text/JavaScript">
    <!--Start hiding JavaScript statements
      Customer1 = new Customer("Robert Robertson", 8043334444);
      Customer1.ShowAlert();
    // End hiding JavaScript statements -->
  </SCRIPT>
  </BODY>
</HTML>
```

Figure 3.18 shows what you will see when you run this script.

Figure 3.18

Displaying your custom object's property values.

Creating Objects with an Object Initializer

An alternative to writing a function that can be called to create new instances of objects is to take advantage of an *object initializer*. In this case, you create the object in the form of an expression by placing properties and methods inside a pair of curly braces, separating the property or method name from its value with a colon. For example, the following statement could be used to create an object called `Customer1`:

```
Customer1 = {name:"Robert Robertson", phone:8043334444,
showAlert:showAlert};
```

The first two entries inside the braces define the following pair of properties and set their values:

```
Customer1.name = "Robert Robertson";
Customer1.phone = 8043334444;
```

The last entry defines a method:

```
Customer1.ShowAlert();
```

If you use an object initializer, you can rewrite the code in the preceding example as shown here:

```
<HTML>
  <HEAD>
    <TITLE>Script 3.15 - Another way to create a custom object</TITLE>
    <SCRIPT LANGUAGE="JavaScript" TYPE="Text/JavaScript">
    <!--Start hiding JavaScript statements
      function ShowAlert() {
        window.alert("Customer: " + this.name + " - Phone: " +
      this.phone);
```

```
      }
    // End hiding JavaScript statements -->
    </SCRIPT>
  </HEAD>
  <BODY>
    <SCRIPT LANGUAGE="JavaScript" TYPE="Text/JavaScript">
    <!--Start hiding JavaScript statements
       Customer1 = {name:"Robert Robertson", phone:8043334444,
       ShowAlert:ShowAlert};
       Customer1.ShowAlert();
    // End hiding JavaScript statements -->
    </SCRIPT>
  </BODY>
</HTML>
```

Deleting Your Object

JavaScript provides a `delete` operator you can use to delete any objects you no longer want. You can add the following line of code to delete the `Customer1` object you've just created:

```
delete Customer1;
```

You can also use the `delete` operator to delete individual object properties or methods without deleting the entire object. For example, to delete the `name` property of the `Customer1` object, type the following:

```
delete Customer1.name;
```

Expanding Object Definitions

You can add additional properties to an object by any of three means:

- Rewrite the function to accommodate the new object property.
- Use the prototype property to add an additional property to all instances of the object.
- Add a new property to an individual object without affecting other objects.

Rewriting the function to accommodate new properties is an obvious option. The *prototype property* can be used to add a new property to all object instances. For example, to add property named `nickname` to all objects of type `customer`, you can write the following statement:

```
customer.prototype.nickname=null;
```

You can then populate an individual object's `nickname` property using the following statement:

```
Customer1.nickname="Leeman";
```

To add a new property to an individual object without adding the property to other instances of the object, type the name of the object, a period, and then the name of the new property and assign its value as shown in the following example. Here a new property, `zipcode`, has been created for the `Customer1` object and assigned a value of `23116`.

```
Customer1.zipcode = 23116;
```

Handling Events

Until now, most of the JavaScripts you have seen have executed in a top-to-bottom manner. By this, I mean that the browser begins executing your script as soon as the page loads, beginning with the first JavaScript statement and moving on to the succeeding statements until the last statement was processed.

The one exception to this was the use of functions placed in the head section of the page or at the top of the body section and which were executed by functions calls later in the script. In some cases, the addition of an `if...then` statement or a `switch` statement might have made the execution of a statement or function optional. But even in these cases where multiple logical paths of script execution exist, the script statements execute logically in a serial fashion.

Defining Events

In JavaScript, an event occurs within the confines of the browser. Events include such activities as mouse clicks, mouse movement, pressing keyboard keys, the opening and closing of windows and frames, and the resizing of windows. Browsers recognize events and perform default actions when those events occur. For example, when a user clicks on a link, the onClick event occurs, and the browser's default action is to load the Web pages specified by the link.

To really make your Web pages interactive, you must add another tool to your scripting skill set: event handlers. An *event handler* is a trap that recognizes the occurrence of a particular type of event. You can write code into your scripts to alter the browser's default response to events. For example, instead of automatically loading the URL specified by a link, you could display a confirmation dialog box that asks the user to agree to certain terms before proceeding.

NOTE The names of event handlers are based on the events that trigger them. Placing the word *on* in front of the event name creates the event handler's name. For example the event handler for the click event is onClick.

Each event is associated with a specific object. When an event occurs for a given object, its event handler executes (assuming that you have written one). For example, the click event occurs whenever a user clicks on a button, document, check box, link, radio option, reset button, or submit button.

Event handlers are surprisingly easy to define considering their power. You place them within HTML tags that define the object. For example, you can define an event to occur whenever a Web page is loaded by placing an onLoad event handler inside the first HTML <BODY> tag as shown here:

```
<BODY onLoad="window.alert('Web page loading: Complete.')">
```

In this example, an alert dialog box appears when the page completes loading. Notice that the event handler comes immediately after the tag, and that its value is placed within quotation marks. You can use any JavaScript statement as the value for the event handler. You can even use multiple statements, provided that you separate them with semicolons. Alternatively, you can use a function call, which allows you to perform more complex actions in response to the event.

You will see plenty of examples of how and where to place event handlers in various types of HTML tags throughout the rest of this session.

> **NOTE** See Appendix B on the CD, "A Summary of JavaScript Events," for a complete list of events, event handlers, and objects to which specific events apply.

The event Object

The event object is populated on every occurrence of an event. The information in its properties can be referenced by event handlers, giving your script access to detailed information about the event.

For example, the event.modifiers property specifies any modifier keys that were associated with a mouse or keyboard event. If the user pressed the Alt key while clicking the mouse button, the event.modifiers property contains the value Alt. The event.type modifier contains a string representing the type of event that occurred, and the event.which modifier contains a number that specifies the mouse button that was pressed or the ASCII value of the keyboard key that was pressed.

Types of Events

JavaScript currently supports 23 different events and event handlers. These events can be broadly divided into a few categories:

- Window and frame events
- Mouse events
- Keyboard events
- Error events

A number of these events and their associated event handlers are demonstrated in the scripts that follow. For a complete list of events and event handlers, see Appendix B on the CD, "A Summary of JavaScript Events."

Window and Frame Events

Events that affect window and frame objects include the load, resize, unload, and move events. The event handlers for these events are the onLoad, onResize, onUnload, and onMove. These event handlers are placed inside the <BODY> tag. The following script uses the alert() method to demonstrate how to execute JavaScript statements in response to occurrences of these events:

```
<HTML>

  <HEAD>

    <TITLE>Script 3.16 - onLoad, onResize, onUnload & onMove

          Example

    </TITLE>

  </HEAD>

  <BODY onLoad="window.alert('Web page loading: Complete.')"

        onResize="window.alert('What is the matter with my current size?')"

        onUnload="window.alert('Oh no, I am melting......')"

        onMove="window.alert('What's wrong with this spot?')">

  </BODY>

</HTML>
```

The first thing you will see when you run this script is a prompt notifying you that the Web page has finished loading (see Figure 3.19). This message is triggered when the onLoad event handler executes in response to the load event.

If you resize the window, the reload event will cause the onReload event handler to execute and display an alert message. Likewise, moving the window results in a similar alert message. The unLoad event handler does not execute until you close the window or load it with another URL.

Figure 3.19

Using the onLoad event handler to notify a user that the entire page has completed loading.

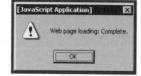

Mouse Events

Mouse events execute whenever you do something with the mouse. This includes any of the following:

- The MouseOver event occurs when the pointer is moved over an object.
- The MouseOut event occurs when the pointer is moved off an object.
- The MouseDown event occurs when a mouse button is pressed.
- The MouseUp event occurs when a mouse button is released.
- The MousePress event occurs whenever the mouse is moved.
- The Click event occurs whenever you single-click on an object.
- The DblClick event occurs whenever you double-click on an object.

The following script demonstrates the use of the onMouseOver/onMouseOut and onMouseDown/onMouseUp events. This script defines two links. Clicking on either link instructs the browser to load the Web page at www.microsoft.com. By adding the onMouseOver and onMouseOut event handlers to the first HTML link tag, I instructed the browser to change the document's background to red when the pointer passes over the link. The onMouseOut event handler then changes the background to white when the pointer moves off the link.

The onMouseDown and onMouseUp event handlers associated with the second link instruct the browser to change the document's background to red when the user clicks on the link (that is, when the user presses down on the mouse button) and to change the background color to white when the user releases the mouse button. Neither the onMouseDown nor the onMouseUp event handler alters the default action of the link. Therefore, if you click on the second link, the Web page at www.microsoft.com is still loaded.

```
<HTML>
  <HEAD>
    <TITLE>Script 3.17 - onMouseover, onMouseOut, onMouseDown &
        onMouseUp Example
    </TITLE>
  </HEAD>
  <BODY>
    <A HREF="http://www.microsoft.com"
```

```
        onMouseOver='document.bgColor="red"';

        onMouseOut='document.bgColor="white"';>

        onMouseOver and onMouseOut example</A><P>

     <A HREF="http://www.microsoft.com"

        onMouseDown='document.bgColor="red"';

        onMouseUp='document.bgColor="white"';>

        onMouseDown and onMouseUp example</A><P>

   </BODY>

</HTML>
```

Figure 3.20 shows the appearance of the browser window when the pointer is not positioned over the first link or the second link.

> **NOTE** One use of the `onMouseOver` and `onMouseOut` event handlers is to create a *rollover effect*, in which a button changes its appearance when the mouse pointer passes over it. You have doubtless seen this effect on many Web sites. I will show you how to create your own button rollover script Sunday morning.

The following script demonstrates the use of the `onClick` and `onDblClick` event handlers. This script creates a form with two buttons. The `onClick` event is assigned to the `<INPUT>` tag of the first button; the `onDblClick` event handler is assigned to the `<INPUT>` tag of the second button.

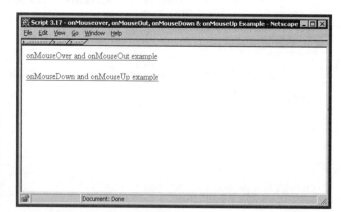

Figure 3.20

Controlling document properties using mouse event handlers.

```
<HTML>

  <HEAD>

    <TITLE>Script 3.18 - onClick & onDblClick Example</TITLE>

  </HEAD>

  <BODY>

    <FORM>

    <INPUT TYPE="button" VALUE="Click on me!"

      onClick="window.alert('You single-clicked.')">

    <INPUT TYPE="button" VALUE="Double-Click on ME"

      onDblClick="window.alert('You double-clicked!')">

    </FORM>

  </BODY>

</HTML>
```

When you load this page and click on one of the buttons, a prompt appears, informing you which button you clicked (see Figure 3.21).

Figure 3.21

Demonstrating `onClick` and `onDblClick` event handling.

Keyboard Events

Keyboard events are like mouse events in that they occur whenever the user presses or releases a keyboard key. There are three keyboard events: `KeyDown`, `KeyUp`, and `KeyPress`. The following example demonstrates how you can use the `onKeyDown` event handler to trap keyboard information from Netscape Navigator.

The script defines a simple form that consists of a single element, a text field. The onKey-Down event handler is included inside the <INPUT> tag and creates an alert dialog box whenever the user presses a key. After the user clicks on the dialog box's OK button, control returns to the script, and the character that the user types is visible in the text box.

```
<HTML>

  <HEAD>

    <TITLE>Script 3.19 - onKeyDown Example</TITLE>

  </HEAD>

  <BODY>

    <FORM>

    <INPUT TYPE="text" VALUE=""

      onKeyDown="window.alert('You pressed: ' +

      String.fromCharCode(event.which))">

    </FORM>

  </BODY>

</HTML>
```

The JavaScript statement associated with the onKeyDown event handler in this example deserves a little extra explanation. Keyboard keystrokes are passed to the script in the form of an ASCII value that is probably of as little value to you as it is to me. To make heads or tails of the value returned by the KeyDown event, I had to convert it back into an English representation. To do this, I used the event object's event.which property. This property provided me with the ASCII value of the key that was pressed to cause this event. I then used the String.fromcharcode() method to convert the ASCII value to a string value.

 NOTE The event object's event.which property specifies the ASCII value of the key pressed or the ASCII value of the mouse button that was clicked.

Figure 3.22 demonstrates what happens when you run the script and type the letter **a**.

Figure 3.22

Using the
`onKeyDown`
event handler to
capture keystrokes.

Error Events

An error event occurs whenever a problem occurs loading a window, frame, or image. The `onError` event handler automatically receives three arguments when it is triggered: the error message itself, the URL of the Web page, and the line number in the script where the error occurred. You can use the `onError` event handler to respond to the error. For example, you can display an alert prompt, redirect the user to another Web page, call a function, advise the user to upgrade the browser or to get a specific plug-in, and so on.

The following script demonstrates how to use the `onError` event handler to display error information. A function called `ErrorTrap()` is defined that accepts three arguments that map to the three arguments passed to the `onError` event handler. The function uses these arguments to format three lines of text that present the error information. The `onError = ErrorTrap` statement tells the browser to call the `ErrorTrap()` function if an error occurs anywhere on the page. To produce an error on the page, I deliberately mistyped the last JavaScript statement by typing an extra *r* in the `document.wrrite()` method call.

```
<HTML>

  <HEAD>

    <TITLE>Script 3.20 - onError Example</TITLE>

  </HEAD>

  <BODY>
```

```
<SCRIPT LANGUAGE="JavaScript" TYPE="Text/JavaScript">
<!--Start hiding JavaScript statements
   function ErrorTrap(msg,url,line_no) {
      document.write("<B>An error has occurred in this script.
   </B><BR>");
      document.write("Error = " + msg + " on line " + line_no +
   "<BR>");
      document.write("URL = " + url + "<BR>");
      return;
   }
   onError = ErrorTrap;
   document.wrrite("This statement will produce an error event");
   // End hiding JavaScript statements -->
   </SCRIPT>
  </BODY>
</HTML>
```

Figure 3.23 shows the results of loading this script. As you can see, the messages written to the window tell you what the error was, where in the Web page the error occurred, and where the page is located.

The following script is also designed to produce an error event. This time, the error is caused because the image file that is referenced does not exist. The onError event hander is used within the image HTML tag in this example. By placing the onError event handler in a particular HTML tag instead of making it a stand-alone JavaScript statement) as was the case in the preceding example), I can define different actions for error events on an object-by-object basis.

```
<HTML>
  <HEAD>
    <TITLE>Script 3.21 - Another onError Example</TITLE>
  </HEAD>
```

```
<BODY>

  <IMG NAME="xxxx" SRC="xxxx.jpg"

     onError="window.alert('Unable to load image!')">

  </BODY>

</HTML>
```

Figure 3.24 shows the results of loading the previous script. An alert prompt is immediately displayed when the browser fails to locate the specified xxxx.jpg image file.

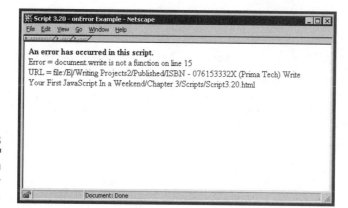

Figure 3.23

Trapping errors with the onError event handler.

Figure 3.24

Using the onError event handler to report problems when loading an image.

Using the onClick Event as a Decision Point

Before wrapping up the afternoon, I want to show you a neat little trick using links and the `onClick` event handler. In the example that follows, I define a link to a Web site to which I add the `onClick` event. Inside the event handler, I use the `window.confirm()` method to ask the user for confirmation before allowing the browser to load the link. The `window.confirm()` prompt gives the user two options. Clicking on OK returns a value of `true` that allows the browser to load the Web page; clicking on Cancel returns a value of `false` that prevents the browser from loading the specified URL and makes processing continue with the next statement after the link.

```
<HTML>

  <HEAD>

    <TITLE>Script 3.22 - Age Verification Example</TITLE>

    <SCRIPT LANGUAGE="JavaScript">

      msg = "You must be older than 30 to" +

        "visit this site. Are you?";

    </SCRIPT>

  </HEAD>

  <BODY>

    <A HREF="http://www.ptpmagazine.com"

      onClick="return(window.confirm(msg))";>

      ptpmagazine.com

    </A>

  </BODY>

</HTML>
```

 TIP
You can use a variation of this example to ask users whether they are sure they want to leave your Web site when they click on links.

Figure 3.25 shows what happens if you load the preceding page.

Figure 3.25

Verifying a user's age before allowing them into your Web site.

What's Next?

Congratulations! You have made it through the most difficult part of the book. Now that you have a JavaScript programming foundation in place, you can really start having fun. Why don't you take a break and get something to eat? When you return this evening, you'll start putting together everything you have learned. By the end of the night, you'll know how to take control of the browser status line, automatically refresh data based on timed intervals, take better advantage of pop-up dialog boxes, detect and work with different types of browsers, and use the `document` object to post edit dates, clear windows, and create links.

Doing Really Cool Things with Your Web Pages

- Controlling the Status Bar
- Improving Browser Navigation
- Taking Advantage of Dialog Boxes
- Working with Different Types of Browsers
- Experimenting with Other Neat Stuff

Now that you have had a nice break, I hope you are ready to jump back into things. You have spent the last 24 hours learning all the basics: HTML tags, JavaScript statements, programming logic, syntax, and so on. Starting tonight, you are going to get the chance to put all this practical knowledge to use.

This evening, you will see example after example of how to apply JavaScript to your Web pages. The emphasis will be on applying what you know to create scripts that are really useful. After all, that's why you started reading this book. Of course, I will have tidbits of new information for you to digest along the way, but the emphasis this evening is more on doing than on learning.

Controlling the Status Bar

One of the simplest and most powerful tricks you can do with JavaScript is to take control of the browser's status bar. You can do this using the `window` object's `status` property. In the next four sections, I will show you examples that include how to post a message to the status bar, how to post a blinking message, how to post a message and have it scroll over and over again, and finally how to use the status bar as a tool for displaying link descriptions.

Just don't get carried away when working with the browser's status bar. You may have seen examples of Web designers going a little overboard with their use of the status bar. Like anything, use these skills in moderation.

Posting a Message to the Status Bar

Ordinarily, the browser uses the status bar to display either the URL of the currently selected link or a description of the selected browser toolbar or menu option. However, as the following example shows, you can change this default behavior.

```
<HTML>
  <HEAD>
    <TITLE>Script 4.1 - Posting a message in the status bar</TITLE>
    <SCRIPT LANGUAGE="JavaScript" TYPE="Text/JavaScript">
    <!-- Start hiding JavaScript statements
      function PostMsg() {
        window.status = "You should see the new message in the
             status bar";
      }
    // End hiding JavaScript statements -->
    </SCRIPT>
  </HEAD>
  <BODY onLoad="window.status = 'Welcome to my status bar script!'">
    <FORM>
      <INPUT NAME="myButton" TYPE="button"
             VALUE="Post Status Bar  Message" onClick="postMsg()">
    </FORM>
  </BODY>
</HTML>
```

The first thing this example does is to create a script in the head section that defines a function named PostMsg(). This function will be used for displaying information in the status bar. The function contains a single statement that uses the window object's status property to post a message on the browser's status bar:

```
function PostMsg() {
  window.status = "You should see the new message in the status bar"
}
```

The <BODY> tag in the example has been modified to include the onLoad event handler:

```
onLoad="window.status = 'Welcome to my status bar script!'"
```

This statement uses the window.status property to place a message on the browser as soon as the page loads. The code next defines a form that contains a single button named myButton. When the user clicks on the button, the button's onClick event handler executes the PostMsg() function, which then writes its message to the browser's status bar.

When you load this page and click on the Post Status Bar Message button, you should see the same results as displayed in Figure 4.1.

Figure 4.1

Manually posting a message in the status bar.

Posting a Blinking Message to the Status Bar

The following example shows you how to get just a bit fancier with messages you post to the status bar. In this case, you are going to place a message in the status bar that blinks every second. You can use this technique to attract the visitor's attention to a message that otherwise might be missed.

```
<HTML>
  <HEAD>
    <TITLE>Script 4.2 - Posting a blinking message
              in the status bar
    </TITLE>
    <SCRIPT LANGUAGE="JavaScript" TYPE="Text/JavaScript">
    <!-- Start hiding JavaScript statements
```

```
window.status="";
msg_on = "yes";
function CycleStatusbar() {
   if (msg_on == "yes") {
     msg_on = "no";
     window.status="This message should be blinking in" +
                  " your status bar!";
   }
   else {
     msg_on = "yes";
     window.status="";
   }
   setTimeout("CycleStatusbar();",1000);
  }
  // End hiding JavaScript statements -->
  </SCRIPT>
 </HEAD>
 <BODY onLoad="CycleStatusbar()">
  <H3>Blinking Status bar Example</H3>
 </BODY>
</HTML>
```

The bulk of the work in this script occurs in the head section. First, the status bar is cleared of any existing messages by the window.status="" statement. Next, a variable named msg_on is assigned an initial value of yes. The CycleStatusbar() function that follows toggles the value of this variable from yes to no with each execution.

As its name implies, the CycleStatusbar() function displays and removes a message over and over again in the status bar to produce a blinking effect. When first called, the function checks the value of msg_on; because the variable equals yes, the function posts its message to the status bar. The function then passes control to the next statement in the script.

The setTimeout("CycleStatusbar();",1000 statement tells the browser to run the CycleStatusbar() function again in 1000 milliseconds (one second). Once it's activated, the setTimeout() method executes the CycleStatusbar() function again. This time when it runs, the value of msg_on will equal no, so the function executes the window.status="" statement (clearing the status bar of any text) and toggles the value of msg_on back to yes. As you can see, the combination of the CycleStatusbar() function and the setTimeout() method produces a looping affect in the script that is used to write and clear a message from the status bar.

NOTE The setTimeout() method belongs to the window object. Its purpose is to automate the execution of JavaScript statements or functions after a scheduled period of time (in milliseconds) has passed. This method does not cause the script to wait until it executes. Instead, it allows the browser to continue processing the page while waiting on its own execution.

The page's <BODY> tag has been modified with the addition of onLoad="CycleStatusbar()", which initiates the looping logic in the head section of the page.

If you run this example, you will see that the message appears in and disappears from the status bar once every second. Figure 4.2 shows what the status bar looks like during an interval in which the message is displayed.

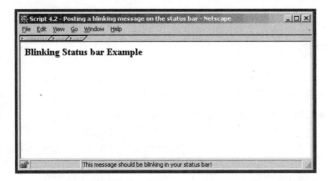

Figure 4.2

Automatically posting a blinking message in the status bar.

Scrolling a Message in the Status Bar

Where the previous example used the window.setTimeout() method to produce a blinking effect in the browser's status bar, this example uses the same method to create a message that scrolls across the status bar. The message appears and then moves off the screen, only to reappear over and over again.

```
<HTML>
  <HEAD>
    <TITLE>Script 4.3 - Scrolling a message in the status bar</TITLE>
    <SCRIPT LANGUAGE="JavaScript" TYPE="Text/JavaScript">
    <!-- Start hiding JavaScript statements
      msg = "                          Let me hypnotize you with this " +
              "message....               ";
      i = 0;
      function CycleMsg() {
        window.status = msg.substring(i, msg.length) +
              msg.substring(0, i);
        i++;
        if (i > msg.length) {
          i = 0;
        }
        window.setTimeout("CycleMsg()",200);
      }
    // End hiding JavaScript statements -->
    </SCRIPT>
  </HEAD>
  <BODY onLoad="CycleMsg()">
    <H3>Scrolling Status Bar Message Example</H3>
  </BODY>
</HTML>
```

As with the preceding examples, the only code in the body section of this page is an onLoad statement that calls a function named CycleMsg():

```
<BODY onLoad="CycleMsg()">
```

This function then initiates a looping process in the head section of the page that manages the scrolling message. The first statement in the script in the head section creates a variable named msg that contains the message to be scrolled. Note that I added a number of blank spaces in front of and following the message text itself. These spaces create a longer message field and allow the message to remain displayed in its entirety for a longer period before it begins to disappear off the left side of the status bar.

```
msg = "                         Let me hypnotize you with this
message....                  ";
```

The script then sets a variable named i equal to 0. The CycleMsg() function that follows uses this variable to control the movement of the message across the status bar. The first statement in the function displays the message; it uses the msg.substring() method to display a portion of the message beginning at position 0 and ending with position msg.length (a number representing the total length of the message). On this first iteration, the entire message is displayed beginning with position 0 and going through the last character in the message (position msg.length). Appended to this string is a substring of the message that begins with position 0 and ends with position 0 on this first iteration.

```
function CycleMsg() {
   window.status = msg.substring(i, msg.length) + msg.substring(0, i);
   i++;
   if (i > msg.length) {
      i = 0;
   }
   window.setTimeout("CycleMsg()",200);
}
```

After displaying this initial message, the function increments the value of i by 1. It also checks to see whether the function has been executed enough times for the value of i to exceed the value stored in msg.length. When this occurs, the function sets i back to 0 so that the whole process can start over. Before it completes its first execution, the function schedules itself to execute again in .2 seconds with the window.setTimeout("CycleMsg()",200) statement.

When the function next executes, the value of i equals 1. When the window.status property is set this time, the first msg.substring() method contains one less character because it starts at character position 1 instead of 0. The second msg.substring() method contains an additional character beginning a 0 and going through to 1. As you can see, with each iteration, the leading character of the message is stripped from the first substring and placed into the second substring. This has the effect of bringing the message's initial character around to the back of the displayed message, creating the scrolling effect. After the entire message has been processed, the value of i is reset to 0, the script is back at its starting point, and everything is repeated.

If you load this page, you will see that the message appears and then slowly scrolls from right to left until it begins to disappear off the left side of the status bar, only to begin reappearing again on the right side of the status bar. Figure 4.3 shows what the message looks like before it begins to scroll away.

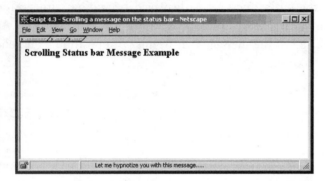

Figure 4.3

Posting a scrolling message in the status bar.

Providing Link Descriptions in the Status Bar

This final status bar example shows you how to post descriptive phrases for the links on your Web pages in the status bar whenever a user moves the mouse pointer over a link on the page.

```
<HTML>

  <HEAD>

    <TITLE> Script 4.4 - Providing link descriptions in the status bar

    </TITLE>

    <SCRIPT LANGUAGE="JavaScript" TYPE="Text/JavaScript">
```

```
<!-- Start hiding JavaScript statements

   function PostMsg(msg) {

     window.status = msg;

   }

   function ClearMsg() {

     window.status="";

   }

// End hiding JavaScript statements -->

</SCRIPT>

</HEAD>

<BODY>

  <A HREF="http://www.netscape.com"

     onMouseOver="PostMsg('Jump to the Netscape home  page');

     return true;" onMouseOut="ClearMsg();"> Netscape</A><P>

  <A HREF="http://www.microsoft.com"

     onMouseOver="PostMsg('Jump to the Microsoft home page');

     return true;" onMouseOut="ClearMsg();"> Microsoft</A><P>

  <A HREF="http://www.myopera.com"

     onMouseOver="PostMsg('Jump to the Opera home page');

     return true;" onMouseOut="ClearMsg();"> Opera</A>

</BODY>

</HTML>
```

This script creates two functions in the head section. One displays a message that is passed to it as an argument in the status bar; the other function clears the message:

```
function PostMsg(msg) {

  window.status = msg;

}

function ClearMsg() {

  window.status="";

  }
```

Three links in the body section of the script execute the onMouseOver and onMouse-Out events to call the status bar functions. When the user moves the mouse pointer over one of these links, its onMouseOver event handler calls the PostMsg() function, passing it a message that describes the link. When the user moves the mouse away from the link, the link's onMouseOut event handler calls the ClearMsg() function and clears the status bar.

```
<A HREF="http://www.netscape.com"

    onMouseOver="PostMsg('Jump to the Netscape

    home page'); return true;" onMouseOut="ClearMsg();">
Netscape</A><P>


<A HREF="http://www.microsoft.com".

    onMouseOver="PostMsg('Jump to the Microsoft home page');

    return true;" onMouseOut="ClearMsg();"> Microsoft</A><P>


<A HREF="http://www.myopera.com"

    onMouseOver="PostMsg('Jump to the Opera home page');

    return true;" onMouseOut="ClearMsg();"> Opera</A>
```

Figure 4.4 shows the results of loading this page and moving the pointer over the Netscape link. Clicking on the link instructs the browser to load the associated URL for that link.

Figure 4.4

Posting descriptive messages in the status bar when the user moves the mouse pointer over a link.

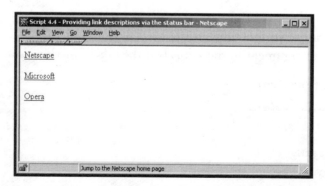

Improving Browser Navigation

Earlier this afternoon, I showed you how to create browser navigation buttons that allow you to imitate the Back, Forward, Reload, and Home buttons on the browser's toolbar. The following sections add a host of new tricks to your tool bag that will allow you to create sophisticated navigation tools for your visitors. You will learn how to do the following:

- ✪ Create a URL field
- ✪ Allow users to jump to places in your Web site or other Web sites using drop-down lists
- ✪ Add buttons that enable users to quickly scroll or jump to other positions in lengthy pages
- ✪ Add rollover effects to your links and graphics

Creating Your Own URL Field

As the following example shows, it does not take a lot of code to create a URL field on your Web page. All that you need is a form with a text field, a button, and the onClick event handler.

```
<HTML>

  <HEAD>

    <TITLE> Script 4.5 - Creating your own URL field</TITLE>

  </HEAD>

  <BODY>

    <H3>Enter a URL and click on Load URL!</H3>

    <FORM NAME="myForm">

      <INPUT NAME="URL_Field" TYPE="text" VALUE="http://"  SIZE="30">

      <INPUT NAME="GoButton" TYPE="button" VALUE="Load URL"

                onClick="window.location=myForm.URL_Field.value">

    </FORM>

  </BODY>

</HTML>
```

The following HTML statements define a form called `myForm` that contains a text field called `URL_Field` and a button named `GoButton`. As you can see, I added an initial value in the text field by adding the `VALUE="http://"` clause to the `<INPUT>` tag:

```
<FORM NAME="myForm">

  <INPUT NAME="URL_Field" TYPE="text" VALUE="http://"  size="30">

  <INPUT NAME="GoButton" TYPE="button" VALUE="Load URL"

          onClick="window.location=myform.URL_Field.value">
```

 NOTE The `window.location` statement automatically loads any assigned URL. Unless you preface the URL with `http://`, the scripts will not be able to load the URL. So make sure that you do not remove the `http://` text that is appended to the beginning of the `URL_Field` or the example will not work.

Adding `onClick="window.location=myform.URL_Field.value"` as the event handler for the button takes the value located in the text field (in this case, `myform.URL_Field.value"`) and assigns it to the `window` object's `location` property. Any time a change is made to `window.location`, the browser immediately tries to load the URL.

Figure 4.5 shows what this URL script looks like when it has been loaded in a browser. By completing the URL address and clicking on the Load URL button, the user can load any Web page into the current window.

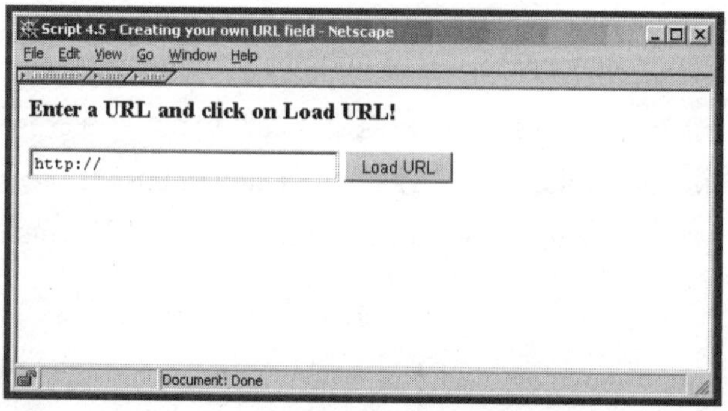

Figure 4.5

Building a custom URL form.

Creating an Automatic Drop-Down Navigation Menu

At times, you many want to offer visitors to your Web site a large number of links to choose from. But creating each one individually can be tiresome and can result in a page that is overly crowded and unattractive. A simple solution to this problem is to use a drop-down list, as shown in this example:

```
<HTML>

  <HEAD>

    <TITLE> Script 4.6 - Creating a drop-down menu - 1</TITLE>

  </HEAD>

  <BODY>

    <FORM NAME="myForm">

      <SELECT NAME="myList" onChange="window.location=

      document.myForm.myList.options[

      document.myForm.myList.selectedIndex].value">

      <OPTION SELECTED VALUE="javascript:void(0)">-- Pick One --

      <OPTION VALUE="http://www.microsoft.com"> Microsoft

      <OPTION VALUE="http://www.netscape.com"> Netscape

      <OPTION VALUE="http://www.myopera.com"> Opera

      </SELECT>

    </FORM>

  </BODY>

</HTML>
```

In the body of the page, a single form is defined and named myForm. Within it, a list called myList is declared. The onChange event handler is used to set the window.location property to the values specified by the following statement:

```
document.myForm.myList.options[
        document.myForm.myList.selectedIndex].value"
```

Each option in the list has an implicit index number. Roughly translated, the preceding statement takes the index number of the option you select from the list (the value in `document.myForm.myList.selectedIndex`) and uses it to assign the value of the selected option to `window.location`.

If you look at the `<OPTION>` tags within the form, you will notice that the first tag looks different. I used `VALUE="javascript:void(0)"` to put an entry into the list that, if selected, is ignored. This tricks allows me to add an instruction at the top of the list that otherwise has no effect. The rest of the options are straightforward. Each `<OPTION>` tag contains a `VALUE` that holds the URL; if this option is selected, the specified URL is opened. Note that each `VALUE` entry is followed by a description that identifies the entry within the list.

Figure 4.6 shows how the list looks when you load this page. Selecting the `-- Pick One --` entry has no effect. Selecting any other entry causes the browser to load the URL associated with that selection.

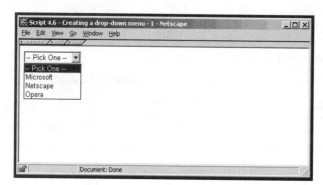

Figure 4.6

Helping users navigate with a drop-down list.

Creating a Drop-Down Menu with a Button Control

The following example builds on the one in the previous section by providing the user with an additional level of control. The following script allows the user to select an entry from a drop-down list without having that entry automatically processed (as was the case in the preceding example). Delaying the processing of a selection is appropriate on forms that require the user to complete a number of activities before the form is processed.

The following code is similar to the code in the preceding section. Note, however, that I removed the `onChange` event handler from the form, which prevents the form from automatically processing the selected option. Instead, I added the `onClick` event handler to the form's button. When the user clicks on the button, the `onClick` event handler sets the `window.location` property to the value of the selected list option, causing the appropriate URL to load.

```
<HTML>

  <HEAD>

    <TITLE> Script 4.7 - Creating a drop-down menu - 2</TITLE>

  </HEAD>

  <BODY>

    <FORM NAME="myForm">

      <SELECT NAME="myList">

        <OPTION SELECTED VALUE="javascript:void(0)">-- Pick One --

        <OPTION SELECTED VALUE="http://www.microsoft.com"> Microsoft

        <OPTION VALUE="http://www.netscape.com"> Netscape

        <OPTION VALUE="http://www.myopera.com"> Opera

      </SELECT>

      <INPUT NAME="Load_URL" TYPE="button" VALUE="Load URL"

          onClick="window.location=document.myForm.myList.options[

          document.myForm.myList.selectedIndex].value">

    </FORM>

  </BODY>

</HTML>
```

Figure 4.7 shows how the list looks when you load this page. Selecting the -- Pick One -- entry still has no effect. Simply selecting any other option no longer causes that option to be loaded. Instead, the Load URL button gives the user control over when and if the entry selected from the list will be processed.

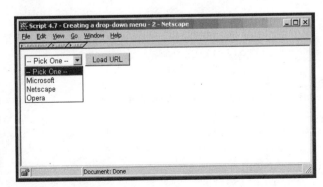

Figure 4.7

Allowing visitors to load pages from a list of predefined URLs.

Scrolling and Jumping

Depending on its contents, a Web page sometimes can grow rather large in size. JavaScript provides the ability to scroll or jump to a predefined location within the page. In addition to making the page easier to navigate, giving the user the ability to jump can also produce a stunning visual effect, as the following example shows:

```
<HTML>

  <HEAD>

    <TITLE> Script 4.8 - Scrolling and jumping example</TITLE>

    <SCRIPT LANGUAGE="JavaScript" TYPE="Text/JavaScript">

    <!-- Start hiding JavaScript statements

      function ScrollDown(){

        for (i=1; i<=600; i++) {

          parent.scrollTo(1,i);

        }

      }

      function ScrollUp(){

        for (i=600; i>=1; i--) {

          parent.scrollTo(1,i);

        }

      }

      function JumpDown(){

        parent.scrollTo(1,600);

      }

      function JumpUp(){

        parent.scrollTo(1,1);

      }

    // End hiding JavaScript statements -->

    </SCRIPT>

  </HEAD>

  <BODY>
```

```
<FORM NAME="myForm">
    <INPUT NAME="scrollButton1" TYPE="button"
        VALUE="Scroll Down" onClick="scrollDown()">
    <INPUT NAME="jumpButton1" TYPE="button"
        VALUE="Jump Down" onClick="jumpDown()">
</FORM>
<BR><BR><BR><BR><BR><BR>
<H3>This is an example...</H3>
<BR><BR><BR><BR><BR><BR>
<H3>of scrolling and jumping...</H3>
<BR><BR><BR><BR><BR><BR>
<H3>from the top to the bottom of a page...</H3>
<BR><BR><BR><BR><BR><BR>
<H3>and back again!!</H3>
<FORM>
    <INPUT NAME="scrollButton2" TYPE="button"
        VALUE="Scroll Up" onClick="scrollUp()">
    <INPUT NAME="jumpButton2" TYPE="button"
        VALUE="Jump Up" onClick="jumpUp()">
</FORM>
</BODY>
</HTML>
```

Four functions are defined in the head section of the page. Two of these functions manage the scrolling effect, and the other two manage the jump affect. Take the ScrollDown() function as an example. The function starts by setting up a for loop that is controlled by a variable called i. The variable i is initially set to a value of 1 and then incremented by 1 until it reaches 600. With each iteration, the loop executes the window object's ScrollTo() method. This method scrolls the window's viewing area to the location specified by the coordinates x and y. In effect, the for loop executes 600 times and scrolls the display down by 1 pixel position on each occurrence. The ScrollUp() function does the same thing in reverse.

```
function ScrollDown(){
  for (i=1; i<=600; i++) {
    parent.scrollTo(1,i);
  }
}
```

The `JumpDown()` function skips the scroll effect altogether by simply specifying the destination coordinate. The `JumpUp()` function does the same thing in reverse.

```
function JumpDown(){
  parent.scrollTo(1,600);
}
```

After establishing the functions, this example script creates two forms and places them at the top and the bottom of the page's body section. Both of these forms define two buttons that call the functions. The buttons in the top form use the `onClick` event handler to execute the `ScrollDown()` and `JumpDown()` functions; the buttons in the bottom form use the `onClick` event handler to execute the `ScrollUp()` and `JumpUp()` functions.

Between the two forms, I placed enough text to make the page long enough to provide an effective demonstration. Loading this page displays the window shown in Figure 4.8. Clicking on either the Scroll Down or Jump Down button scrolls or jumps the viewing area down to the bottom of the page, where the Scroll Up and Jump Up buttons have been placed.

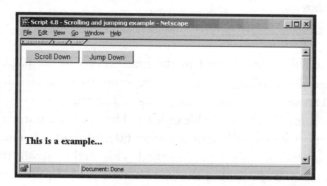

Figure 4.8

Adding scroll and jump buttons to help visitors navigate your Web page faster.

Working with Rollovers

My personal favorite JavaScript effect is the rollover. A *rollover* is a image that changes when the mouse pointer passes over it. All the rollover really does is use the onMouseOver and onMouseOut event handlers to toggle between two similar links or images, giving the appearance that the image is changing. This very popular technique has become common on the Web.

 NOTE Make sure that both copies of the rollover images you use are the same size. Otherwise, the effect is lost because the second image will look distorted.

In the following example, you will see an example that uses the rollover effect to animate three images. Although the images appear to the user to be text, they are actually graphic images. Unfortunately, the rollover technique only applies to graphics.

```
<HTML>
  <HEAD>
    <TITLE> Script 4.9 - Working with rollovers</TITLE>
    <SCRIPT LANGUAGE="JavaScript" TYPE="Text/JavaScript">
    <!-- Start hiding JavaScript statements
        netscape1        =new Image;
        netscape2        =new Image;
        microsoft1       =new Image;
        microsoft2       =new Image;
        opera1           =new Image;
        opera2           =new Image;
        netscape1.src    ="netscape1.jpg";
        netscape2.src    ="netscape2.jpg";
        microsoft1.src   ="microsoft1.jpg";
        microsoft2.src   ="microsoft2.jpg";
        opera1.src       ="opera1.jpg";
        opera2.src       ="opera2.jpg";
    // End hiding JavaScript statements -->
```

```
      </SCRIPT>
   </HEAD>
   <BODY>
     <A HREF="http://www.netscape.com"
       onMouseover="document.mybutton1.src=netscape2.src"
       onMouseout="document.mybutton1.src=netscape1.src">
      <IMG SRC="netscape1.jpg" BORDER="0" NAME="mybutton1"></A><P>
      <A HREF="http://www.microsoft.com"
       onMouseover="document.mybutton2.src=microsoft2.src"
       onMouseout="document.mybutton2.src=microsoft1.src">
      <IMG SRC="microsoft1.jpg" BORDER="0" NAME="mybutton2"></A><P>
      <A HREF="http://www.myopera.com"
       onMouseover="document.mybutton3.src=opera2.src"
       onMouseout="document.mybutton3.src=opera1.src">
      <IMG SRC="opera1.jpg" BORDER="0" NAME="mybutton3"></A>
   </BODY>
</HTML>
```

The trick to making your rollovers work is to preload the images into the user's cache so that when they are referenced in the script, they can be instantly displayed. The script in the head section of the page does this. The rollover menu is comprised of three images, each of which requires a second but slightly different version of each of the three images. I must therefore define six images. The following statements define each image object and preload them into cache as soon as the page starts loading:

```
netscape1        =new Image;

netscape2        =new Image;

microsoft1       =new Image;

microsoft2       =new Image;

opera1           =new Image;

opera2           =new Image;

netscape1.src    ="netscape1.jpg";

netscape2.src    ="netscape2.jpg";
```

```
microsoft1.src        ="microsoft1.jpg";

microsoft2.src        ="microsoft2.jpg";

opera1.src            ="opera1.jpg";

opera2.src            ="opera2.jpg";
```

When the page is first loaded, three images are displayed. Each of these images is defined by links in the body section. The following HTML tag shows the first link:

```
<A HREF=http://www.netscape.com
   onMouseover="document.mybutton1.src=netscape2.src"
   onMouseout="document.mybutton1.src=netscape1.src">
   <IMG SRC="netscape1.jpg" BORDER="0" NAME="mybutton1"></A><P>
```

As you can see, the onMouseOver event handler automatically loads the other version of the image when the mouse pointer passes over the image; the onMouseOut event handler puts the original image back when the mouse pointer moves away from the image. The other two links are defined in a similar fashion.

Figure 4.9 shows how the page looks after the user has placed the pointer over the Opera link. If the user clicks on the link, the URL associated with the link is loaded. Otherwise, when the user moves the pointer away the original graphic for the Opera link is reloaded.

● ●
 NOTE In order to really appreciate the rollover example, you need to load and run it for yourself. It is on the book's accompanying CD-ROM along with all the other examples that you see in this book.
● ●

Figure 4.9

Adding rollover effects to menu graphics.

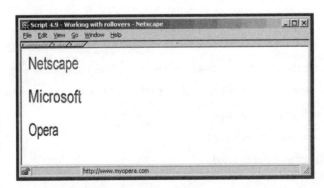

Take a Break

Now is as good a time as any to take a break. You've earned it. When you return, I will share more information about the `window` object's dialog methods and give you some advice about how to prepare to deal with all the different versions of Internet browsers that are out there. As a little bonus, I will show you how to add a clock to your Web pages and set up banners you can use to advertise your own or other people's Web sites. See you in a few minutes!

Taking Advantage of Dialog Boxes

Welcome back. I hope you had a nice break. The evening will be over before you know it, so let's get started. In addition to opening a window and displaying HTML, JavaScript provides you with access to several predefined pop-up dialog boxes you can use to interact with visitors. The three types of dialog boxes are listed here:

- Alert dialog box
- Prompt dialog box
- Confirm dialog box

You have already seen these dialog boxes in use in previous examples. The following sections explain in detail just how you can use the `window` object's `alert()`, `prompt()`, and `confirm()` methods to take full advantage of these dialog boxes.

Testing Pop-Up Dialog Boxes

The example that follows shows how you can use all three of the `window` object's methods to create pop-up dialog boxes:

```
<HTML>
  <HEAD>
    <TITLE> Script 4.10 - Testing pop-up dialog boxes</TITLE>
    <SCRIPT LANGUAGE="JavaScript" TYPE="Text/JavaScript">
    <!-- Start hiding JavaScript statements
      function AlertUsr(msg) {
          window.alert(msg);
```

```
        }
        function PromptUsr(msg) {
            age = window.prompt(msg,55);
        }
        function ConfirmUsr(msg) {
            answer = window.confirm(msg);
        }
    // End hiding JavaScript statements -->
    </SCRIPT>
  </HEAD>
  <BODY>
    <FORM>
      <INPUT NAME="button1" TYPE="button" VALUE="Alert"
        onClick="AlertUsr('This is an alert prompt!')">
      <INPUT NAME="button2" TYPE="button" VALUE="Prompt"
        onClick="PromptUsr('This is a prompt. How old are you?')">
      <INPUT NAME="button3" TYPE="button" VALUE="Confirm"
        onClick="ConfirmUsr('This is a confirmation!')">
    </FORM>
  </BODY>
</HTML>
```

The script in the head section defines three functions, one for each method. The `AlertUsr()` function executes the `window` object's `alert()` method by passing the message that it receives as an argument. No other arguments are supported.

```
function AlertUsr(msg) {
 window.alert(msg);
}
```

The `PromptUsr()` function executes the `window` object's `prompt()` method and passes it two arguments. The first argument is the message to be displayed in the prompt, and the second argument is a default value that is automatically displayed in the dialog box's text field. If you want to leave the text field empty, you should type empty quotation marks ("") in place of the argument. If you choose not to include the second argument, the word undefined appears in the text field when the dialog box pops up. This is both unattractive and inconvenient for the user.

```
function PromptUsr(msg) {
    age = window.prompt(msg,55);
}
```

The ConfirmUsr() function executes the window object's confirm() method, passing it the message it receives as an argument. No other arguments are supported.

```
function ConfirmUsr(msg) {
    answer = window.confirm(msg);
}
```

To test each function, I next defined a form with three buttons in the body section of the code. I added an onClick event handler to each button and assigned the event handler to one of the functions. For example, for the button named button1, the onClick event handler executes the AlertUsr() function and passes it the text 'This is an alert prompt!' as shown here:

```
<INPUT NAME="button1" TYPE="button"
    VALUE="Alert" onClick="AlertUsr('This is an alert prompt!')">
```

 NOTE   Notice the use of the single quotes around the message text in the onClick event handler. The single quotes are used because the JavaScript statement assigned to the onClick event handler must itself be placed within double quotes. Any time you have quotes inside other quotes, you must differentiate the pairs of quotes. I could have reversed things and used single quotes on the outside and double quotes on the inside; the result would have been the same.

Figure 4.10 shows what the page will look like if you load it using Netscape Navigator.

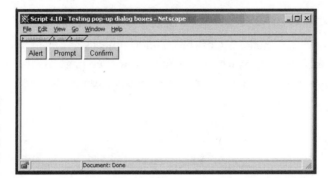

Figure 4.10

Testing the window object's pop-up dialog boxes.

Each browser displays the dialog boxes that are opened by the `window` object's `alert()`, `prompt()`, and `confirm()` methods a little differently. For example Figure 4.11 shows what the alert dialog box looks like when it opens in Internet Explorer. Figure 4.12 shows what the prompt dialog box looks like when it opens in Netscape Navigator. Figure 4.13 shows what the confirm dialog box looks like when it opens in Opera. As you can see, there are differences in the appearance of each browser's title bar.

Figure 4.11

An alert dialog box as it appears in Internet Explorer 5.

Figure 4.12

A prompt dialog box as it appears in Netscape Navigator 4.

Figure 4.13

A confirm dialog box as it appears in Opera 4.x.

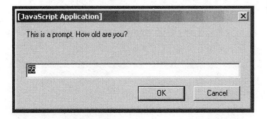

Adding a Welcome Message

One very polite way to make use of the `window` object's `alert()` method is to display a welcome message to visitors when they visit your Web page. As the following example shows, placing an `alert()` statement in the body section of the page can be done easily:

```html
<HTML>
  <HEAD>
    <TITLE>Script 4.11 - Adding a simple welcome message</TITLE>
  </HEAD>
  <BODY>
    <SCRIPT LANGUAGE="JavaScript" TYPE="Text/JavaScript">
    <!-- Start hiding JavaScript statements
      window.alert('Welcome to my Web Site!');
    // End hiding JavaScript statements -->
    </SCRIPT>
  </BODY>
</HTML>
```

NOTE Greeting messages are commonly created by using the `onLoad` event handler inside the `<BODY>` tags.

Figure 4.14 shows the result of loading the previous example in Netscape Navigator.

Figure 4.14

Displaying a generic greeting when visitors first enter your Web site.

Using the Visitor's Name in a Message

A more sophisticated greeting involves using the `window` object's `prompt()` method to ask the user to type his or her name and then to display a greeting that uses that name. The following example demonstrates this technique:

```
<HTML>
  <HEAD>
    <TITLE> Script 4.12 - Using the visitor's
           name in a message
    </TITLE>
  </HEAD>
  <BODY>
    <SCRIPT LANGUAGE="JavaScript" TYPE="Text/JavaScript">
    <!-- Start hiding JavaScript statements
      your_name =
        window.prompt('Welcome to my Web Site! What is your name?','');
      window.alert('Thanks for visiting us ' + your_name +
        '.  We hope that you enjoy your experience!');
    // End hiding JavaScript statements -->
    </SCRIPT>
  </BODY>
</HTML>
```

This example uses both the `prompt()` and the `alert()` methods to communicate with the user. The `prompt()` method is used to gather information that is then used by the `alert()` method to thank the user for visiting.

Figure 4.15 shows the first part of the interaction that the user sees when this page loads. Notice that the prompt dialog box does not display an initial message or an undefined message.

If the user clicks on OK, the alert dialog box appears as shown in Figure 4.16.

Figure 4.15

Using the
window object's
prompt()
method to collect
user input.

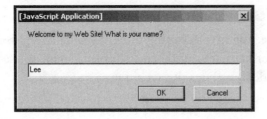

Figure 4.16

Using the window
object's alert()
method to send
the user an
informational
message.

Of course, there are many other benefits to asking for the user's name. For example, you can store it in a variable and reference it repeatedly to interact with the user or to thank the user for visiting when the onUnload event handler executes to signify that the user is leaving or closing the page. If your page also includes a form, you can use the user's name to fill in a name field and save the user some typing.

NOTE Have you ever wondered how it is that some Web sites seem to remember who you are and can greet you by name every time you visit? Well, it's because they have been baking cookies. Tomorrow, I will show you how to bake some cookies of your own. *Cookies* are small, harmless pieces of information you can store on the user's computer and retrieve the next time the user returns. For example, after you collect the user's name, you can store that information as a cookie. The next time the user returns to your Web page, you can check to see whether the user has been to your Web site before by looking to see whether the user's computer has stored one of your cookies. If you find the cookie, you can greet the user by name. If your script cannot find your cookie, the script can prompt for the user's name and save it for the next visit.

Working with Different Types of Browsers

Throughout this book, I have stated again and again that because of the constantly evolving nature of JavaScript and Internet browsers, writing Web pages that everyone can use is a bit of a chore. This task continues to be made more difficult by the appearance of new technologies such as small handheld devices and appliances that are now beginning to access the Internet but that have no JavaScript support whatsoever.

The next two sections describe how to interrogate every visitor's browser for information about its JavaScript capabilities and show ways in which you might try to support the various browsers.

Gathering Browser Information

The following example shows how to determine the type of browser and the version number of that browser that a visitor is using to load your Web page. The script uses the `navigator` object to collect browser-specific information.

```
<HTML>
  <HEAD>
    <TITLE> Script 4.13 - Gathering Browser information</TITLE>
  </HEAD>
  <BODY>
    <SCRIPT LANGUAGE="JavaScript" TYPE="Text/JavaScript">
    <!-- Start hiding JavaScript statements
      document.write("You are using the " + navigator.appName +
        " browser <BR>");
      document.write("Version: " + navigator.appVersion);
    // End hiding JavaScript statements -->
    </SCRIPT>
  </BODY>
</HTML>
```

The script consists of just two statements. The first statement uses the `document.write()` method to display a message. The message uses the `navigator.appName` property to display the name of the browser viewing the page:

```
document.write("You are using the " + navigator.appName +

    " browser <BR>");
```

A second `document.write()` statement displays another message using the `naviga-tor.appVersion` property:

```
document.write("Version: " + navigator.appVersion);
```

When you load this example, you will see results similar to those in Figure 4.17, depending on the browser you are using.

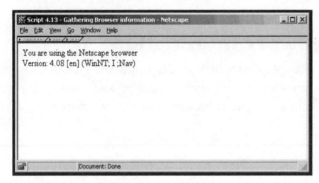

Figure 4.17

Using `navigator` object properties to gather information about the browser that loaded the Web page.

A Browser Redirection Example

Once you know how to use the properties of the `navigator` object to capture browser information, you can write scripts that redirect visitors to pages you have written to support those particular browsers. The following example shows one manner in which you can do this:

```
<HTML>
  <HEAD>
    <TITLE> Script 4.14 - A browser redirection example</TITLE>
  </HEAD>
  <BODY>
    <SCRIPT LANGUAGE="JavaScript" TYPE="Text/JavaScript">
    <!-- Start hiding JavaScript statements
      browser_name=navigator.appName;
```

```
browser_ver=parseInt(navigator.appVersion);
if ((browser_name=="Netscape") ||
    (browser_name=="Microsoft Internet Explorer")) {
  if (browser_name=="Netscape") {
    if (browser_ver==2) {
      //window.location="http://fillthispartin.com/NSver2.html";
      document.write("NS Vers 2");
    }
    if (browser_ver==3) {
      //window.location="http://fillthispartin.com/NSver3.html";
      document.write("NS Vers 3");
    }
    if (browser_ver==4) {
      //window.location="http://fillthispartin.com/NSver4.html";
      document.write("NS Vers 4");
    }
  }
  else {
    if (browser_name=="Microsoft Internet Explorer") {
      if (browser_ver==3) {
        //window.location="http://fillthispartin.com/ver3.html";
        document.write("IE Vers 3");
      }
      if (browser_ver==4) {
        //window.location="http://fillthispartin.com/ver4.html";
        document.write("IE Vers 4");
      }
      if (browser_ver==5) {
        //window.location="http://fillthispartin.com/ver5.html";
        document.write("IE Vers 5");
```

```
                }
              }
            }
          }
      else {
          //window.location=
          //"http://fillthispartin.com/unsupported.html";
          document.write("Other browsers will see this message.");
      }
    // End hiding JavaScript statements -->
    </SCRIPT>
  </BODY>
</HTML>
```

First the script creates two variables and assigns them the values of the navigator object's properties appName and appVersion.

 NOTE Did you notice that the statement that set the browser_ver variable includes the parseInt() method? This method parses a string and returns an integer value. The parseInt() method ignores all remaining characters after it finds a nonnumeric character. My version of Netscape Navigator is at 4.08. The statement browser_ver=parseInt(navigator.appVersion) returns the value 4 because the parseInt() method stopped when it came across the period.

Next, the script executes an if statement that checks to see whether the browser's appName is either Netscape or Microsoft Internet Explorer:

```
if ((browser_name=="Netscape") ||
    (browser_name=="Microsoft Internet Explorer")) {
........
}
```

If this statement proves `false`, the `else` statement associated with this `if` statement executes and displays a message on the browser. Immediately following the `else` statement is a `window.location` statement that has been commented out; this statement provides an example of how to redirect non-Netscape and non-Internet Explorer browsers to a generic page:

```
else {
    document.write("You are not using a Netscape " +
        "or Internet Explorer.");
    //window.location="http://fillthispartin.com/unsupported.html";
}
```

If the browser that opened the page was a version of Netscape Navigator, the first `if` statement would prove `true`, and the following section of code is processed. Because the browser is a Netscape Navigator browser, the next `if` statement also proves `true`. If this were not the case (that is, if the browser was not a version of Netscape Navigator), a similarly structured section of code would have tested for various versions of Internet Explorer. As the following section of code shows, a test is performed for versions 2, 3, and 4 of Netscape Navigator until a match is found. After a match is found, a message is written to the window. A comment statement provides a template you can modify to redirect the user's browser to an appropriate page.

```
if (browser_name=="Netscape") {
    if (browser_ver==2) {
        //window.location="http://fillthispartin.com/NSver2.html";
        document.write("NS Vers 2");
    }
    if (browser_ver==3) {
        //window.location="http://fillthispartin.com/NSver3.html";
        document.write("NS Vers 3");
    }
    if (browser_ver==4) {
        //window.location="http://fillthispartin.com/NSver4.html";
        document.write("NS Vers 4");
```

```
    }

}
```

Figure 4.18 shows the result of loading this page using the Opera browser. As you can see, the browser claims to be Netscape version 4, which means that the browser should be able provide the same level of JavaScript support as a Netscape Navigator version 4 browser.

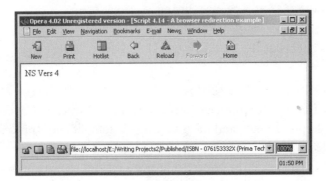

Figure 4.18

Redirecting the visitor to an alternative Web page based on the version of the browser that has been used to load the page.

Experimenting with Other Neat Stuff

In this last portion of this evening session, you will learn three very useful tricks. First, I will show you how easy it is to add a clock to your Web pages. A clock is especially useful if you create pages with which visitors are likely to spend a great deal of time. For example, you might write a page that reloads itself every few minutes so that you can provide your visitors with the real-time information you are positing on the Web site. Placing a digital clock on your pages allows your visitors to see how long they have been visiting as well as how current the existing information is.

The second example you will look at shows an option for working around one of JavaScript main weaknesses: its inability to provide meaningful, password-protected access to your Web pages. This example shows you a way to apply a relatively simple password scheme that will suffice to keep the average unauthorized Web surfer away from your site.

The last thing I will show you tonight is how to create your own banners. *Banners* are a great way to advertise other parts of your site or to make money by leasing banner space to people who want to advertise on your Web pages.

Building a JavaScript Clock

Adding a digital clock to your Web pages is a relatively simple task. All it takes is the Date object and the setTimeout() method. You can create a clock in its most simple form by using the document.write() method to display the clock. However, this example adds a finishing touch by displaying the clock inside a form text field.

```html
<HTML>
  <HEAD>
    <TITLE> Script 4.15 - Building a JavaScript Clock</TITLE>
    <SCRIPT LANGUAGE="JavaScript" TYPE="Text/JavaScript">
    <!-- Start hiding JavaScript statements
      function ShowClock() {
        the_time_is = new Date;
        the_minute = the_time_is.getMinutes();
        the_hour = the_time_is.getHours();
        the_second = the_time_is.getSeconds();
        if (the_minute < 10) {
          the_minute = "0" + the_minute;
        }
        if (the_hour < 10) {
          the_hour = "0" + the_hour;
        }
        if (the_second < 10) {
          the_second = "0" + the_second;
        }
        document.myForm.displayTime.value = the_hour + ":"  +
            the_minute + ":" + the_second;
        setTimeout("ShowClock()",1000);
      }
    // End hiding JavaScript statements -->
    </SCRIPT>
  </HEAD>
```

```
<BODY onLoad="ShowClock()">
  <FORM NAME="myForm">
    <B>The time is:</B>
    <INPUT NAME="displayTime" TYPE="TEXT" SIZE="8">
  </FORM>
</BODY>
</HTML>
```

This example places the script in the head section. The first thing the script does is to establish a function named ShowClock() that is used to acquire, format, and display the clock's data.

The first thing the ShowClock() function does is to set the value of a variable named the_time_is to the current date. It then uses the getMinutes(), getHours(), and getSeconds() methods of the Date object to extract the individual elements of time:

```
the_time_is = new Date
the_minute = the_time_is.getMinutes()
the_hour = the_time_is.getHours()
the_second = the_time_is.getSeconds()
```

To provide a consistent display, the script examines each element to make sure that it is two digits long. If the minute, hour, or second value is between 0 and 9, the script pads the value with a 0. Therefore 0 hours becomes 00 hours, 6 seconds becomes 06 seconds, and so on.

```
if (the_minute < 10) {
  the_minute = "0" + the_minute
}
if (the_hour < 10) {
  the_hour = "0" + the_hour
}
if (the_second < 10) {
  the_second = "0" + the_second
}
```

After each element has been properly formatted, the script assembles and displays the elements in the text field `displayTime` on the form `myForm` as shown here:

```
document.myForm.displayTime.value = the_hour + ":"  +

     the_minute + ":" + the_second
```

To keep the clock running, the `ShowClock()` function ends by scheduling its own execution in one second using the `setTimeout()` method:

```
setTimeout("ShowClock()",1000)
```

Figure 4.19 shows what this example looks like when you load the page.

Figure 4.19

Creating a simple digital clock.

A Simple Password Script

As I have already stated, client-side JavaScript lacks the capability to implement a true password-protection scheme for a Web site. However, when used in conjunction with a Web server-based program, JavaScript can provide a front end that collects the user's name and password, sends the user's information to the server program, and displays an HTML page that the server returns. Figure 4.20 shows this process. In this example, the server executes a CGI program that validates the user against a database and then returns an HTML page based on the success or failure of the validation process.

But by itself, a client-side JavaScript cannot accomplish this type of password validation. Of course, you could always write a script and embed user names and passwords in the code. Although this approach might stop some unwanted visitors, anyone who knows how to view HTML source code could read it and discover the names and passwords. To be a little more clever, you could place the user names and passwords in an external .js file, which would probably be enough to stop the average unauthorized user.

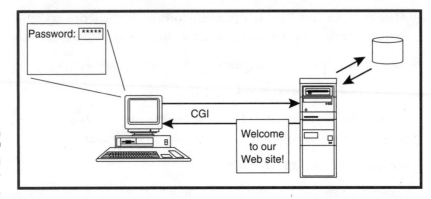

Figure 4.20

A depiction of a
typical password-
validation process.

One trick you can do to provide a measure of password protection for your Web site is to publish an intermediary Web page that requires the visitor to provide a password before loading your site's real home page. The trick is to make the required password the same as the name of your home page.

Figure 4.21 shows an example in which the visitor finds his or her way to your intermediary page and is confronted by a password form. The user must enter `ivworld` in the Password field to gain access to your site. Of course, if users become aware that the password is the name of the site's real home page, they could just as easily load that page instead of opening the intermediary password page and typing the password. However, unless you provide your users with the password, they cannot find the page; if you gave the password to them, it's probably okay for them to load the page directly anyway.

Following is the script required to implement the example in Figure 4.21:

```
<HTML>
  <HEAD>
    <TITLE> Script 4.16 - A simple password-protection example</TITLE>
    <SCRIPT LANGUAGE="JavaScript" TYPE="Text/JavaScript">
    <!-- Start hiding JavaScript statements
      function LoadTheURL() {
        document.location.href = "http://www.xxxxxxxx.com/" +
            document.myForm.psswdField.value + ".html";
      }
```

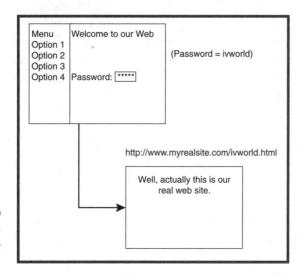

Figure 4.21

Requiring a password to access to your Web site.

```
    // End hiding JavaScript statements -->
    </SCRIPT>
  </HEAD>
  <BODY>
    <B>Please type your password:</B>
    <FORM NAME="myForm">
      <INPUT NAME="psswdField" TYPE="password" size="15">
      <INPUT NAME="Login" TYPE="button" VALUE="Login"
        onClick="LoadTheURL()">
    </FORM>
  </BODY>
</HTML>
```

NOTE For the previous example to work you need to substitute `http://www.xxxxxxxx.com` with the URL of a real web site.

First a function named LoadTheURL() is defined in the head section. The function consists of one statement. The href property of the location object, a child of the document object, is set to the to the value of a URL address. This address is a concatenated string that includes the value of document.myForm.passwdField.value. This value contains the password typed by the user.

```
function LoadTheURL() {

    document.location.href = "http://www.yourwebsite.com/" +
    document.myForm.psswdField.value + ".html"

}
```

The value of document.myForm.passwdField.value is established in the page's form. The form is named myForm and contains two elements. The first element is a password field named passwdField. This field is similar to the text field you have seen in other form examples except that it automatically hides the characters as the user types them, thus hiding the password from prying eyes. The second form element is a button with an onClick event handler that calls the LoadTheURL() function when the button is clicked.

```
<FORM NAME="myForm">

    <INPUT NAME="psswdField" TYPE="password" size="15">

    <INPUT NAME="Login" TYPE="button" VALUE="Login"

        onClick="loadTheURL()">

</FORM>
```

The result is that as soon as the script sets the document.location.href property, the browser tries to load the target URL. If the user types the wrong password, an error appears, otherwise your home page loads.

NOTE This is a very simple script. In real life, you would probably want to add code that validates the contents of the form before processing it. For example, you could make sure that the user does not leave the Password field blank. I will go into great detail tomorrow about how to validate your forms.

Figure 4.22 shows what the preceding script looks like when it is loaded by the browser.

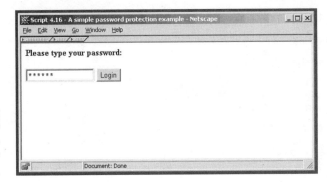

Figure 4.22

Password-protecting your Web site.

A Rotating Banner Example

The final example for the night shows you one way to create a cycling banner on your Web site. In this case, the script cycles through four banners; the script can be easily modified to accommodate as many or as few banners as you want to display.

 NOTE An alternative to using JavaScript to create banners is to use a graphics application to create an animated GIF image that automatically cycles through a collection of GIF files. However, creating banners using JavaScript gives you several advantages over using animated GIFs: With JavaScript, you can easily adjust the behavior of the banner. With JavaScript, you can use JPEG files, which produce clearer images and are smaller than their GIF counterparts, making them download faster. You can bet that people who visit your Web site will appreciate that!

```
<HTML>
  <HEAD>
    <TITLE> Script 4.17 - A Rotating Banner Example</TITLE>
    <SCRIPT LANGUAGE="JavaScript" TYPE="Text/JavaScript">
    <!-- Start hiding JavaScript statements
      MyBannerArray = new Array(4);
      MyBannerArray[0]="banner0.jpg";
      MyBannerArray[1]="banner1.jpg";
```

```
            MyBannerArray[2]="banner2.jpg";

            MyBannerArray[3]="banner3.jpg";

            current_banner=0;

            no_of_banners=MyBannerArray.length;

            function CycleBanner() {

                if (current_banner==no_of_banners) {

                    current_banner=0;

                }

                document.myBanner.src=MyBannerArray[current_banner];

                current_banner ++;

                setTimeout("CycleBanner()", 5*1000);

            }

        // End hiding JavaScript statements -->

        </SCRIPT>

    </HEAD>

    <BODY onLoad="CycleBanner()">

        <CENTER> <IMG NAME="myBanner" SRC="banner0.jpg"> </CENTER>

    </BODY>

</HTML>
```

The first thing the script does is to define and populate an array named `MyBannerArray` with the four JPEG images files:

```
MyBannerArray = new Array(4);

MyBannerArray[0]="banner0.jpg";

MyBannerArray[1]="banner1.jpg";

MyBannerArray[2]="banner2.jpg";

MyBannerArray[3]="banner3.jpg";
```

Next, two variables are created. The first variable is used to track the currently selected element in the array. The second variable represents the total number of elements in the array:

```
current_banner=0;

no_of_banners=MyBannerArray.length;
```

Then a function called `CycleBanner()` is created. It contains an `if` statement that compares the value of `current_banner` to `no_of_banners`. With each iteration of this function, the value of `current_banner` is incremented by 1. When `current_banner` equals `no_of_banners`, every banner will have been displayed. The `if` statement then sets `current_banner` back to 0, thus preparing the next cycle of the banner rotation.

```
if (current_banner==no_of_banners) {

   current_banner=0;

}
```

The script then sets the image source for the `myBanner` image (`document.myBanner.src`) equal to the current banner (`MyBannerArray[current_banner]`). Then it increments the value of `current_banner` to represent the next JPEG in the array:

```
document.myBanner.src=MyBannerArray[current_banner];

current_banner++;
```

The last thing the function does is to use the `setTimeout()` method to call itself again in 5 seconds, thus establishing an indefinite loop:

```
setTimeout("CycleBanner()", 5*1000);
```

 NOTE To ensure a smooth and attractive effect as the banners roll by, make sure that all the banner images have the same physical dimensions.

Figure 4.23 shows the results of loading this script in a browser. The first of four banners appears in the body of the page; it will be replaced in five seconds by the second image in the array.

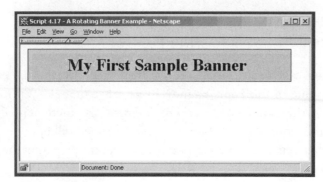

Figure 4.23

Making money by renting banner space on your Web pages.

What's Next?

Whew! That was a lot to cover in a single session. By now, you should be feeling pretty good about your JavaScript skills. I'll bet that, based on what you have learned so far, you already have plenty of ideas for things you want to try on your Web pages.

Tomorrow, you will learn how JavaScript can work with frames, forms, plug-ins, debugging, and cookies. Yes, I will even show you how to bake your first JavaScript cookie. So go get a good night's sleep, and we'll get started again in the morning.

Enhancing Web Pages with Frames and Forms

- ✿ Introducing Frames
- ✿ Creating Frames with HTML
- ✿ Using JavaScript to Manage Frames
- ✿ Introducing Forms
- ✿ Creating Forms with HTML
- ✿ Using JavaScript to Manage Forms

Good morning, and welcome back. Last night, you learned how to do a lot with JavaScript, including how to take control of the browser's status bar, improve browser navigation, create and control dialog boxes, and detect and work with different types of browsers. You even learned how to create a JavaScript clock, a password script, and an advertisement banner.

This morning, you will focus on two topics: forms and frames. The pace this morning might seem a little slower than yesterday's because you won't be moving from topic to topic like you did yesterday. However, I know you will find this morning's material just as valuable and interesting as yesterday's.

NOTE You might be wondering why I did not cover the HTML portion of this chapter in the Appendix E, "A Basic HTML Overview," that is included on this book's CD. The HTML review provided in Appendix E is provided to ensure that everyone who reads this book has at least a basic understanding of HTML. For many, a review of this appendix might be unnecessary. Frames and forms are more advanced topics, and I wanted to go over them in conjunction with the JavaScript coverage of these topics to ensure the most thorough coverage possible. If you are already familiar with working with HTML forms or frames, you might want to just skim over the portions of this morning's session that review these topics and focus your attention on the JavaScript topics.

By the time the morning is over, you will be able to organize and control your Web pages using frames managed by JavaScript. You will learn how to load other people's Web pages inside your frames and how to prevent others from doing the same thing with your Web pages. You will also learn a great deal about forms, including how to create them, validate their contents, and submit them using e-mail.

Here's an overview of what you'll cover in this session:

- Organizing you Web site with frames
- Managing your frame with JavaScript
- Incorporating forms into your HTML
- Managing your forms with JavaScript

Introducing Frames

So far, everything I have shown you has been in the form of a window. In other words, all the Web pages you have worked with have the window object at the top of the page's object hierarchy. In addition, every HTML page so far has contained a head and a body section. You have embedded JavaScripts in both of these sections.

Modern browsers provide an alternative approach to organizing and presenting data within the browser. Using *frames*, HTML can divide a window into multiple smaller windows, each of which is its own entity with its own URL. In fact, as far as JavaScript is concerned, a frame is simply a variation of the window object. So even though there is a JavaScript frame object, this object is really just a convenient way of referring to a specialized window object. Because a frame is a window object, frame objects support the same methods and properties that window objects do. When you use frames, you will have one frame object for every frame defined on the page.

Frames are an advanced HTML programming technique. Not everybody uses them, although you do see them a lot in professional Web sites. As you will see, frames are very easy to create and manage, and they provide you with a great tool for presenting and managing your Web site.

Creating Frames with HTML

Frames are created using the HTML <FRAMESET> and <FRAME> tags. The <FRAMESET> tag replaces the body section in an HTML page. This tag defines how your frames will be laid out and how space will be allocated to each frame.

Because the <FRAMESET> and <FRAME> tags are so closely tied to one another, it is difficult to discuss one without mentioning the other. Therefore I am going to present them simultaneously. The syntax of the <FRAMESET> tag is as follows:

```
<FRAMESET ROWS="" COLS="" onLoad="" onUnload="">
    .
    .
    .

</FRAMESET>
```

A frameset can contain any number of frames; it can even contain other framesets. The frameset can also contain the <NOFRAMES> tag, which supports browsers that are not enabled to work with frames by displaying alternative text information.

All the frameset's attributes are optional. The frameset's ROWS and COLS attributes allow you to specify the physical dimensions of the frames that make up the frameset. For example, specifying a frameset that contains two rows and two columns yields a total of four frames. Both of these attributes accept a comma-delineated list of lengths. Each length value represents the amount of space to be assigned to a frame. You can specify the length value in any of these three formats:

- **Percentage:** Assigns a length to one of the dimensions based on the amount of space available. For example, ROWS="50%,50%" defines two rows and allocates 50 percent of all available space to the first row and the remaining 50 percent of space to the second row.

- **Pixels:** Specifies the number of pixels to be assigned. For example, COLS="162,738" defines two columns and assigns the first column a width of 162 pixels and the second a column a width of 738 pixels.

- **Relative:** Allows you to specify relative values. For example, COLS="2*,*" tells the browser to allocate twice as much space to the first column as it assigns to the second column.

NOTE You can also mix and match length formats. For example, COLS="140,*" assigns 140 pixels to the first column and all of the remaining space to the second column.

By default, the browser assumes that 100 percent of available space should be used when displaying the frames in the frameset. When specific COLS and ROWS attributes are specified, the browser builds the frames by assigning the specified length values on a top-down and left-to-right basis.

NOTE If you overestimate the amount of space when defining the COLS and ROWS attributes, the browser automatically scales down that dimension of the frames. For example, if you accidentally specified COLS="80%,80%", the browser automatically scales down the dimensions of the two columns to 50 percent each.

The onLoad and onUnload event handlers allow you to assign the JavaScript statements or functions you want to be executed whenever all the frames on the page are loaded or unloaded.

NOTE You should always consider adding <NOFRAMES> tags to your pages. In addition to being polite, these tags help ensure that everyone can get some value from your Web pages. The following example demonstrates how to display a message that browsers that do not support frames will display. Notice that the <BODY> and </BODY> tags were included inside the <NOFRAMES> and </NOFRAMES> tags.

```
<NOFRAMES>
  <BODY>
    Browsers that do not support frames will show this message.
</NOFRAMES>
  </BODY>
</NOFRAMES>
```

<FRAME> tags exist only inside <FRAMESET> tags; they specify a rectangular area within the frameset. By default a frame occupies the entire area of the frameset that is has been assigned too. The <FRAME> tag can include a number of attributes:

○ NAME: The name used when referencing the frame.

○ SRC: The URL that is loaded into the frame.

○ LONGDESC: An optional long description that further describes the frame's contents.

- ✿ FRAMEBORDER: A value of either 0 or 1. A value of 1 places a visible border around the frame.

- ✿ MARGINWIDTH: A value that pads the width portion of the area assigned to the frame with the specified number of pixels.

- ✿ MARGINHEIGHT: A value that pads the height portion of the area assigned to the frame with the specified number of pixels.

- ✿ NORESIZE: If this parameter is specified, it prevents the user from resizing the frame.

- ✿ SCROLLING: If this parameter is specified, it allows you to determine when scrollbars are added to the frame (your options are yes, no, or auto). If this parameter is not specified, the default is auto.

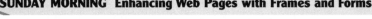

TIP

Removing a frame's borders by setting the FRAMEBORDER attribute to 0 automatically prevents users from being able to resize the frame and eliminates the need to specify the NORESIZE attribute.

NOTE

Even if you specify FRAMEBORDER=1, an adjacent frame that has its FRAMEBORDER set to 0 can still establish a border between the two frames.

Building Your First Frame

In its simplest form, an example using frames involves three different HTML pages. The first page contains the <FRAMESET> and <FRAME> tags and defines the layout in which the other pages will be displayed. The other two pages provide the content that is loaded into the frames; each of these pages is composed of typical HTML and JavaScript statements.

Following is such an example. The first page contains two <FRAME> tags inside a single <FRAMESET> tag. The <FRAMESET> tag defines two frames using the COLS="*,*" attribute, which instructs the browser to assign all available space to the frames. The first frame is named left and loads the specified page. Because the frameset used the COLS attribute to define two column frames, the first frame is the left column. The second frame is named right and is assigned a different page to load.

```
<HTML>

  <HEAD>

    <TITLE>Script 5.1a - Building your first frame </TITLE>

  </HEAD>

  <FRAMESET COLS="*,*">

    <FRAME SRC="Script5.1b.html" NAME="left">

    <FRAME SRC="Script5.1c.html" NAME="right">

  </FRAMESET>

</HTML>
```

 NOTE Not every HTML file referenced in this chapter will be shown. However, they can be found on the book's accompanying CD.

The page in the left frame contains a simple HTML header tag that displays a message that makes it easy to identify which frame the page is loaded into, as shown in the following example.

```
<HTML>

  <HEAD>

    <TITLE>Script 5.1b - left.html</TITLE>

  </HEAD>

  <BODY>

    <H3>This is the left frame.</H3>

  </BODY>

</HTML>
```

Likewise, the page in the right frame contains an HTML heading tag that displays a message that makes it easy to tell which frame that page is loaded into:

```
<HTML>

  <HEAD>

    <TITLE>Script 5.1c - right.html</TITLE>
```

```
  </HEAD>

  <BODY>

    <H3>This is the right frame.</H3>

  </BODY>

</HTML>
```

Figure 5.1 shows what the frames will look like if you load the example using Netscape Navigator.

NOTE The previous example loaded pages that were located on the same server as the page that contained the frameset definition. Alternatively, you can load any URL address into a frame. For example, `<FRAME SRC="http://www.netscape.com" NAME="left">` and `<FRAME SRC="http://www.microsoft.com" NAME="right">` load the Netscape and Microsoft home pages into the left and right frames.

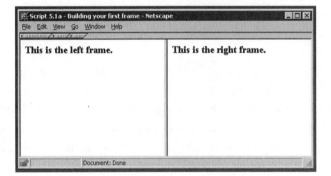

Figure 5.1

A simple pair of frames displaying the contents of two different Web pages.

Creating a Navigation Frame

Perhaps the most common use of frames is to provide a navigation menu on a Web site. In this case, a small frame is defined on the left side of the page that contains a series of links. When one of these links is clicked, content is loaded into the right frame. You create this arrangement in a very similar manner as in the previous example, except that the left frame contains specially formatted links that load the specified URL into the right frame instead of into its own frame.

The following three HTML pages demonstrate how you can create a Web site using this frame navigation technique. The first page contains two <FRAME> tags inside a single <FRAMESET> tag. The <FRAMESET> tag defines two frames as specified by the COLS="162,*" parameter, which tells the browser to create a window with two frames-based columns. The first column is 162 pixels wide. All available remaining space is assigned to the second column and its frame.

```
<HTML>

  <HEAD>

    <TITLE>Script 5.2a - Building a Web site with a

                navigation frame

    </TITLE>

  </HEAD>

  <FRAMESET COLS="162,*">

    <FRAME SRC="Script5.2b.html" NAME="left" SCROLLING="auto">

    <FRAME SRC="Script5.2c.html" NAME="right" SCROLLING="auto">

  </FRAMESET>

</HTML>
```

The two <FRAME> tags in this page load initial contents into each frame. The following page is loaded into the left frame and serves as the navigation menu for the Web site. It contains three links, each of which loads a new page into the right frame when selected. The link's TARGET="" attribute directs the browser to override the default action of loading the page into the currently selected frame and instead loads it into the specified frame—in this case, the frame named right.

```
<HTML>

  <HEAD>

    <TITLE>Script 5.2b - The Web site's navigation page</TITLE>

  </HEAD>

  <BODY>

    <P><B>Sample Index</B></P>
```

```
        <A HREF="Script5.2d.html" TARGET="right">Sample Link 1</A><BR>

        <A HREF="Script5.2e.html" TARGET="right">Sample Link 2</A><BR>

        <A HREF="Script5.2f.html" TARGET="right">Sample Link 3</A><BR>

    </BODY>

</HTML>
```

The third page in this example is simply the initial main page that is loaded into the right frame when the browser opens the frame page (see Figure 5.2). This page is unloaded as soon as the user clicks on one of the links in the navigation page.

```
<HTML>

    <HEAD>

        <TITLE>Script 5.2c - The main page for the Web site</TITLE>

    </HEAD>

    <BODY>

        <H3>This is the initial content page that is

                displayed in the right frame.

        </H3>

    </BODY>

</HTML>
```

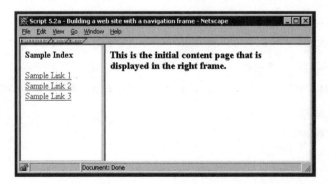

Figure 5.2

An example of using frames to provide a navigation menu for a Web site.

Nesting Framesets

Of course, you can have more than two frames on a single page. In fact, you can have as many frames on the page as you want (although there is an obvious practical limit to the amount of space available on the screen).

The following example demonstrates how to nest one frameset inside another to create pages with frames based on multiple rows and columns. In this example, four frames are created.

The first <FRAMESET> tag defines two frames and assigns 20 percent of the available space to the first frame and 80 percent of the available space to the second frame. The next line defines a frame named left. This frame provides a navigation index for the rest of the page. Next, a new <FRAMESET> tag is added; this frameset takes the space that would have gone to the second frame and assigns it to three new frames. The first and second frames are each assigned one-third of the available space and the third frame is assigned the remaining 34 percent of space. The final three lines contain <FRAME> statements that name each frame and load their initial content.

```
<HTML>
  <HEAD>
    <TITLE> Script 5.3a -Example of a Nested Frameset</TITLE>
  </HEAD>
  <FRAMESET COLS="20%,80%">
    <FRAME SRC="Script5.3b.html" NAME="left" SCROLLING="auto">
    <FRAMESET ROWS="33%,33%,34%">
      <FRAME SRC="Script5.3c.html" NAME="right1" SCROLLING="auto">
      <FRAME SRC="Script5.3d.html" NAME="right2" SCROLLING="auto">
      <FRAME SRC="Script5.3e.html" NAME="right3" SCROLLING="auto">
    </FRAMESET>
  </FRAMESET>
</HTML>
```

The following is the code for the navigation page that is loaded in the left frame. Notice that the TARGET attribute for each link is set up to load a page into a different frame.

```
<HTML>

  <HEAD>

    <TITLE> Script 5.3b- The navigation page for

                 the nested FRAMESET example

    </TITLE>

  </HEAD>

  <BODY>

    <P><B>Sample Index</B></P>

      <A HREF="Script5.3f.html" TARGET="right1">Replace frame 1</A>

      <BR>

      <A HREF="Script5.3g.html" TARGET="right2">Replace frame 2</A>

      <BR>

      <A HREF="Script5.3h.html" TARGET="right3">Replace frame 3</A>

      <BR>

  </BODY>

</HTML>
```

The rest of the pages that make up this example are simple HTML pages containing messages formatted as HTML headings. These pages are named Script5.3c through Script5.3h and are available for review on the CD that accompanies this book. Figure 5.3 shows what the page with its four frames looks like when it's loaded in a browser.

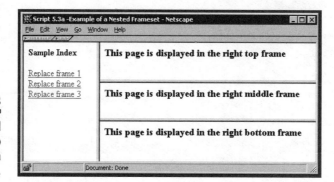

Figure 5.3

Using nested framesets to organize a Web site.

Taking Care of Browsers That Cannot Display Frames

Many older browsers do not support frames. In addition, some browsers allow their owners to disable frame support. For example, you can disable frame support in the Opera browser by choosing File, Preferences; when the Preferences dialog box opens as shown in Figure 5.4, click the Documents option in the Category list and then disable the Enable Frames checkbox.

To anticipate the possibility that such a browser will try to open your framed page, you can use the <NOFRAMES> tag to display alternative content. <NOFRAMES> tags are placed within <FRAMESET> tags and must include <BODY> tags using the following syntax:

```
<FRAMESET>

   <NOFRAMES>

     <BODY>

          .

          .

          .

     </BODY>

   </NOFRAMES>

</FRAMESET>
```

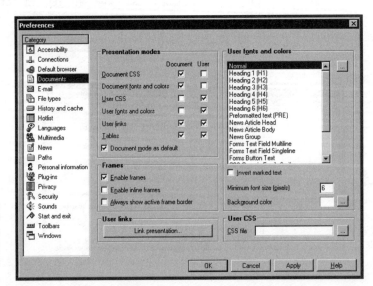

Figure 5.4

Select Documents before disabling frame support in Opera 4.02.

The following example shows how you might employ the <NOFRAMES> tag to communicate with your visitors who use frame-impaired browsers:

```
<HTML>

  <HEAD>

    <TITLE>Script 5.4a- Displaying alternate content

                   for frame impaired browsers

    </TITLE>

  </HEAD>

  <FRAMESET COLS="162,*">

    <FRAME SRC="Script5.4b.html" NAME="left" SCROLLING="auto">

    <FRAME SRC="Script5.4c.html" NAME="right" SCROLLING="auto">

    <NOFRAMES>

      <BODY>

        <P>This text provides alternative content for browsers

              without frame support.

        </P>

      </BODY>

    </NOFRAMES>

  </FRAMESET>

</HTML>
```

NOTE You might be tempted to include a message instructing visitors with frame-impaired browsers to download and install a more current browser. Just remember that your visitors' browsers may be capable of displaying frames but that they have simply chosen to disable frame support. Consider phrasing any message you display so that it addresses both possibilities for why the browser cannot display frames.

Figure 5.5 shows what the frame-disabled Opera browser displays when this script is loaded.

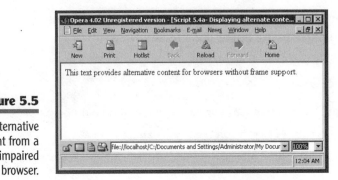

Figure 5.5

Viewing alternative content from a frame-impaired browser.

TIP

It is generally considered good programming practice to include <NOFRAMES> tags every time you use frames. Doing so ensures that your visitors can benefit from your Web pages regardless of their browsers' support for frames. One option is to place a link to either your main page or to the Web page that serves as the navigation index.

Using JavaScript to Manage Frames

So far, you have looked at frames only within the context of HTML programming. However, you also can use JavaScript to control frames and frame content. JavaScript provides you with the capability of controlling more than one frame at a time—something that cannot be accomplished with HTML.

Before you can take advantage of JavaScript's capability to control frames, you must first understand something about how the browsers build a frame hierarchy into your Web pages. Every frame belongs to a frameset that can be referred to as the frame's `parent` or `top`. Each frame in the frameset is listed in an array named `frames[]` based on the order in which the page is loaded. The first frame in the array is `frames[0]`, the second is `frames[1]`, and so on.

For example, the following page defines a simple two-frame display:

```
<HTML>

  <HEAD>

    <TITLE> Script 5.5a- Demonstrating frame hierarchy</TITLE>

  </HEAD>
```

```
<FRAMESET COLS="*,*">

  <FRAME SRC="Script5.5b.html" NAME="left">

  <FRAME SRC="Script5.5c.html" NAME="right">

</FRAMESET>

</HTML>
```

Structurally, the browser that loads this page will create a frame hierarchy that is logically organized as shown in Figure 5.6.

As you can see, the `top` or `parent` frameset is at the top of the hierarchy, and each frame in the frameset is listed in the order in which it is defined. Now that you understand how the browser creates this frame hierarchy, you can use JavaScript to reference and control frames. For example, `parent.frame[0]` and `top.frame[0]` both refer to the first frame; `parent.frame[1]` and `top.frame[1]` reference the second frame. An array is automatically created that contains an entry for each form on the Web page beginning with an index of 0 based on the order in which the frames are defined.

NOTE If you add the `NAME=""` attribute to the `<FRAME>` tag, you can also refer to individual frames by their assigned name. In the preceding example, which names the frames `left` and `right`, you could reference the first frame in the hierarchy with either the `parent.left` or `top.left` statement.

Figure 5.6

Viewing the logical structure of a page frame hierarchy.

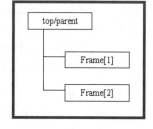

Creating Frame Content Using JavaScript

HTML provides only static content. One of the benefits of using JavaScript with frames is that you can provide dynamic content on a frame. In other words, you can write directly to a frame instead of loading a Web page into it. The following example demonstrates this technique.

The first page in this example contains <FRAMESET> and <FRAME> tags that define the structure for the Web site. In this case, two frames are defined in column format and assigned equal amounts of space. To keep things simple, I named the frames left and right.

```
<HTML>
  <HEAD>
    <TITLE>Script 5.6a- Using JavaScript to add
                dynamic content to frames
    </TITLE>
  </HEAD>
  <FRAMESET COLS="*,*">
    <FRAME SRC="Script5.6b.html" NAME="left">
    <FRAME SRC="Script5.6c.html" NAME="right">
  </FRAMESET>
</HTML>
```

The left frame contains a form with a button that, when clicked, executes the JavaScript statement top.right.document.write('Hello world!') and, as a result, displays the message *Hello world!* in the right frame. You might remember that the top or parent reference represents the top of the frame hierarchy. The top.right call refers to the frame named right in the same frameset as the left frame (its "sibling" frame, and the frame that contains the top.right statement). Had you left the top.right reference off the document.write() statement, the message would have been written in the left frame.

```
<HTML>
  <HEAD>
    <TITLE>Script 5.6b- Writing dynamic content</TITLE>
  </HEAD>
  <BODY>
```

```
<FORM>

  <INPUT TYPE="button" NAME="button1" VALUE="Click Me"

     onClick="top.right.document.write('<H3>Hello world!</H3>')">

  </FORM>

 </BODY>

</HTML>
```

The following page shows you the structure of the `right` frame:

```
<HTML>

 <HEAD>

  <TITLE>Script 5.6c- The initial content displayed

              in the right frame

  </TITLE>

 </HEAD>

 <BODY>

  <H3>This is the right frame.</H3>

 </BODY>

</HTML>
```

Figure 5.7 shows how things look after you load the frame and click on the Click Me button.

Figure 5.7

An example of using JavaScript to post messages onto frames instead of unloading and loading new pages.

Controlling Frames with JavaScript

You already know that you can load Web pages into target frames using the HTML link tag as shown here:

```
<A HREF="link1.html" TARGET="right_pane">Sample Link 1</A><BR>
```

Alternatively, you can use JavaScript to load pages into your frames. Because of the JavaScript programming logic, you can exercise greater control over how and when the frames are unloaded and loaded. The following example shows how you can replace your HTML links with JavaScript to manage your frames. The example consists of four pages. The first page contains the <FRAMESET> and <FRAME> tags and defines the overall structure of the Web site. In this case, two frames are defined and named left and right; both are assigned 50 percent of the available display area in the browser.

```
<HTML>

  <HEAD>

    <TITLE> Script 5.7a- Controlling frames with JavaScript</TITLE>

  </HEAD>

  <FRAMESET COLS="*,*">

    <FRAME SRC="Script5.7b.html" NAME="left">

    <FRAME SRC="Script5.7c.html" NAME="right">

  </FRAMESET>

</HTML>
```

The left frame contains a form that defines a button named button1 that displays the text *Click Me*. When clicked, the button's onClick event handler is executed. Using the browser hierarchy, the JavaScript statement in the event handler first references the top (or parent) of the hierarchy. Next, the statement specifies the frame in which the new page will be loaded. Instead of referencing the frame as parent.right, the frame is identified using its location in the frames[] array. Because the target frame is the second frame that was defined and the frames[] array starts with an index value of 0, parent.frames[1] is used to reference the second frame. Next, the location property is added. Finally, the HTML page that is to be loaded is specified.

```
<HTML>

  <HEAD>

    <TITLE> Script 5.7b- Adding the JavaScript control</TITLE>
```

```
    </HEAD>
    <BODY>
      <FORM>
        <INPUT TYPE="button" NAME="button1" VALUE="Click Me"
          onClick="parent.frames[1].location='Script5.7d.html'">
      </FORM>
    </BODY>
</HTML>
```

The page that is initially loaded into the right frame is very straightforward:

```
<HTML>
  <HEAD>
    <TITLE> Script 5.7c- Initial content loaded
                    into the right frame
    </TITLE>
  </HEAD>
  <BODY>
    <H3>This is the right frame.</H3>
  </BODY>
</HTML>
```

The page that will be loaded into the right frame when the button is clicked is equally straightforward, containing a single message formatted as an HTML heading:

```
<HTML>
  <HEAD>
    <TITLE> Script 5.7d- The new page</TITLE>
  </HEAD>
  <BODY>
    <H3>This is the new frame you just loaded!</H3>
  </BODY>
</HTML>
```

Figure 5.8 shows the result of loading this example and clicking on the Click Me button. In the next example, I will show you how to use JavaScript to do something that HTML alone cannot do: control more than one frame at a time.

Figure 5.8

An example of loading pages under the control of JavaScript.

Controlling More than One Frame at a Time

The next example shows how easy it is to use JavaScript to control more than one frame at a time. In this case, I have modified the form in the `left` frame from the previous example. As you can see, the `onClick` event handler now specifies a second JavaScript statement. I was able to add the second statement to the event handler by placing a semicolon at the end of the first statement. Had I wanted to add yet another statement to the event handler, I probably would have elected to create a function, placed all the statements within the function brackets, and then called the function from within the `onClick` event handler.

The structure of the second statement is the same as that of the first statement except that it references a difference frame (the `parent.frame[1]` frame, or the `right` frame).

```
<HTML>

  <HEAD>

    <TITLE> Script 5.8b- Controlling more than one

                  frame at a time with JavaScript

    </TITLE>

  </HEAD>

  <BODY>

    <FORM>
```

```
<INPUT TYPE="button" NAME="button1" VALUE="Click Me"
    onClick="parent.frames[0].location='Script5.8d.html';
               parent.frames[1].location='Script5.8e.html'">
   </FORM>
  </BODY>
</HTML>
```

Displaying Other Web Sites Using Frames

In this example, I will show you how to provide your visitors with links to other sites and to allow them to visit these sites without ever leaving your site.

One of the disadvantages of providing your visitors with links to other sites is that they may follow them and never come back to your site. However, if you use frames, you can have the best of both worlds. In addition to keeping your visitors in your site and providing a very slick interface, you can give even small Web sites the impression of being huge megasites by doing nothing more than loading other URLs into your frames.

The following example creates a Web site using frames. The frame on the left provides a navigation menu; the frame on the top right displays your Web site's title or other useful information. The remaining frame is used to display the URLs of other Web sites.

The first page defines the layout of the frames. In this case, a <FRAMESET> tag divides the display into two columns, assigning 15 percent of the space to the first column and the remaining 85 percent to the second column. Next, a <FRAME> tag specifies the page that will serve as the navigation index. A second nested <FRAMESET> tag divides the space allocated to the second column into two rows and assigns eight percent to the first row and the remaining 92 percent to the second row. Two frames are then defined. The first loads a local Web page into the small top frame, and the second loads the URL for a popular Internet search engine, www.yahoo.com, into the larger frame.

```
<HTML>
  <HEAD>
    <TITLE> Script 5.9a- Loading other URLs into your frames</TITLE>
  </HEAD>
  <FRAMESET COLS="15%,85%">
```

```
<FRAME SRC="Script5.9b.html" NAME="left" SCROLLING="auto">
<FRAMESET ROWS="8%,92%">
  <FRAME SRC="Script5.9c.html" NAME="right1" SCROLLING="auto">
  <FRAME SRC="http://www.yahoo.com" NAME="right2"
      SCROLLING="auto">
</FRAMESET>
</FRAMESET>
</HTML>
```

The navigation page loaded into the `left` frame defines several links to other popular Internet search engines. In this case, since the links to these URLs are all loaded into the same frame, I choose to use HTML link tags with the `target` attribute:

```
<HTML>
  <HEAD>
    <TITLE> Script 5.9b- Using the left frame as
                a navigation page
    </TITLE>
  </HEAD>
  <BODY>
    <P><B>Search Engines:</B></P>
      <A HREF="http://www.excite.com" TARGET="right2">Excite</A>
      <BR>
      <A HREF="http://www.alta-vista.com" TARGET="right2">AltaVista</A>
      <BR>
      <A HREF="http://www.yahoo.com" TARGET="right2">Yahoo</A>
      <BR>
  </BODY>
</HTML>
```

The next page will be loaded into the `top` frame and is used to display the name of the Web site; this frame helps to give a polished look and feel to the Web site.

```
<HTML>

  <HEAD>

    <TITLE> Script 5.9c- Adding a title frame to your Web
site</TITLE>

  </HEAD>

  <BODY>

    <CENTER>

    <H2>Welcome to my Internet Search Engine Web Site.</H2>

    </CENTER>

  </BODY>

</HTML>
```

Figure 5.9 shows what the initial display looks like when you first load this example. As you can see, by using frames and three simple scripts, you can create a Web site that provides users with access to a collection of popular URLs.

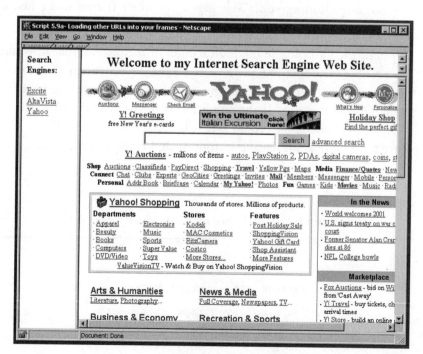

Figure 5.9

Using JavaScript to simultaneously control multiple frames.

NOTE   There are lots of ways to make money on the Internet. One way is to join associate programs with various Internet companies. In these programs, you get paid for every customer who you lead to their Web site and who then makes a purchase. For example, using a modified version of the previous example, you could easily create your own online bookstore with several pages that highlight books you think will attract customers and that provide links to other online bookstores whose affiliate programs you have joined. Visitors to your site can purchase books or anything thing else that the other online company sells. In fact, in tonight's final lesson, I'll demonstrate how to build such a bookstore.

Frames...No Thank You

Although you might appreciate how easy it is to load other URLs into your frames, you might not want to have your own Web pages show up in other people's frames—especially if your pages are loaded into frames that are too small and that make your site look bad.

That's where this frame example comes in handy. It shows you how to prevent other people from loading your Web pages into their frames using just a couple lines of JavaScript.

I placed the script inside the head section of the page so that it would execute as soon as possible. The first line in the script is an `if` statement that checks to see whether somebody is trying to load the page into a frame by checking the value of `top.frames.length`. If the condition is 0 or `true`, then the statement `top.location=self.document.location` tells the browser to set the page's `location` property to itself, thus preventing it from being loaded into a frame.

```
<HTML>

  <HEAD>

    <TITLE>Script 5.10- Preventing your Web page
                 from being loaded into a frame

    </TITLE>

    <SCRIPT LANGUAGE="JavaScript" TYPE="Text/JavasSript">

    <!-- Start hiding JavaScript statements

      if (top.frames.length!=0) {
```

```
        top.location=self.document.location;

    }
  // End hiding JavaScript statements -->

  </SCRIPT>

</HEAD>

<BODY>

  <CENTER>

    <H1>Welcome to my page!</H1><BR>

    <H3>Thanks for visiting!!!</H3>

  </CENTER>

</BODY>

</HTML>
```

Anyone who tries to load this Web page into their frame will be surprised to see that your page is not only not loaded, but also that it has completely replaced their own Web page as shown in Figure 5.10.

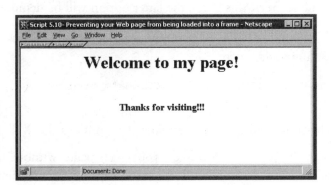

Figure 5.10

Preventing your Web pages from loading into a frame.

Take a Break

Frames are a great tool for presenting and managing information on your Web pages, and I could go on and on about them. However, there is only so much time left in the weekend, and you have plenty of new material left to cover. Why not get up to stretch your legs for a minute? When you return, I will show you how to create forms so that you can collect and process information from the people who visit your Web site.

Introducing Forms

Of course you know what a form is, so I won't bore you with a technical explanation. Within the context of an HTML page, a form is created using the <FORM> tags. Within the <FORM> tags, individual form elements such as checkboxes or text fields are defined. The syntax for an HTML form is outlined here:

```
<FORM NAME="" METHOD="" ACTION="">
```

In this syntax, the following parameters are used:

○ NAME: An optional name that you can assign to the form.

○ METHOD: Either get or post. These are two commands that can be used to send and received documents to and from Web servers. The get method is used to send a request for a document to a Web server. The post method is used to send the contents of a form to the Web server. Both of these options are beyond the scope of this book.

○ ACTION: Either the URL address that identifies the Web server and program that is to receive the form's contents or mailto, which is an option that allows you to send the form's contents in the form of an e-mail message. The former option is beyond the scope of this book; the latter option will be demonstrated at the end of the morning.

Consider this example statement:

```
<FORM NAME="myForm" METHOD="POST" ACTION="myprog.cgi">
```

This statement sends the contents of the form myForm to a CGI program called myprog.cgi that is located in the same folder that contains the Web page.

You can leverage the power of forms on your Web pages without using JavaScript. However, JavaScript provides powerful validation capabilities and allows you to interact with visitors as they fill out the forms.

The form Object

The browser creates a form object for every form element defined by <FORM> tags. You can assign a name to each element using the optional NAME="" attribute for each element, or you can use the forms[] array, which contains an index listing of every form element on the page beginning with a value index of 0. In addition, each form contains its own `elements[]` array that contains an entry for each form element on that particular form. For example, the fourth form element on a form called `myForm` can be referenced as `myForm.elements[3]`.

The `form` object has a number of properties, many of which are objects in their own right:

- ✿ `action`: Created based on the `<FORM>` tag's `ACTION` attribute.
- ✿ `button`: An object that users can click to initiate an action.
- ✿ `checkbox`: An object that allows users to select or clear its value.
- ✿ `elements[]`: An array of all the form elements.
- ✿ `encoding`: Created based on the `<FORM>` tag's `ENCTYPE` attribute.
- ✿ `fileUpload`: An object used to specify a file that can be included as form data.
- ✿ `hidden`: An object that does not appear on the form but that you can programmatically fill with data.
- ✿ `length`: A property that specifies the number of elements in the `forms[]` array.
- ✿ `method`: Created based on the `<FORM>` tag's `METHOD` attribute.
- ✿ `name`: Created based on the `<FORM>` tag's `NAME` attribute.
- ✿ `password`: An object that masks any text that is typed into it.
- ✿ `radio`: An object that is organized into a collection of similar objects, only one of which can be selected.
- ✿ `reset`: A button object that allows you to clear and reset a form to its default values.
- ✿ `select`: An object that provides a list of selectable options.
- ✿ `submit`: A button object that allows you to submit the form for processing.
- ✿ `target`: Created based on the `<FORM>` tag's `TARGET` attribute.
- ✿ `text`: An object used to hold a single line of text.
- ✿ `textarea`: An object similar to the `text` object except that it accepts multiple lines of text.

The `form` object also has several methods that can be applied to it:

- ✿ `handleEvent()`: Allows you to simulate a specific event on the specified object such as `click` or `dblclick` events.

✿ reset(): Allows you to programmatically clear and reset a form to its default values.

✿ submit(): Allows you to programmatically submit a form for processing.

NOTE Of the three form methods, only the form handleEvent() method allows you to pass it an argument. For example, handleEvent(click).

Form Components

Three different types of tags can be placed within the <FORM> tags:

✿ <INPUT>: Allows you to specify a range of form elements including text and password fields, buttons, and radio and checkbox options.

✿ <SELECT>: Allows you to create a list of selectable options.

✿ <TEXTAREA>: Specifies a multiline text field.

You will see examples of each of these tags throughout the rest of the morning.

Creating Forms with HTML

Throughout this book, you have seen example after example of forms. The rest of the morning is dedicated to explaining in greater detail how those forms work. My intention is to explain each major form element individually using short examples and then, at the end of the morning, to demonstrate how to build a larger and more complex form that ties all the pieces and parts together.

The button Element

The button form element is created by specifying the TYPE="button" attribute in the <INPUT> tag. By default, a rectangular button is displayed on the form. However, the <INPUT> tag allows you to use a graphic image in place of the default button by placing an IMG element within the tag. The <INPUT> tag's implementation of the button supports the following attributes:

✿ NAME: The name of the button.

- ✿ TYPE: The type is equal to `"button"` for this element.
- ✿ VALUE: Specifies the text that appears on the button.

The following page defines a form that contains a single button named `myButton` with the label *Click Here*. An `onClick` event handler has been added to the button so that when the button is clicked, an alert prompt appears to display a welcome message.

```
<HTML>

  <HEAD>

    <TITLE>Script 5.11- Form: A button example</TITLE>

  </HEAD>

  <BODY>

    <FORM>

      <INPUT NAME="myButton" TYPE="button" VALUE="Click Here"
             onClick="window.alert('Welcome!')">

    </FORM>

  </BODY>

</HTML>
```

Figure 5.11 shows the results of loading the previous example and displaying the Click Here button.

Figure 5.11

Displaying an alert dialog using a form's button object.

The checkbox Element

The `checkbox` form element is created by specifying the `TYPE="checkbox"` attribute in the `<INPUT>` tag. It is used to display a checkbox on the form that has only two possible values: checked or cleared. The value of the `checkbox` element is independent of any other form element. The `<INPUT>` tag's implementation of the checkbox supports the following options:

- ❖ CHECKED: When this option is specified, it sets the default value for the checkbox element to CHECKED. By default, all checkbox elements are created in the cleared state.
- ❖ NAME: The name of the checkbox element.
- ❖ VALUE: Specifies a value that is assigned when the checkbox is selected.

The following page defines a form that contains three checkboxes named checkbox1, checkbox2, and checkbox3. The CHECKED attribute that has been assigned to the second and third checkboxes results in these checkboxes being selected when the form loads. Whenever a checkbox is selected, it is assigned a value. For example, when the first checkbox is selected, the value retired is assigned to checkbox1.

```
<HTML>
  <HEAD>
    <TITLE>Script 5.12- Form: A checkbox example</TITLE>
  </HEAD>
  <BODY>
    <FORM>
    <P><B>Select any of the following options that apply to you:</B>
    </P>
    Are you older than 65?
    <INPUT NAME="checkbox1" TYPE="checkbox" VALUE="retired">
    <BR>
    Do you vacation more than twice a year?
    <INPUT NAME="checkbox2" TYPE="checkbox" VALUE="rich" CHECKED>
    <BR>
    Have you ever been on a cruise?
    <INPUT NAME="checkbox3" TYPE="checkbox" VALUE="very_rich" CHECKED>
    </FORM>
  </BODY>
</HTML>
```

Figure 5.12 shows what this form looks like when the page is first loaded by the browser.

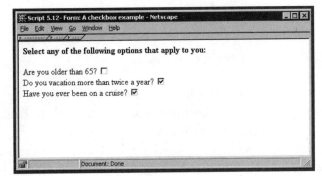

Figure 5.12

Adding
checkbox
elements to a form.

The fileUpload Element

The `fileUpload` form element is created by specifying the `TYPE="file"` attribute in the `<INPUT>` tag. The `fileUpload` element allows the user to specify a file that will serve as form input. The `<INPUT>` tag's implementation of the `fileUpload` element supports the following attributes:

- ✪ NAME: The name of the `fileUpload` field.
- ✪ TYPE: The type is equal to `"file"` for this element.
- ✪ VALUE: Specifies the name of the selected file.

The following page defines a form named `myForm` that contains two elements. First, the `<FORM>` tag uses the `METHOD` and `ACTION` attributes to identify the server-based program that will process the form after it has been submitted. The first `<INPUT>` tag defines a `fileUpload` element named `selectedFile`; the second `<INPUT>` tag creates a button that, when clicked, submits the form for processing.

```
<HTML>

  <HEAD>

    <TITLE>Script 5.13- Form: A fileUpload example</TITLE>

  </HEAD>

  <BODY>

    <FORM NAME="myform" METHOD="post" ACTION="cgi-bin/myscript">

      <INPUT NAME="selectedFile" TYPE="file"><BR>

      <INPUT NAME="myButton" TYPE="submit">
```

```
    </FORM>

  </BODY>

</HTML>
```

Figure 5.13 shows what this form looks like when the page is first loaded by the browser. Clicking on the Browse button opens the File Upload dialog box shown in Figure 5.14. From this dialog box, you can select a file and click on Open. The name and path of the file you selected is displayed in the `fileUpload` element's display field. Clicking on the Submit Query button in the form calls the specified server program and passes the form's contents to the program.

NOTE The Browse button in the previous example was automatically created by the `fileUpload` element. You cannot change the wording of this button. However, if you prefer you can change the text that is displayed on the Submit button by adding the `VALUE` attribute and setting it equal to the text that you wish to be displayed.

NOTE If you run the previous example as is, you will receive an error because the example expects to be able to find a CGI program named `cgi-bin/myscript`, which you do not have. This example is only intended to show you how you could integrate your Web pages with server-based programs. There are several more examples in this chapter that behave in the same fashion. If you prefer, you can set `ACTION=""` to test these scripts without viewing the error message.

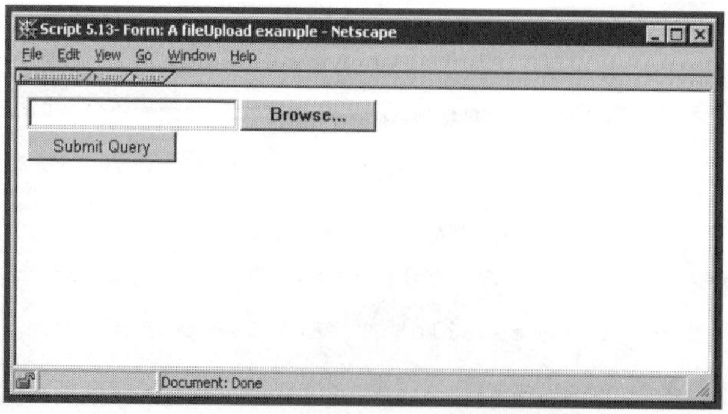

Figure 5.13

The `fileUpload` form element allows you to submit entire files as part of a form.

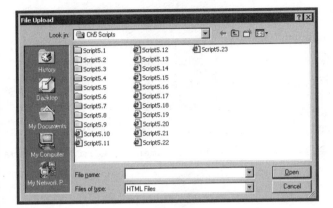

Figure 5.14

The File Upload dialog box allows you to find and select the file you want to add as form data.

The hidden Element

The `hidden` form element is created by specifying the `TYPE="hidden"` attribute in the `<INPUT>` tag. A hidden element is one that that cannot be physically seen on the form, although it can be used to hold data that is programmatically added to the form. The `<INPUT>` tag's implementation of the `hidden` element supports the following attributes:

- ✿ NAME: The name of the hidden field.
- ✿ TYPE: The type is equal to `"hidden"` for this element.
- ✿ VALUE: Specifies a value that is assigned to the hidden field.

The following page defines a form named `myForm`. The first form element is named `myField` and is a hidden form element. The next two elements are buttons. Clicking on the first button causes the button's `onClick` event handler to set the value of `myField` to the text string `User_did_not_listen`. Clicking on the second button executes its `onClick` event handler and results in an alert dialog box that displays the value of the `myField form element`. If you load this page and click on the second button first, the page displays a value of `empty` because `document.myForm.myField.value` has not yet been set.

```
<HTML>
  <HEAD>
    <TITLE>Script 5.14- Form: A hidden field example</TITLE>
  </HEAD>
```

```
<BODY>

  <FORM NAME="myForm">

    <INPUT NAME="myField" TYPE="hidden" VALUE="empty">

    <INPUT NAME="myButton1" TYPE="button" VALUE="Do not click me!"

       onClick="document.myForm.myField.value='User_did_not_listen'">

    <INPUT NAME="myButton2" TYPE="button" VALUE="Show Hidden"

        onClick="window.alert(document.myForm.myField.value)">

  </FORM>

  </BODY>

</HTML>
```

Figure 5.15 shows the results of loading this example and clicking on the first button and then clicking on the second button.

Figure 5.15

Adding a hidden object to your form.

The password Element

The password form element is created by specifying the TYPE="password" attribute in the <INPUT> tag. The password element masks the characters that the user types as asterisks to prevent the characters from being displayed. As the name implies, a common use for this form element is to hide passwords as they are being typed. Other uses might include hiding private information such as credit card or social security numbers. The <INPUT> tag's implementation of the password element supports the following attributes:

✪ NAME: The name of the password field.

- ✿ MAXLENGTH: The maximum number of characters that can be entered into the field.
- ✿ SIZE: The number of characters that the field can display.
- ✿ TYPE: The type is equal to "password" for this element.
- ✿ VALUE: Specifies an initial default value for the field.

The following page defines a form that contains a single password field named myPasswd. The SIZE="20" attribute allows the field to display 20 characters of text, while the MAXLENGTH="30" attribute limits the total number of characters that the field can accept to 30 characters.

```
<HTML>

  <HEAD>

    <TITLE>Script 5.15- Form - A password field example</TITLE>

  </HEAD>

  <BODY>

    <FORM>

    Type your password:

    <INPUT NAME="myPasswd" TYPE="password" SIZE="20" MAXLENGTH="30">

    </FORM>

  </BODY>

</HTML>
```

Figure 5.16 shows what this example looks like when you load it and type a few characters of text. As you can see, whatever text you type is masked behind asterisk characters.

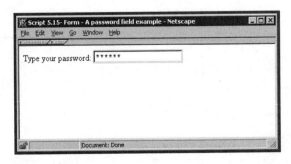

Figure 5.16

Using the password object to hide confidential information on forms.

The radio Element

The radio form element is created by specifying the TYPE="radio" attribute on the <INPUT> tag. The radio element is used to display radio buttons on the form. The selected option can have only one of two possible values: checked or cleared. Although the radio element is very similar to the checkbox element, radio elements are placed in groups, only one of which can be selected at a time. You can group radio elements by setting the NAME="" attribute of all the radio elements in the group to the same value. If you want to create a second group of radio elements, you assign all the radio elements in the second group a different name.

The <INPUT> tag's implementation of the radio element supports the following attributes:

- ✪ CHECKED: When specified, this attribute sets the default value for the radio option to CHECKED.
- ✪ NAME: The name of the group to which this individual radio button belongs.
- ✪ VALUE: Specifies the value assigned to the group when this particular radio button option is selected.

The following page defines a form that contains four radio buttons, all of which belong to the group named radio_option1. Each of the four radio buttons contains a different value. The radio button that is selected determines the value assigned to the radio_option1 group. When this page is first loaded, the third radio button is automatically selected as indicated by the CHECKED attribute in the <INPUT> tag that defines that radio button.

```
<HTML>
  <HEAD>
    <TITLE>Script 5.16- Form: A radio option example</TITLE>
  </HEAD>
  <BODY>
    <FORM>
    <P><B>Select the option that applies to you:</B></P>
    Less than 20:
    <INPUT NAME="radio_option1" TYPE="radio" VALUE="Selection1"><BR>
    Between 21-35:
    <INPUT NAME="radio_option1" TYPE="radio" VALUE=Selection2"><BR>
```

```
Between 36-55:

<INPUT NAME="radio_option1" TYPE="radio"

     VALUE="Selection3" CHECKED><BR>

Older than 56:

<INPUT NAME="radio_option1" TYPE="radio" VALUE="Selection4">

</FORM>

  </BODY>

</HTML>
```

Figure 5.17 shows what this example looks like when it is first loaded by the browser.

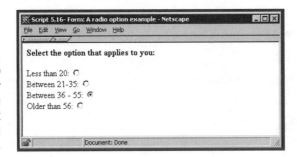

Figure 5.17

Allowing the user
to choose one
option from a list
of options using
radio buttons.

The reset Element

The `reset` form element is created by specifying the `TYPE="reset"` attribute in the `<INPUT>` tag. The `reset` element appears on the form as a rectangular button with the label *Reset*. The `reset` element comes with a built-in method for resetting the contents of the form to their default values. The `<INPUT>` tag's implementation of the `reset` element supports the following attribute:

✿ `VALUE`: Specifies the descriptive text to be displayed on the Reset button.

The following page defines a form that contains four radio buttons, all of which belong to the group named `radio_option1`. The third radio button is set as the default. The last element in the form is the `reset` element.

```
<HTML>

  <HEAD>
```

```
          <TITLE>Script 5.17- Form: A reset button example</TITLE>
     </HEAD>
     <BODY>
       <FORM NAME="myForm">
       <P><B>Select the option that applies to you:</B></P>
       Less than 20:
       <INPUT NAME="radio_option1" TYPE="radio" VALUE="Selection1"><BR>
       Between 21-35:
       <INPUT NAME="radio_option1" TYPE="radio" VALUE=Selection2"><BR>
       Between 36-55:
       <INPUT NAME="radio_option1" TYPE="radio"
             VALUE="Selection3" CHECKED><BR>
       Older than 56:
       <INPUT NAME="radio_option1" TYPE="radio" VALUE="Selection4">
       <P>
       <INPUT TYPE="reset">
       </P>
       </FORM>
     </BODY>
</HTML>
```

Figure 5.18 shows how the form looks when the page is first loaded or after the Reset button has been clicked.

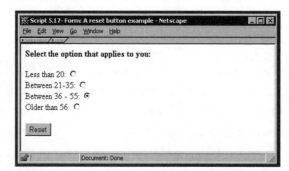

Figure 5.18

Resetting a form's contents to their initial values using the `reset` element.

The select Element

The `select` form element presents a list of options in the form of a drop-down menu or a scrollable list from which individual options can be selected. The `select` element supports the following attributes:

- `MULTIPLE`: When specified, allows multiple options to be selected from the list.
- `NAME`: The name assigned to the selected element.
- `SIZE`: The number of choices displayed in the list.

 NOTE If you do not include the `select` element's `SIZE` attribute or if you set this attribute equal to 1, the choices in the `select` element are presented in the form of a drop-down list. If you set `SIZE` to 2 or more, the choices are displayed in the form of a scrollable list instead.

Starting and ending `<SELECT>` and `</SELECT>` tags identify the `select` element. All the choices that appear in the list are specified with individual `<OPTION>` tags. The `<OPTION>` tag supports these two attributes:

- `SELECTED`: Specifies the default choice.
- `VALUE`: Specifies the value associated with this choice.

The following page defines a form that contains a drop-down list named `myList` that presents four choices. The first choice has been set as the default selection. Each choice in the list has been assigned a different value and displays a different description.

```
<HTML>
  <HEAD>
    <TITLE>Script 5.18- Form: A drop-down menu example</TITLE>
  </HEAD>
  <BODY>
    <FORM NAME="myForm">
      Please select the type of account that you
      would like to open today:
      <SELECT NAME="myList">
```

```
            <OPTION SELECTED VALUE="ccAccount">Credit Card

            <OPTION VALUE="chkAccount">Checking

            <OPTION VALUE="savAccount">Savings

            <OPTION VALUE="mmAccount">Money Market

            </SELECT>

        </FORM>

    </BODY>

</HTML>
```

Figure 5.19 shows how the form looks when the page is loaded and after you click on the arrow in the drop-down field.

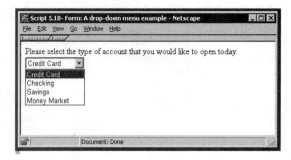

Figure 5.19

Adding a drop-down list of options to a form.

The submit Element

The submit form element is created by specifying the TYPE="submit" attribute on the <INPUT> tag. The submit element supplies a built-in method for submitting the contents of a form to the server-based program specified in the <FORM> tag. The <INPUT> tag's implementation of the submit element supports the following attribute:

✪ VALUE: Specifies the descriptive text to be displayed on the Submit button.

The action taken when the Submit button is clicked depends on the METHOD and ACTION attributes in the <FORM> tag.

The following example modifies an earlier script. In this case, I have modified two lines. The first modification was to the <FORM> tag, which I changed to look like the following:

```
<FORM NAME="myform" METHOD="post" ACTION="cgi-bin/myscript">
```

The <FORM> tag now includes METHOD and ACTION attributes that tell the browser what to do with the form when the Submit button is clicked. The second modification is the addition of a Submit button. The <INPUT> tag that defines the button is a very simple tag whose only attribute allows you to label the Submit button:

```
<INPUT TYPE="submit" VALUE="Click here to submit your answers">
```

The modified script is shown here. As you can see, aside from the change made to the <FORM> tag and the addition of the <INPUT> tag that defines the Submit button, the script remains unchanged from its earlier incarnation:

```
<HTML>
  <HEAD>
    <TITLE>Script 5.19- Form: A submit button example</TITLE>
  </HEAD>
  <BODY>
    <FORM NAME="myform" METHOD="post" ACTION="cgi-bin/myscript">
    <P><B>Select the option that applies to you:</B></P>
    Less than 20:
    <INPUT NAME="radio_option1" TYPE="radio" VALUE="Selection1"><BR>
    Between 21-35:
    <INPUT NAME="radio_option1" TYPE="radio" VALUE=Selection2"><BR>
    Between 36-55:
    <INPUT NAME="radio_option1" TYPE="radio"
          VALUE="Selection3" CHECKED><BR>
    Older than 56:
    <INPUT NAME="radio_option1" TYPE="radio" VALUE="Selection4">
    <P>
    <INPUT TYPE="submit" VALUE="Click here to submit your answers">
    </P>
    </FORM>
  </BODY>
</HTML>
```

Figure 5.20 shows what the page looks after the browser has loaded it.

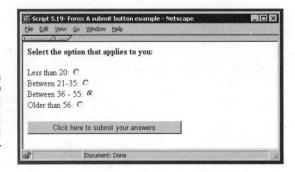

Figure 5.20

Submitting form
contents to a
server-based
program for further
processing.

The text Element

The text form element is created by specifying the TYPE="text" attribute in the
<INPUT> tag. The <INPUT> tag's implementation of the text element supports the fol-
lowing attributes:

O NAME: The name of the text field.

O MAXLENGTH: The maximum number of characters that can be entered in the field.

O SIZE: The number of characters that the field can display.

O TYPE: The type is equal to "text" for this element.

O VALUE: Specifies an initial default value.

The following page defines a form that contains a single text field named myText. The
SIZE="25" attribute setting allows the field to display 25 characters of text, while the
MAXLENGTH="40" attribute limits the amount of text that the field can accept to 40
characters. An initial value is placed in the text field using VALUE="http://".

```
<HTML>
  <HEAD>
    <TITLE>Script 5.20- Form: A text field example</TITLE>
  </HEAD>
  <BODY>
    <FORM>
    <INPUT NAME="myText" TYPE="text" SIZE="25"
        MAXLENGTH="40" VALUE="http://">
```

```
        </FORM>

      </BODY>

    </HTML>
```

Figure 5.21 shows what the form looks like when the page is loaded by the browser. Although you cannot prevent users from typing over the `http://` text in the field, you can validate the text they enter. I will talk more about validation of data in a few minutes.

Figure 5.21

Adding text fields to your forms allows you to collect and process the widest possible range of data.

The textarea Element

The `textarea` form element is created using its own tag. It works like the `text` field element except that it permits you to collect multiple lines of information in your forms. It supports the following options:

- ✪ NAME: The name of the `textarea` field.
- ✪ TYPE: The type is equal to `"textarea"` for this element.
- ✪ ROWS: The number of rows that make up the `textarea` element.
- ✪ COLS: The number of columns that make up the `textarea` element.

The following example demonstrates how to add a `textarea` field to a form. The element you are adding is 4 rows deep and 40 characters wide, allowing it to collect as many as 160 characters of information. As you can see, an initial value can be added by typing it between the `<TEXTAREA>` tags.

```
<HTML>

  <HEAD>

    <TITLE>Script 5.21- Form: A textarea example</TITLE>
```

```
   </HEAD>

   <BODY>

     <FORM>

     <TEXTAREA NAME="myTextarea" ROWS="4" COLS="40">

       Filler........

     </TEXTAREA>

     </FORM>

   </BODY>

</HTML>
```

Figure 5.22 shows the results of loading this page in a browser.

NOTE You might have noticed the appearance of the scroll bars in the previous example. The browser automatically displays them as past of the `textarea` field and activates them as necessary.

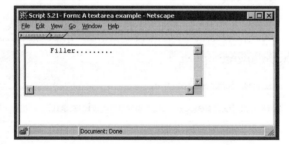

Figure 5.22

The `textarea` object is ideal for collecting large amounts of user input.

Using JavaScript to Manage Forms

Most form elements provide a number of methods you can use to programmatically work with the elements. These methods allow you to invoke events without depending on the user. For example, you might create a form that includes several text fields and a Reset button. In the event that the user decides to click on the Reset button and start filling the form out all over again, you could add the `focus()` method to the Reset

button's `onClick` event to automatically assist the user by placing the cursor back in the first text field. A list of methods supported by form elements includes:

✿ The `click()` method has the same effect as though the user clicked on the object.

✿ The `blur()` method moves the focus away from the object.

✿ The `focus()` method places the focus on the object.

✿ The `select()` method highlights the text in the form elements that contain text.

Form Events

In addition to event handlers supplied by individual form elements, the `form` object provides the following two event handlers:

✿ The `onReset` event handler allows you to execute JavaScript statements or call a function before the form is reset.

✿ The `onSubmit` event handler allows you to execute JavaScript statements or call a function before the form is submitted.

These event handlers allow you to execute commands or call subroutines before performing the reset or submit action requested by the user. As the examples that follow will demonstrate, this enables you to create warning messages that inform the user of the consequences of their actions, to validate form contents, and to assist the user in properly filling out the form while making sure only valid data is provided.

The following list identifies which events are associated with each form element and can be used as a reference to see what events each form element allows you to leverage when you are developing your forms:

Event	Form Elements Affected
Click	button, checkbox, radio, reset, submit
Blur	button, checkbox, fileUpload, password, radio, reset, select, submit, text, textarea
Focus	button, checkbox, fileUpload, password, radio, reset, select, submit, text, textarea
Select	fileUpload, password, text, textarea

In the next section, I show you how to take advantage of event handlers so that you can trigger validation of user input on your forms.

Form Validation

The real benefit of using JavaScript with your forms is to perform validation of user input. Validation allows you to ensure that the user has filled in all required fields and that valid data has been entered in those fields. When the user makes a mistake, you can display alert messages explaining the error and asking the user to correct the problem before submitting the form again.

The following example creates a form for a bicycle shop that allows Internet customers to place online orders for new bikes. Customers are given a list of options to choose from and are asked to specify what method of payment they plan to use when they pick up their new bikes.

First, I will show the full example, and then I will break it down and explain it piece by piece:

```
<HTML>

  <HEAD>

    <TITLE>Script 5.22- A form validation example</TITLE>

    <SCRIPT LANGUAGE="JavaScript" TYPE="Text/JavaScript">

    <!-- Start hiding JavaScript statements

      function ValidateOrder() {

        if (document.myForm.firstName.value.length < 1) {

          window.alert("Missing First name! Please correct");

          return;

        }

        if (document.myForm.lastName.value.length < 1) {

          window.alert("Missing Last name! Please correct");

          return;

        }

        if (document.myForm.address.value.length < 1) {

          window.alert("Missing Address! Please correct");

          return;
```

```
        }
      option_selected = "no";
      for (i=0; i < document.myForm.radio_option1.length; i++) {
        if (document.myForm.radio_option1[i].checked) {
          option_selected = "yes";
        }
      }
      if (option_selected == "no") {
        window.alert("You must select the bike " +
              "model that you wish to order! Please correct");
        return;
      }
      window.alert("Your order looks good. Click on Submit!");
    }
  // End hiding JavaScript statements -->
  </SCRIPT>
</HEAD>
<BODY>
  <CENTER>
    <H2>Welcome to Jerry's Custom Bike Shop</H2>
    <H5>Payment due at pickup</H5>
  </CENTER>
  <FORM NAME="myForm" METHOD="post" ACTION="cgi-bin/myscript">
    <B>First name:</B> <INPUT NAME="firstName" TYPE="text" SIZE="15"
      MAXLENGTH="20" VALUE=""><BR>
    <B>Last name:</B> <INPUT NAME="lastName" TYPE="text" SIZE="15"
      MAXLENGTH="20">
    <P><B>Mailing Address:</B>
    <INPUT NAME="address" TYPE="text" SIZE="30" MAXLENGTH="50"></P>
    <P><B>Select the bike you wish to order:</B></P>
```

```
10 Speed Deluxe:
<INPUT NAME="radio_option1" TYPE="radio" VALUE="10Speed"><BR>
15 Speed Racer:
<INPUT NAME="radio_option1" TYPE="radio" VALUE=15Speed><BR>
<P><B>Additional Comments: (Optional)</B></P>
<TEXTAREA NAME="myTextarea" TYPE="textarea" ROWS="4" COLS="40">
</TEXTAREA>
<P><B>Please specify method of payment:</B>
<SELECT NAME="myList">
   <OPTION SELECTED VALUE="check">Personal Check
   <OPTION VALUE="creditCard">Credit Card
   <OPTION VALUE="moneyOrder">Money Order
</SELECT></P>
<INPUT TYPE="reset" VALUE="Reset Form">
<INPUT TYPE="submit" VALUE="Submit Order"
    onClick="window.alert('Your bike will be ready in 5 days')">
<INPUT TYPE="button" VALUE=Validate Order"
    onClick="ValidateOrder()">
    </FORM>
  </BODY>
</HTML>
```

You start out by examining the contents of the body section of the page. This section begins with two headers and defines the form that will use the post method to send the form's contents to a CGI program named myscript. Because the CGI ACTION attribute does not specify a URL or path, you know that the program must reside in the same location as the example page.

```
<FORM NAME="myForm" METHOD="post" ACTION="cgi-bin/myscript">
```

Next, create three text fields that will contain first name, last name, and address information. The two name fields are 15 characters wide, and each can collect up to 20 characters of information. The address field is 30 characters long and can contain up to 50 characters.

```
<INPUT NAME="firstName" TYPE="text" SIZE="15" MAXLENGTH="20" VALUE="">
<INPUT NAME="lastName" TYPE="text" SIZE="15" MAXLENGTH="20">
<INPUT NAME="address" TYPE="text" SIZE="30" MAXLENGTH="50">
```

A pair of radio buttons is then defined and grouped using the group name radio_option1. The first radio button is assigned a value of 10Speed and the second radio button is assigned a value of 15Speed.

```
<INPUT NAME="radio_option1" TYPE="radio" VALUE="10Speed">
<INPUT NAME="radio_option1" TYPE="radio" VALUE=15Speed">
```

The next form element is a textarea. It can contain up to 160 characters of additional information regarding the bicycle order:

```
<TEXTAREA NAME="myTextarea" TYPE="textarea" ROWS="4" COLS="40"></TEXTAREA>
```

A drop-down list named myList defines three options for payment. Each option is specified by an <OPTION> tag and includes a VALUE and a description:

```
<SELECT NAME="myList">
   <OPTION SELECTED VALUE="check">Personal Check
   <OPTION VALUE="creditCard">Credit Card
   <OPTION VALUE="moneyOrder">Money Order
</SELECT>
```

The final form elements are three buttons. The first button is a Reset button that clears the form and restores all its default settings. The second button is a Submit button. Before submitting the form for processing, the Submit button's onClick event handler displays an alert message telling the customer that the selected bike will be ready for pick up in five days. The form is submitted when the customer clicks on OK. The last button allows the customer to validate the order before submitting it. When clicked, this button calls the function ValidateOrder().

```
<INPUT TYPE="reset" VALUE="Reset Form">
<INPUT TYPE="submit" VALUE="Submit Order"
       onClick="window.alert('Your bike will be ready in 5 days')">
<INPUT TYPE="button" VALUE=Validate Order" onClick="ValidateOrder()">
```

The `ValidateOrder()` function consists of a series of `if` statements that check the value of specific form elements to ensure that they have been properly completed.

The first `if` statement checks the value of the `length` property for the form's `first-Name` text field. If this field contains no character information, an alert pop-up dialog box appears, instructing the user to fill in that field. The `return` statement that follows the `alert()` statement prevents further processing of the `ValidateOrder()` function.

```
if (document.myForm.firstName.value.length < 1) {

  window.alert("Missing First name! Please correct");

  return;

}
```

The next section of the `ValidateOrder()` function checks to see whether one of the radio options has been selected to specify the kind of bike being ordered. You might have noticed that when the form defined the `radio` elements, it did not set one of them as the default answer; it is possible that the customer might forget to select one of these two options. To check all the radio elements on the form, a `for` loop is set up that loops through all `radio` elements beginning at 0 and incrementing by 1 until all the radio options have been processed. The `length` property of the `radio_option1` object specifies the total number of radio buttons that are a part of the group and provides this upper limit.

For each iteration of the loop, an `if` statement checks each radio button to see whether its `CHECKED` property has been set; if it has, a variable named `option_selected` is set equal to `yes`. Otherwise, this variable remains set equal to `no`. After every `radio` element has been examined, another `if` statement checks to see whether the value of `option_selected` was ever set to `yes`; if this is not the case, an alert pop-up dialog box appears, instructing the user to pick one of the radio options. This `if` statement also ends with a `return` statement that prevents further processing of the `Validate-Order()` function.

```
option_selected = "no"

for (i=0; i < document.myForm.radio_option1.length; i++) {

  if (document.myForm.radio_option1[i].checked) {

    option_selected = "yes";

  }
```

```
  }

if (option_selected == "no") {

  window.alert("You must select the bike model that " +

            "you wish to order! Please correct");

  return;

}
```

The final statement in the `ValidateOrder()` function is executed only if all of the function's preceding validation logic finds that the form has been correctly filled in. This last statement displays a pop-up dialog box informing the customer that the order is ready for processing.

```
alert("Your order looks good. Click on Submit!")
```

Figure 5.23 shows what the form looks like when you load the page.

Of course, depending on the customer to initiate the validation of their order might not be the best course of action. Instead, you probably want to automatically execute the

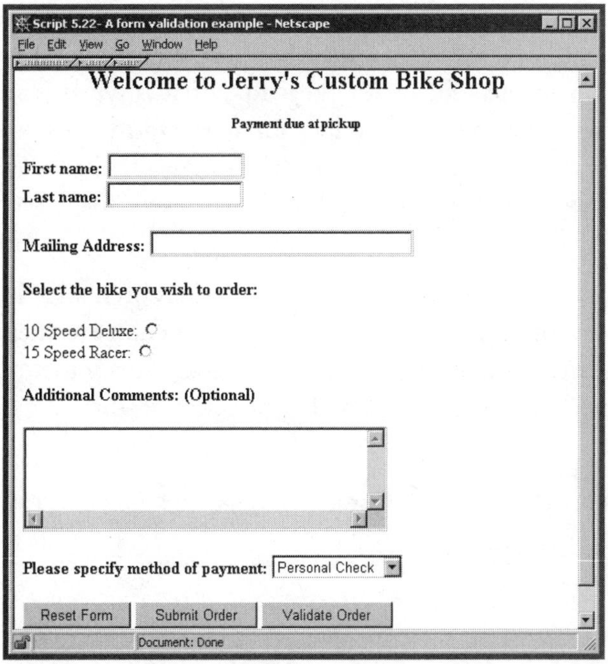

Figure 5.23

An example of validating the contents of a form before allowing it to be submitted for processing.

`ValidateOrder()` function when the user clicks on the Submit button. You can accomplish this goal by modifying the `<FORM>` to include a call to `ValidateOrder()` using the `onSubmit` event handler:

```
<FORM NAME="myForm" METHOD="post" ACTION="cgi-bin/myscript"
   onSubmit="return ValidateOrder();">
```

Before this validation technique will work, you also must modify the `return` statement on all of the `if` statements in the function to say `return false` as shown in the following example. This modification not only stops the processing of the `ValidateOrder()` function as soon as a validation error is discovered, but will also prevent the `submit` event from executing.

```
if (document.myForm.firstName.value.length < 1) {
   window.alert("Missing First name! Please correct");
   return false;
}
```

Another validation technique you might want to consider is to validate each form element as the customer completes it. To use this technique, you must understand the concepts of *focus* and *blur*. When a cursor has been placed in a text field, that field is said to have the document's focus. Any keystroke that is typed is sent to that field. If you then move the cursor to a different location in the form, the text field loses focus— a situation known as *blur*. Selecting a form element executes its focus event and moving the focus to another form element executes the blur event for the form object that has lost focus.

In the following example, the `onBlur` even handler has been added to an `<INPUT>` tag that defines a `text` object. The `ValidateOrder()` function executes after the customer selects the `text` field and then changes the form's focus to another object. Of course, if the customer forgets to fill in this field and never selects it, this validation technique will not help.

```
<INPUT NAME="firstName" TYPE="text" SIZE="15" MAXLENGTH="20" VALUE=""
   onBlur="ValidateOrder()">
```

One validation technique you can use to make things as easy as possible for your users is to add a statement that places the focus on the form object that has not been properly completed. For example, you might modify the `if` statement that validates the customer's first name as shown here:

```
if (document.myForm.firstName.value.length < 1) {

  window.alert("Missing First name! Please correct");

  document.myForm.firstName.focus();

}
```

E-Mailing Form Results

You do not have to have access to the CGI programs of a Web server to be able to collect the contents of forms that visitors to your Web site fill out. In this final example of the morning, you learn how to use e-mail as a method for retrieving the contents of your forms. The trick to making this work is to modify the `<FORM>` tag as shown here:

```
<HTML>

  <HEAD>

    <TITLE> Script 5.23- E-mailing form contents</TITLE>

  </HEAD>

  <BODY>

    <FORM NAME="myForm" ACTION="mailto:jlf04@yahoo.com"

      ENCTYPE="text/plain">

      <INPUT NAME="selectedFile" TYPE="file"><BR>

      <INPUT NAME="myButton" TYPE="submit">

    </FORM>

  </BODY>

</HTML>
```

As you can see, the `<FORM>` tag includes the `ACTION` and `ENCTYPE` attributes. The `ACTION="mailto:jlf04@yahoo.com"` attribute setting tells the browser to submit the form's contents in an e-mail message to the e-mail address specified by the `mailto:` setting. The `ENCTYPE="text/plain"` attribute sends the text in a plain non-encoded format.

Figure 5.24 shows the results of loading and executing the previous example. As you can see, the browser will always require confirmation from the user before it will attempt to submit the form's contents in an e-mail message. Once confirmed, the contents of the form are sent to the specified e-mail account as the body of the e-mail message.

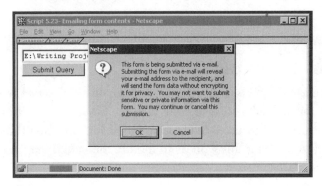

Figure 5.24

Sending form contents using e-mail.

What's Next?

Okay, lunch time! Go get a bite to eat and relax your mind. When you come back, you will learn how to leverage plug-ins to provide a richer experience for the visitors to your Web site. You will also look at how to spruce things up with basic graphical animation. As I promised yesterday, I will show you how to bake your first JavaScript cookie. At the end of the afternoon, I will give you some tips on how to debug your scripts and make your programming experience as efficient and enjoyable as possible.

Advanced JavaScript Programming

- ✿ Leveraging plug-ins
- ✿ Understanding basic graphics and animation
- ✿ Baking JavaScript cookies
- ✿ Debugging your JavaScripts

Welcome back. I hope that you had a good break and are ready to get back to work. This morning, you learned all about working with frames and forms—including how to create sites with navigation frames that allow you to load your own and other people's Web pages. You also learned all about forms. By now, you should be able to design forms, validate their contents, and e-mail the results back to yourself.

Now it's time to move on to the last set of topics. First, you'll learn how to work with plug-ins. *Plug-ins* are specialized programs designed to work with your browser and extend its capabilities. Then you will expand on your knowledge of basic JavaScript animation. Finally, you will get your chance to bake that cookie I have been promising you as a reward for all your hard work.

After completing all these topics, you'll spend the remaining portion of the afternoon on a discussion about debugging your JavaScripts. I will provide you with an assortment of good programming tips and tricks. Then I will show you how to work with the Netscape JavaScript console to troubleshoot JavaScript errors. You'll end the afternoon by looking at how to leverage other JavaScript debugging tools available from Netscape and Microsoft.

By the time this afternoon is over, you will have worked your way through two full days of JavaScript material and should be feeling pretty good about all you have learned. Tonight, you will finish up by building a Web site that makes use of your new JavaScript programming skills.

Leveraging Plug-Ins

The plug-in technology was invented by Netscape to allow you to install small program extensions to the browser that provide it with additional capabilities to do things such as play video and audio. Plug-ins allow third-party software developers to integrate new technologies into existing browsers.

Sounds great, doesn't it? Well, it is—but like everything else associated with Web development, there are some drawbacks to the use of plug-ins. First of all, you cannot count on all your visitors having the same plug-ins. Nor can you hope that they will be willing to download and install them even if you direct them to the appropriate URL. The biggest drawback to relying on plug-ins is that in some cases they may not work on Microsoft browsers. For example, although some plug-ins may work with Internet Explorer, the LiveAudio plug-in that is used in one of the examples that follows is not supported by Internet Explorer. Instead of fully adopting support for plug-in technology on Internet Explorer, Microsoft has focused its efforts on developing its own proprietary Active X technology. Unfortunately, Active X does not work in the Netscape Navigator browser.

Currently, hundreds of plug-ins are available, all of which are easily downloadable from the Web. This abundance of available technology makes your job more difficult because it increases the chances that your visitors will have plug-ins installed that you do not support instead of the ones that you do.

 NOTE Plug-ins are stored in a folder called `plugins`. For Netscape 3 browsers, look in `\progam_files\netscape\navigator\program\plugins`. For Netscape 4 browsers, look in `\program_files\netscape\communicator\program\plugins`. For Internet Explorer browsers, look in `\progam_files\plus!\microsoft_internet\plugins`.

Examining the Plug-Ins Stored on Visitors' Computers

If you want to use a plug-in in your code, you should include some additional code that checks your visitor's computer for the existence of the plug-in. If it is not installed, you can advise the user to download and install the plug-in. Alternatively, you might want to redirect the visitor to pages that provide alternative content.

The following example demonstrates how to obtain a list of all the plug-ins installed on a visitor's computer. As you will see, the script uses the navigator object and the plugins object (a child object of the navigator object) to display the installed plug-ins.

```
<HTML>
  <HEAD>
    <TITLE>Script6.1 - Plug-in analysis example</TITLE>
  </HEAD>
  <BODY>
    <SCRIPT LANGUAGE="JavaScript" TYPE="Text/JavaScript">
    <!-- Start hiding JavaScript statements
      document.write("<H3>Plug-in analysis:</H3>");
      for (i = 0; i < navigator.plugins.length; i++) {
        document.write("<B>Name:</B> " + navigator.plugins[i].name +
            "<BR>");
      }
      document.write("<P>Total Number of installed plug-ins = " +
          navigator.plugins.length + "</P>");
    // End hiding JavaScript statements -->
    </SCRIPT>
  </BODY>
</HTML>
```

The plugins object is an array that contains one entry for each installed plug-in. The script uses a for loop to spin through the list of elements in the plugins array and display the contents. As shown here, the for loop begins with the first element in the plugins array and uses the navigator.plugins.length property to determine when every element has been examined:

```
for (i = 0; i < navigator.plugins.length; i++) {
  document.write("<B>Name:</B> " + navigator.plugins[i].name +
      "<BR>");
}
```

Figure 6.1 shows the results of the example when I ran it on my computer.

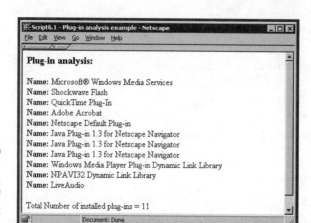

Figure 6.1

Analyzing the plug-ins stored on the computers of people who visit your Web site.

In most cases, you only want to know whether a visitor is running a specific plug-in and do not need to examine the entire `plugins` array. The following example shows how you can check for the installation of a specific plug-in. In this case, I am looking for the Adobe Acrobat plug-in:

```
my_plugin = navigator.plugins["Adobe Acrobat"]

if (my_plugin) {

   document.write("Adobe Acrobat is installed")

}

else {

   document.write("Adobe Acrobat is not installed")

}
```

NOTE You may be wondering how I knew that the when I wanted to check for the Adobe Acrobat plug-in that I needed to check for "Adobe Acrobat" and not "Adobe", "ADBAcrobat", or some or the spelling. Well, in this case I simply installed the plug-in and ran the previous script. Finding documentation about individual plug-ins can sometimes be difficult. The best place to look is on the Web site of the software vendor that wrote the plug-in.

> **TIP**
>
> ■
>
> Anytime a software vendor releases a new version of a product, things change. The same is true for plug-ins. You never know when the vendor is going to change the plug-in's name, so remember to keep an eye out and to change your scripts accordingly.
>
> ■

Using the Netscape LiveAudio Plug-In

This example uses the built-in Netscape LiveAudio plug-in to play a .wav file when the user clicks on a button. The LiveAudio plug-in is included by default with the installation of Netscape. But as I said earlier, this example will not work with the Internet Explorer browser because Internet Explorer uses ActiveX technology and not plug-ins.

>
>
> **NOTE**
>
> You can find documentation about the LiveAudio plug-in in the Client-Side JavaScript Guide that as of the writing of this book is available for free at `http://developer.netscape.com/docs/manuals/javascript.html`.

The script starts by defining a function that first checks to make sure that the visitor has the LiveAudio plug-in installed. If it is not installed, an alert dialog is displayed. If it is installed, what happens next depends on the argument that is passed to the function. Valid options are `play`, `pause`, and `stop`. The argument is analyzed by a `switch` statement. When a match occurs in one of the `case` statements, the appropriate action is taken. For example, when the `pause` option is selected, the `document.myWav.pause()` statement executes. This statement references a method that belongs to the `myWav` object that is defined in the body section of the HTML page.

The LiveAudio plug-in provides the `myWav` object's methods. The three methods provided by the LiveAudio plug-in that this example uses are `play()`, `pause()`, and `stop()`. As you might expect, these three methods provide control over the playing of the audio file. The `stop()` and `pause()` methods do not support arguments. `False` is passed to the `play()` method as an instruction not to play the audio file continually in a loop. Had a value of `true` been passed as the argument to the `play()` method, the file would have played continually.

```
<HTML>
  <HEAD>
    <TITLE>Script6.2 - A example using the
                 Netscape LiveAudio plug-in
    </TITLE>
    <SCRIPT LANGUAGE="JavaScript" TYPE="Text/JavaScript">
    <!-- Start hiding JavaScript statements
      function Jukebox(instruction) {
        my_plugin = navigator.plugins["LiveAudio"];
        if (my_plugin) {
          switch (instruction) {
            case "play":
              document.myWav.play(false);
              break;
            case "pause":
              document.myWav.pause();
              break;
            case "stop":
              document.myWav.stop();
              break;
          }
        }
        else {
          window.alert("Sorry. Your browser does not " +
                "support the Netscape LiveAudio plug-in.");
        }
      }
    // End hiding JavaScript statements -->
    </SCRIPT>
  </HEAD>
  <BODY>
```

```
<EMBED SRC="testing.wav" NAME="myWav" HIDDEN="true" MASTERSOUND>
</EMBED>
<FORM NAME="myForm">
  <INPUT TYPE="button" VALUE="Start" onClick="Jukebox('play')">
  <INPUT TYPE="button" VALUE="Pause" onClick="Jukebox('pause')">
  <INPUT TYPE="button" VALUE="Stop" onClick="Jukebox('stop')">
</FORM>
</BODY>
</HTML>
```

The <EMBED> tag is used to associate the object with the page. The NAME=myWav attribute is specified so that the script in the head section can reference the object and its methods. The HIDDEN=true attribute prevents the object from being displayed by the browser. The MASTERSOUND option is a required attribute.

The remainder of the page defines a form with three buttons whose onClick event handlers make calls to the Jukebox() function when clicked. Figure 6.2 demonstrates the appearance of the example when it is loaded into Netscape Navigator.

Figure 6.2

The LiveAudio plug-in is automatically installed with Netscape Navigator and allows you to play audio files.

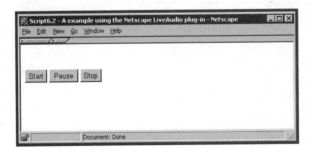

Understanding Basic Graphics and Animation

You have already seen examples of how JavaScript can be used to control animation and graphics in a browser. The examples you saw earlier in the weekend showed you how to create menu rollovers and rotating banners. The next three examples further demonstrate ways in which you can use JavaScript to manipulate graphics and animation on your Web pages.

The first example shows how to use JavaScript to create animated effects. The second example demonstrates how you can provide the user with control over a document's background color. The final example sets up an online photo album so that you can share your favorite pictures with the world.

The Blinking Eye

Using JavaScript and a series of like-sized images, you can create basic graphic animations. This example displays a blinking eye that opens and closes as it stares at your visitors. The actual effect is very simple: First, you need to create a collection of image files that have the same physical dimensions and that are each slightly different from each other as shown in Figure 6.3.

In the following example, I will demonstrate how to create a simple graphic animation using JavaScript. In this example the script will use a series of eight slightly different images to produce the illusion of a blinking eye.

```
<HTML>

  <HEAD>

    <TITLE>Script6.3 - Blinking eye example</TITLE>

    <SCRIPT LANGUAGE="JavaScript" TYPE="Text/JavaScript">

    <!-- Start hiding JavaScript statements


      current_img = 0;


      function BlinkEye() {
        current_img++;
        if (current_img > images.length - 1) {
          current_img=0;
```

Figure 6.3

The eight images that make up the blinking eye animation example.

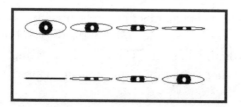

```
      }
      document.myEye.src = images[current_img];
      setTimeout('BlinkEye()',100);
   }


   image1 = new Image; image1.src = "eye1.jpg";
   image2 = new Image; image2.src = "eye2.jpg";
   image3 = new Image; image3.src = "eye3.jpg";
   image4 = new Image; image4.src = "eye4.jpg";
   image5 = new Image; image5.src = "eye5.jpg";
   image6 = new Image; image6.src = "eye6.jpg";
   image7 = new Image; image7.src = "eye7.jpg";
   image8 = new Image; image8.src = "eye8.jpg";


   images= new Array(8);
   images[0] = image1.src;
   images[1] = image2.src;
   images[2] = image3.src;
   images[3] = image4.src;
   images[4] = image5.src;
   images[5] = image6.src;
   images[6] = image7.src;
   images[7] = image8.src;
  // End hiding JavaScript statements -->
  </SCRIPT>
</HEAD>
<BODY>
  <IMG SRC="images[0]" WIDTH="100" HEIGHT="100" BORDER="0"
        NAME="myEye">
  <SCRIPT LANGUAGE="JavaScript" TYPE="Text/JavaScript">
```

```
<!-- Start hiding JavaScript statements
   BlinkEye();
// End hiding JavaScript statements -->
</SCRIPT>
</BODY>
</HTML>
```

The first thing the script does is define a variable that tracks the current image:

```
currentImg = 0;
```

Next the script defines a function named `BlinkEye()` that, when called, increments the current image by 1. The function then sets `document.myEye.scr` equal to the current image (as specified by the array position `images[current_img]`); this statement has the affect of changing the image displayed in the `<IMG>` tag named `myEye` in the body section of the page. The function then sets itself up to execute again in .1 seconds with the statement `setTimeout('BlinkEye()',100)`.

```
function BlinkEye() {
  current_img++;
    if (current_img > images.length - 1) {
      current_img=0;
    }
  document.myEye.src = images[current_img];
  setTimeout('BlinkEye()',100);
}
```

To ensure that the graphics load quickly, you should preload them into the user's cache. As the following line demonstrates, the script defines an `image` object for each graphic and then associates it with a graphic. The end result is that all the images are downloaded and placed into the user's cache before the effect begins to execute.

```
image1 = new Image; image1.src = "eye1.jpg";
```

Of course, for the `BlinkEye()` function to cycle through the images, the images must be loaded into an array:

```
images= new Array(8);
images[0]  =  image1.src;
images[1]  =  image2.src;
images[2]  =  image3.src;
images[3]  =  image4.src;
images[4]  =  image5.src;
images[5]  =  image6.src;
images[6]  =  image7.src;
images[7]  =  image8.src;
```

The `<IMG>` tag in the body section defines the initial graphic that is displayed when the page first loads as well as its physical dimensions and characteristics. The `BlinkEye()` statement starts the whole animation process in motion. Figure 6.4 demonstrates the effect of the animation as the eye is beginning to close.

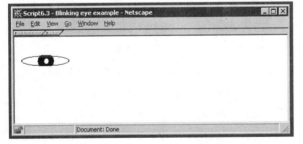

Figure 6.4

Using JavaScript to produce simple animated graphics.

The Background Changer

This next example demonstrates how to allow the user to control the document's background color. By adapting this example, you can allow your visitors to customize their views of your pages. If you then combine this approach with the use of cookie technology, you can store this information and retrieve it every time that user visits your Web pages.

This example provides the user with two options for setting background color. The first method is to choose from a list of predefined options, and the second method is to type their color preference.

```
<HTML>

  <HEAD>

    <TITLE>Script 6.4 - Background animation example</TITLE>

  </HEAD>

  <BODY>

    <SCRIPT LANGUAGE="JavaScript" TYPE="Text/JavaScript">

    <!-- Start hiding JavaScript statements

      function Change_Background(color_num) {

        document.bgColor = color_num;

      }

    // End hiding JavaScript statements -->

    </SCRIPT>

    <H3>Select your background preference:</H3>

    <FORM NAME="myForm">

      <SELECT NAME="myList"

        onChange="change_Background(

        document.myForm.myList.options[

        document.myForm.myList.selectedIndex].value)"

        <OPTION VALUE="red"> Red

        <OPTION VALUE="green"> Green

        <OPTION VALUE="yellow"> Yellow

        <OPTION VALUE="blue"> Blue

        <OPTION VALUE="pink"> Pink

        <OPTION VALUE="purple"> Purple

        <OPTION VALUE="orange"> Orange

        <OPTION VALUE="brown"> Brown

        <OPTION VALUE="white"> White

      </SELECT>

      <H3>Or type your own color here:</H3>

      <INPUT NAME="myText" TYPE="text" SIZE="10" MAXLENGTH="15"

             VALUE="">
```

```
<INPUT NAME="myButton1" TYPE="button" VALUE="Change"
    onClick="Change_Background(document.myForm.myText.value)">
</FORM>
</BODY>
</HTML/>
```

This example defines a function named `Change_Background()` that changes the documents `bgColor` property to match the argument that it receives:

```
function Change_Background(color_num) {
  document.bgColor = color_num;
}
```

The script defines a drop-down list of color options that the visitor can select from and uses the `<SELECT>` tag's `onChange` event to call the `Change_Background()` function if the user selects one of the options:

```
onChange="Change_Background(
    document.myForm.myList.options[
    document.myForm.myList.selectedIndex].value)"
```

The final portion of the script allows your more discerning visitors to specify their own preferred background color by first defining a text field in which the user can type his or her color choice and a button that, when clicked, executes the `Change_Background()` function and passes the color the user specified (for example, `document.myForm.myText.value`).

Figure 6.5 shows how this example looks when first loaded into the browser.

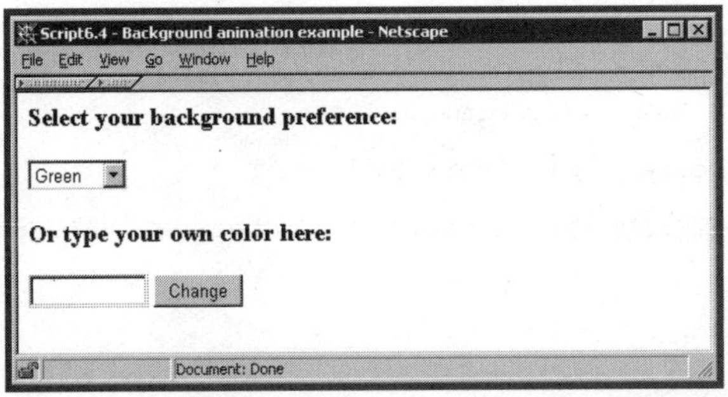

Figure 6.5

An example of a script that allows your visitors to set a background color preference.

The Picture Viewer

This final graphic example uses a combination of frames and JavaScript to deliver an impressive but simple online picture viewer. As the following example shows, the script located in the head section defines and loads all the images into the visitor's cache.

```
<HTML>
  <HEAD>
    <TITLE>Script 6.5 - Example of a picture viewer</TITLE>
    <SCRIPT LANGUAGE="JavaScript" TYPE="Text/JavaScript">
    <!-- Start hiding JavaScript statements
       birthday = new Image(); birthday.src = "birthday.jpg";
       puppydog = new Image(); puppydog.src = "puppydog.jpg";
       stuffed  = new Image(); stuffed.src  = "stuffed.jpg";
    // End hiding JavaScript statements -->
    </SCRIPT>
  </HEAD>
  <BODY>
    <CENTER>
    <TABLE BORDER="10">
      <TR>
        <TD>
          <H3>Hello and welcome to my personal photo album!</H3>
        </TD>
      </TR>
      <TR>
        <TD>
          <FORM NAME = myForm>
          <B>Choose a picture:</B>
          <INPUT NAME="myButton1" TYPE="button" VALUE="birthday"
```

```
        onClick = "document.myImage.src = birthday.src">
   <INPUT NAME="myButton2" TYPE="button" VALUE="puppydog"
        onClick = "document.myImage.src = puppydog.src">
   <INPUT NAME="myButton3" TYPE="button" VALUE="stuffed"
        onClick = "document.myImage.src = stuffed.src">
   </FORM>
   </TD>
  </TR>
  <TR>
   <TD>
     <IMG NAME="myImage" SRC="welcome.jpg" WIDTH="440"
          HEIGHT="292">
   </TD>
  <TR>
 </TABLE>
 </CENTER>
 </BODY>
</HTML>
```

In the body section, a TABLE of one column and three rows is defined. The first row contains a welcome message formatted with the level 3 HTML header <H3>. The second row contains a form with three buttons, each of which has an onClick event handler that changes the src property of the image to a different picture.

```
<INPUT NAME="myButton1" TYPE="button" VALUE="birthday"
    onClick = "document.myImage.src = birthday.src">
<INPUT NAME="myButton2" TYPE="button" VALUE="puppydog"
    onClick = "document.myImage.src = puppydog.src">
<INPUT NAME="myButton3" TYPE="button" VALUE="stuffed"
    onClick = "document.myImage.src = stuffed.src">
```

The last row in the table contains a simple `<IMG>` tag that loads an initial image and defines the display's physical dimensions. Figure 6.6 shows what this example looks like when it is first loaded.

Figure 6.6

By combining JavaScript and frames, you can create very powerful presentations.

Baking JavaScript Cookies

Cookies are little pieces of information you can store on and retrieve from your visitors' computers. Whether you realize it or not, you work with cookies every day. Just about any time you visit a professional Web site, a cookie is stored on your computer. These sites use cookies to record small pieces of information about you, such as your name or the time of your last visit.

Cookies are stored in plain text files on the user's computer. Cookie technology is very limited. It cannot be used to plant viruses or to harm the user's computer. The cookie is a property of the `document` object. Assigning a value to the `document.cookie` property creates a cookie. For example, the following statement defines a cookie that stores the visitor's name:

```
document.cookie = "name=" + name + ";expires=" +

                expirationDate.toGMTString();
```

The `expires` field is required and tells the browser how long to store the cookie before deleting it. If you forget to add this field, the cookie expires as soon as the current session ends.

In a similar fashion, you can retrieve the cookie the next time the visitor loads your Web page with the following statement:

```
myCookie = document.cookie;
```

In the two examples that follow, I will show you how to create and retrieve a simple cookie.

 NOTE Netscape Communicator browsers store cookies in one file named cookies.txt. Internet Explorer stores cookies as individual files inside a folder named cookies. There is no way to override where the browser stores its cookies.

Creating a Cookie

This first cookie example displays a form and asks visitors to type their names. It then creates a cookie that includes the visitor's name and an expiration date of one month from the current date.

 NOTE This very simple example does not include logic to first make sure that the visitor does not already have a cookie from you before bothering to ask for his or her name. The example also does not contain logic to check whether the cookie is about to expire so that it can replace it with a new one. I leave that code to you to devise.

```
<HTML>
  <HEAD>
    <TITLE>Script 6.6 - Baking your first cookie</TITLE>
    <SCRIPT LANGUAGE="JavaScript" TYPE="Text/JavaScript">
    <!-- Start hiding JavaScript statements
        expiration_date = new Date;
        expiration_date.setMonth(expiration_date.getMonth() + 1);
```

```
    function BakeTheCookie(name) {
        document.cookie = "name=" + name + ";expires=" +
                expiration_date.toGMTString();
    }
  // End hiding JavaScript statements -->
  </SCRIPT>
</HEAD>
<BODY>
  <H3>Cookie Information Collector</H3>
  <FORM NAME="myForm">
    <B>What is your name? </B>
    <INPUT TYPE="text" NAME="visitorName">
    <INPUT NAME="myButton" TYPE="button" VALUE="Save Cookie"
        onClick="BakeTheCookie(document.myForm.visitorName.value)">
  </FORM>
</BODY>
</HTML>
```

This cookie example contains a script in the head section. The first thing it does is to define a data object called `expiration_date`. Next it sets the expiration date for the cookie using the `Date` object's `setMonth()` method to add one month to the current date:

```
expiration_date = new Date;
expiration_date.setMonth(expiration_date.getMonth() + 1);
```

The logic to "bake" the cookie is located in a function named `BakeTheCookie()` that accepts the name of the visitor as an argument:

```
function BakeTheCookie(name) {
  document.cookie = "name=" + name + ";expires=" +
            expiration_date.toGMTString();
}
```

The rest of the example is a form that collects the visitor's name and then calls the `BakeTheCookie()` function. Figure 6.7 demonstrates what the example looks like when it is first loaded into your browser.

```
onClick="BakeTheCookie(document.myForm.visitorName.value)"
```

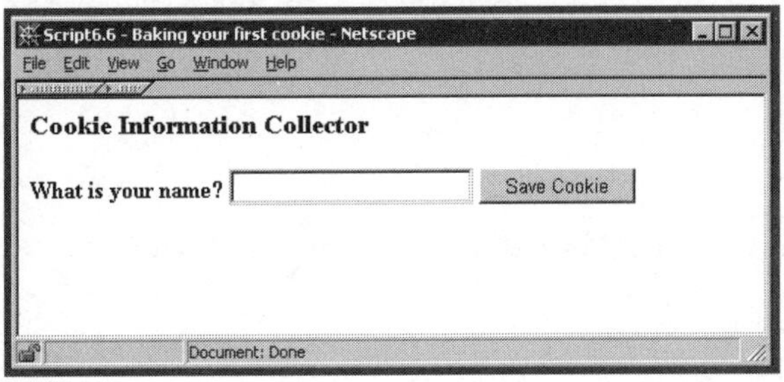

Figure 6.7

You can use a cookie to store information about your visitors that you can reuse every time they visit your Web site.

Viewing Your Cookie

Okay, so you have baked your cookie and saved it on your visitor's computer. What next? The answer is *not much*. You just wait for the visitor to return. When the visitor does return, you can check to see whether he or she has one of your cookies. An example of how to do this follows.

NOTE In actual practice, you will want to write a script that combines the cookie logic of this and the previous example so that you first check to see whether the user has one of your cookies before you assign another cookie.

```
<HTML>
  <HEAD>
    <TITLE>Script 6.7 - Retrieving your cookie</TITLE>
    <SCRIPT LANGUAGE="JavaScript" TYPE="Text/JavaScript">
    <!-- Start hiding JavaScript statements

      function CookieCheck() {
        visitor_name = "";
```

```
          cookie_name = "";
        if (document.cookie != "") {
          cookie_name = document.cookie.split("=")[0];
          visitor_name = document.cookie.split("=")[1];
            window.alert("cookie_name = " + cookie_name +
                "\nCookie Contents = " + visitor_name);
        }
        else {
          window.alert("Your cookie was not found!");
        }
      }


    // End hiding JavaScript statements -->
    </SCRIPT>
  </HEAD>
  <BODY onLoad="CookieCheck()">
  </BODY>
</HTML>
```

The cookie logic for this example is located in a function named `CookieCheck()` located in a script in the head section. The function is called by the `onLoad` event in the `<BODY>` tag.

The first thing the script does is to check whether the visitor already has one of your cookies:

```
if (document.cookie != "")
```

If the visitor does not have one of your cookies, the `document` object's `alert()` method is used to display a pop-up dialog box stating that a cookie was not found. However, if a cookie *was* found, the script retrieves the value of the cookie using the `cookie` object's `split()` method. The `split()` method breaks the cookie into fields. The first statement sets a variable named `cookie_name` equal to the name the cookie was saved as. The second statement sets another variable named `visitor_name` to the name that is stored in the cookie.

```
cookie_name = document.cookie.split("=")[0];
visitor_name = document.cookie.split("=")[1];
```

The script then uses the `document` object's `alert()` method to display the contents of the cookie:

```
window.alert("cookie_name = " + cookie_name +
        "\nCookie Contents = " + visitor_name);
```

NOTE Although this example shows you how to retrieve and display your cookie, a more effective use of this information might be to display a welcome message that greets the visitor by his or her name.

Figure 6.8 demonstrates how the script formats the results when it finds a cookie.

NOTE One of the most important security rules governing the creation and retrieval of cookies is that only their creators should be able to retrieve them. Every time a cookie is created, an attribute known as a `domain` is added to the cookie. The `domain` attribute is set equal to the name of the Internet domain URL belonging to the computer that created the cookie. For example, the domain attribute for a cookie from Netscape might look like `.netscape.com`. Whenever a cookie retrieval request is received, a comparison is made against the Internet domain URL of the requesting computer and the domain attribute listed for each cookie to see whether a match is found.

Figure 6.8

By retrieving cookie information, you can avoid having to ask visitors repeatedly for the same information, and can greet them by name when they return to your site.

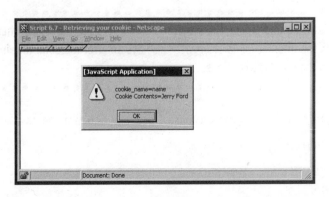

Take a Break

Time to take a break. Why don't you take a walk, stretch your legs, and then get a snack to build up your energy? When you return, you'll jump right into JavaScript debugging. After all, debugging is perhaps the longest and most difficult part of the script development process. Fortunately, as you will see, there are some tricks, techniques, and tools you can use to minimize the amount of time you spend debugging.

Debugging Your JavaScripts

In programming, there is one universal truth: Everyone makes mistakes. In programming, a mistake in a program code is referred to as a *bug*. The process of finding and fixing bugs is called *debugging* and is a normal part of the development process. Even if you write a script that seems to work well right from the start, you should still perform a certain amount of testing and debugging to verify that the JavaScript will work as expected in different scenarios.

In most cases, JavaScript supplies you with clues about where problems lie. But there will be times when things are not working and JavaScript will not provide you with any error messages—leaving it totally up to you to resolve the problem. In both cases, you can follow a number of processes to help you debug the code and find the error. This is what the remainder of the afternoon will cover.

Debugging is not very glamorous or fun, and it usually seems to take longer than you anticipated. The bad news is that the longer your program is, the more errors you will see. The good news is that with time, experience, programming discipline, and a sound debugging process, you will become proficient at debugging your scripts.

 NOTE In Netscape and Opera, the browser stops processing the script when it encounters an error. The Internet Explorer browser displays an error message that includes the offer to allow the scripts to continue.

You are going to come across three types of errors when writing JavaScripts:

- ✿ Load-time errors
- ✿ Runtime errors
- ✿ Logic errors

Load-Time Errors

Load-time errors occur when you attempt to load your Web pages into the browser. These errors tend to be fairly obvious and typically involve basic syntax issues. A *syntax error* occurs because the browser is unable to determine what the script is trying to do. Unlike human communications, a small syntactical error in computer code is enough to break down all communications. Remember that JavaScript is case sensitive and that you must be consistent in the manner in which you define and reference variables, functions, objects, methods, properties, and events.

Netscape Navigator and Microsoft Internet Explorer used to display pop-up error dialog boxes that provided you with information about errors. The current versions of both of these browsers now hide error messages from view because the typical user neither needs nor wants to see them. The only person who really needs to see the error messages is the programmer because after a script has been fully debugged and made available on the Internet, it shouldn't have any errors anyway (and even if there are errors, no one but the programmer can do anything about them). Netscape and Microsoft's philosophy is to minimize the possible impact of a script's bugs on the user. Later this afternoon, I will show you how to view Netscape and Internet Explorer error messages.

TIP

The best way to deal with syntax errors is to avoid them in the first place. Type carefully and double-check your scripts before running them to make sure that everything is in order. For example, make sure that you have avoided using reserved words as variable names or that you do not forget to match up all opening and closing parentheses and braces. Remember to separate the attributes of the various loop statements with commas—except for the `for` statement, which uses the semicolon to separate its arguments.

Often the error message tells you everything you need to know to find and fix the problem—including a brief problem description and perhaps even the actual portion of code that caused the error. For example, when loading the following script, a syntax error will occur:

```
1.   <HTML>
2.     <HEAD>
3.       <TITLE>Script 6.8 - Sample syntax error</TITLE>
```

```
4.      </HEAD>
5.      <BODY>
6.        <SCRIPT LANGUAGE="JavaScript" TYPE="Text/JavaScript">
7.        <!-- Start hiding JavaScript statements
8.          var test_color = "blue";
9.          if (test_color == "blue" {
10.            document.write("We have a match");
11.          }
12.      // End hiding JavaScript statements -->
13.      </SCRIPT>
14.    </BODY>
15. </HTML>
```

Can you spot the error by eyeballing the script? The script consists of only a few lines of code, but the error still may not jump out at you. When I loaded this script, Netscape recorded the following error message:

```
JavaScript Error: file:/A|/JavaScript Syntax error 1.html,
line 9:


missing ) after condition.

    if (test_color == "blue" {
.........................^
```

With this information in hand, the job of debugging the script is much easier. As you can see, several very useful pieces of information were provided in the error message:

- **Line number on which the error occurred:** `line 9`
- **Error message itself:** `missing ) after condition`
- **Error text (the actual line of code that generated the error):** `if (test_color == "blue" {`

■ ■
To better show the value of the line number information provided in the error message,
I added line numbers to the left of the previous example. These numbers are not a part
of the sample code that you normally type. When you are looking for a JavaScript editor,
you may want to look for one that automatically provides line numbering.
■ ■

As you can see, the error message indicates that a right parenthesis is missing on line 9.
If you look at the error text portion of the error message, you will see where the) should
have been inserted:

```
if (test_color == "blue" ) {
  document.write("We have a match");
}
```

Runtime Errors

A *runtime error* occurs as a result of an attempt by your script to do something that is
against the rules. For example, if the script attempts to reference an undeclared variable
or to call a function that has not yet been defined, a runtime error occurs. Other examples include using JavaScript commands incorrectly. For example, the following script
will produce a runtime error:

```
1.    <HTML>
2.      <HEAD>
3.        <TITLE>Script 6.9 - Sample runtime error</TITLE>
4.      </HEAD>
5.      <BODY>
6.        <SCRIPT LANGUAGE="JavaScript" TYPE="Text/JavaScript">
7.        <!-- Start hiding JavaScript statements
8.          myFunction();
9.          function Myfunction() {
10.           document.write("Hello World!");
11.         }
12.      // End hiding JavaScript statements -->
```

```
13.    </SCRIPT>
14.   </BODY>
15. </HTML>
```

The error message that follows tells you the line number where the browser thinks the error occurred and gives you a brief description of the error. In the preceding example, I intended to create and call a function named MyFunction(). Even though the error message points me to line 8, the actual error is on line 9 where I mistyped the function name as Myfunction().

```
JavaScript Error: file:/A|/JavaScript runtime error 2.html,
line 8:


myFunction is not defined.
```

TIP

As the previous example demonstrates, the line number in the error message is not always accurate. But generally speaking, it comes pretty close to pinpointing the error. If the line indicated in the error message does not contain the error, you often will find it within a few lines before or after the line number stated.

Logic Errors

Logic errors can be the most difficult type of errors to find. These errors are not the result of a syntax or runtime error. Instead, they occur when you make a mistake in the logic that drives your script and you do not get results you expected. Unfortunately, as far as JavaScript is concerned, the script is running well and the browser generates no errors. So you will not receive any help in honing in on where the problem lies.

For example, the following script contains a logic error. The script was supposed to count from 1 to 10 and then terminate. However, when writing the for statement that controls the looping logic, I accidentally typed i-- instead of i++. Instead of starting at 1 and going to 10, the script started at 1 and began counting backwards into negative numbers. Because the value of i never reaches 11, the script never stops running. Although the script did exactly what it was *told* to do, it did not do what I *intended* it to do.

```
1.    <HTML>
2.      <HEAD>
3.        <TITLE>Script 6.10 - Sample logical error</TITLE>
4.      </HEAD>
5.      <BODY>
6.        <SCRIPT LANGUAGE="JavaScript" TYPE="Text/JavaScript">
7.        <!-- Start hiding JavaScript statements
8.          document.write(" Let's count from 1 to 10 <BR>")
9.          for (i=1;i<11;i--) {
10.            document.write(i + "<BR>")
11.          }
12.        // End hiding JavaScript statements -->
13.        </SCRIPT>
14.      </BODY>
15.    </HTML>
```

Another common example of a logic error is one that everybody gets wrong and involves the misuse of the assignment operator in place of the = comparison operator. For example, the following script displays the "We have a match" message even though the values of the apples and oranges variables are not the same. Clearly, this is not the logic I intended. When I rewrote the if statement as if (apples = oranges) and loaded it, the example worked as expected, and the "We do not have a match" message was displayed.

```
<HTML>
  <HEAD>
    <TITLE>Script 6.11 - A second sample logical error</TITLE>
  </HEAD>
  <BODY>
    <SCRIPT LANGUAGE="JavaScript" TYPE="Text/JavaScript">
    <!-- Start hiding JavaScript statements
      apples = 5;
```

```
    oranges = 15;
    if (apples = oranges) {
      document.write("We have a match");
    }
    else {
      document.write("We do not have a match");
    }
  // End hiding JavaScript statements -->
  </SCRIPT>
  </BODY>
</HTML>
```

TIP

One of the ways I could have debugged the preceding example would have been to add a checkpoint in the script just before the `if` statement. A *checkpoint* is a statement that displays the value of a variable so that you know what it has been set to. I will describe this debugging technique in more detail in a few minutes.

Habits of Highly Effective Programmers

Before I delve further into the discussion of debugging your scripts, I thought I'd talk about things that you can do to reduce the number of errors in your scripts and that can make the debugging process a little easier.

- ✿ **Remember to use plenty of comments.** Comments allow you to explain why you wrote the script the way you did and to explain particularly difficult sections of code. Comments make it much easier for others to follow behind you and for you to understand your own code months or years later.

- ✿ **Always use indentation to make your code easy to read.** Indenting statements also makes it easier for you to match up beginning and ending tags, curly braces, and other HTML and script elements.

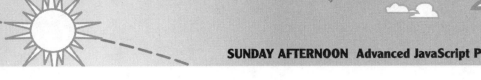

- **Write modular code.** Whenever possible, group your code statements into functions. Functions allow you to group related statements and to test and reuse portions of code with minimal effort. Simplify your design by assigning only one task to a function.

- **Declare functions and variables at the top of your scripts.** This approach makes these elements easy to find and modify and is a lot less confusing than embedding them throughout different portions of lengthy scripts. This technique also helps to ensure that the functions and variables are defined before they are referenced.

- **Be consistent in the way you name variables and functions.** Try using names that are long enough to be meaningful and that describe the contents of the variable or the purpose of the function.

- **Use consistent syntax when naming variables and functions.** In other words, keep them all lowercase or all uppercase; if you prefer CamelBack notation, use it consistently.

- **Do not assume that just because your script ran once without an error it is bug free.** Make sure that you test the script using different browsers and, if possible, with different versions of the same browser.

- **Make sure that you test your script using browsers that do not support JavaScript to ensure that your script properly provides alternative content.** Try disabling support in your browsers for such things as frames to make sure that all browsers display your information as you intend it to be displayed.

- **Test all possible scenarios.** This includes testing with good and bad data. If your pages have forms, try to type invalid data and check to make sure that the validation routines work like you think they will. Test every link and click on every button.

- **Test long scripts in a modular fashion.** In other words, do not try to write the entire script before testing any portion of it. Write a piece and get it to work before adding the next portion of code.

- **Load your pages using different resolutions to make sure that they look like you expect them to at any size.** Also try resizing your browser windows to see how they look at different sizes.

- **Test every event handler to ensure that it executes as expected.**

- **Explicitly declare variables using the var keyword.**

- **Use descriptive variable and function names and avoid using single-character names.**

- **Pay attention when using object names.** Only core JavaScript objects begin with capitalized letters (for example, `Array`, `Boolean`, `Date`, `Function`, `Math`, `Number`, `Object`, `RegExp`, and `String`).

- **Watch your quotation marks.** Remember that quotation marks are used in pairs around strings and that both quotation marks must be of the same style (either single or double). If you want to show quotation marks as part of the text message, embed them inside quotation marks of the alternate type (for example, place single quotation marks inside double quotation marks and vice versa).

Using Checkpoints

One very simple debugging technique is to place checkpoints into your script when you are writing and testing it. You can do this by taking advantage of the `document` object's `alert()` method to display the value of variables before and after they are evaluated or changed within the script to make sure that they are being set to what you think they are. Another use for checkpoints is to monitor the execution flow of your scripts to make sure that they are executing in the order you anticipate. For example, you can place an `alert()` statement in every function that displays a message each time the function is called.

 NOTE Alternatively, you can display a message in the current window using the `document.write()` method or open up a new window and write to it. It really does not matter which of these checkpoint techniques you use. Some may work better than others depending on the circumstances.

Just remember one important thing: Save your visitors some frustration by remembering to remove or comment out all your checkpoints when you are done testing.

Testing Before You Write

One of the most difficult things about programming in any language is figuring out the right syntax for a command that you want to execute in your script. One really neat trick you can do using Netscape is to type `javascript:` followed by the statement you want to test in the browser's URL field (see Figure 6.9).

Figure 6.9

You can type
JavaScript
commands and
statements into
the Netscape URL
field to test their
results before you
use the statements
in your scripts.

Trapping Errors with onError

The JavaScript error event executes every time a script encounters a problem loading a window, frame, or image. A JavaScript `onError` event handler routine can be set up to handle these situations. Three arguments are automatically passed to the `onError` event handler:

- ✪ Error message
- ✪ URL information
- ✪ Line number

The following script demonstrates how to write a function you can place in any of your scripts to display information associated with an occurrence of the error event. A function named `errorTrap()` is defined in the head section of the page; the function accepts three arguments. These arguments correspond to the three arguments that are automatically passed to the `onError` event handler. The `errorTrap()` function then formats the error information in an alert pop-up dialog box.

The statement `onError = errorTrap` in the script in the body section tells the browsers to call the function for any error event. I added a line after this statement that contains a spelling error to demonstrate how this all works.

```
<HTML>

  <HEAD>

    <TITLE>Script6.12 - Capturing errors with the

                onError event handler

    </TITLE>
```

```
<SCRIPT LANGUAGE="JavaScript" TYPE="Text/JavaScript">
<!-- Start hiding JavaScript statements
   function ErrorTrap(msg,url,line_no) {
      window.alert("Error: " + msg + "\nLine: " + line_no +
            "\nULR: " + url);

   }
// End hiding JavaScript statements -->
</SCRIPT>
</HEAD>
<BODY>
<SCRIPT LANGUAGE="JavaScript" TYPE="Text/JavaScript">
<!-- Start hiding JavaScript statements
   onError = ErrorTrap;
   document.wrrite("");
// End hiding JavaScript statements -->
</SCRIPT>
</BODY>
</HTML>
```

Figure 6.10 shows the alert pop-up dialog box that is displayed as a result of loading this script. As you can see, all the error information is displayed—and in this case, it points you to the exact location of the problem.

Figure 6.10

The onError event handler can be used in conjunction with the document's alert() method to display debugging information.

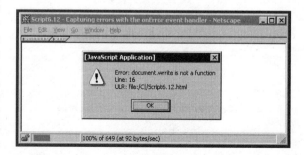

> **TIP**
>
> You may have noticed that I used the `/n` character in the `alert()` statement to format the message output. This special formatting character causes a carriage return.

Understanding Internet Explorer Error Messages

Internet Explorer can suppress or display JavaScript error messages. This feature is configured on the Advanced property sheet on the Internet Options dialog box (see Figure 6.11) found in the Tools menu. By default, Internet Explorer 5 does not display JavaScript error messages. To turn on this feature, enable the Display a Notification about Every Script Error check box and click on OK.

The next time you load a Web page that contains a JavaScript error, you will see an Internet Explorer error dialog box similar to the one shown in Figure 6.12. As you can see, you can control the amount of information that is displayed by clicking on the Hide Details button.

You can safely prevent the display of Internet Explorer error messages by clearing the Display a Notification about Every Script Error check box and clicking on OK without loosing convenient access to error information. Instead, when an error is encountered, a small alert icon is displayed in the lower-left corner of the browser as shown in Figure 6.13. Double-click on the icon to view the error dialog box shown in Figure 6.12.

Display a Notification about every script error

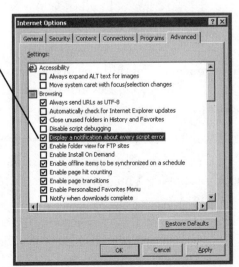

Figure 6.11

Configuring Internet Explorer 5 to automatically display script errors when they occur.

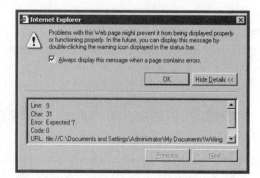

Figure 6.12

Viewing all the details of an Internet Explorer error message.

Figure 6.13

When error notification is enabled, you can view Internet Explorer script error messages by double-clicking on the alert icon in the status bar.

Working with the Netscape JavaScript Console

Netscape comes with an integrated JavaScript tool known as the Netscape JavaScript Console. There is no equivalent tool in Internet Explorer.

You have undoubtedly noticed that I have used Netscape Navigator predominately throughout this book. There are two reasons for this: The first is that I personally prefer Netscape to the other major browsers. The second reason is because I like to work with the Netscape JavaScript Console when writing and debugging my scripts.

Netscape sends all messages to the JavaScript Console. I like this for several reasons:

○ When I am not writing JavaScripts, I use Netscape to browse the Internet, Because all the JavaScripts error message I might run across when surfing are sent to the JavaScript Console, I don't have to see them.

○ When I am writing JavaScripts, I do not always need to see the error messages. If my script fails to load, I can usually spot the error in a few moments without assistance.

- When I am ready to do some serious debugging, I can open the JavaScript Console and leave it displayed at all times. I prefer this arrangement to the Internet Explorer pop-up error messages.

- I also like to take advantage of the JavaScript Console typein field when I want to test a command's syntax or see how a command works.

The Netscape JavaScript Console, shown in Figure 6.14, is organized into two frames. The upper frame displays a scrollable list of error messages. This frame allows you to view current and previous errors. Start the JavaScript Console by typing **javascript:** in the URL field in Netscape Navigator. I think that you will find the Console's running history of errors very helpful, but if you prefer, you can click on the Clear Console button to clear out the messages in the display area.

NOTE The JavaScript Console is sometimes also called the Communicator Console. In fact, the JavaScript Console window actually displays Communicator Console in its title bar.

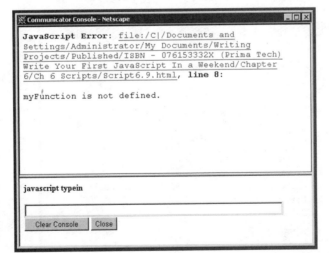

Figure 6.14

Netscape Navigator provides a built-in JavaScript debugger that allows you to view error messages and test command syntax.

Testing JavaScript Statements

The bottom frame in the JavaScript Console contains the typein field where you can type JavaScript statements and test their results. For example, if you wanted to test the syntax of two commands that sets a variable and then use that variable in an alert()

statement, you could type the two commands separated by a semicolon and view the results as shown in Figure 6.15.

You can also use the `typein` field to test JavaScript expressions and to perform mathematical calculations to make sure that your formulas will return expected results before you add them to your scripts.

For example, the following line demonstrates how to test the syntax of a function and its statements. As you can see, the statement tests a small function named `DisplayMsg()` by calling it and passing a single argument. When this statement executes, you should see an alert dialog box appear.

```
function DisplayMsg(var1) { window.alert(var1) }; DisplayMsg("Hi");
```

The next example contains three statements. The first statement defines a variable, the second statement changes its value, and the third statement displays an alert dialog box if its conditional test evaluates to `true`.

```
var oranges = 5; oranges = oranges + 5;

if (oranges < 12) window.alert("Order more oranges");
```

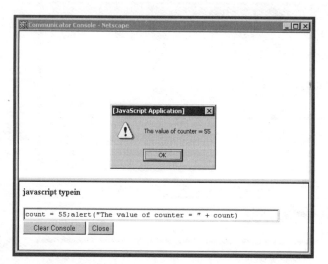

Figure 6.15

You can type JavaScript commands into the Netscape JavaScript Console to test their results.

Displaying Pop-Up Error Messages

In the days before Netscape 4.06, pop-up dialog boxes were used to report errors. Since then, the JavaScript Console has been the default location for all Netscape JavaScript

error messages. If you prefer to work with the old pop-up style error dialog boxes instead of the Netscape JavaScript Console, you can configure Navigator to accommodate this preference by modifying the Navigator preference file. This file is named `prefs.js` and is usually located in a directory under your username located in the Program Files\netscape\users\ directory. Use the following procedure to modify this file so that pop-up error dialog boxes are automatically displayed:

1. Close all active Netscape Navigator sessions.
2. Open the `prefs.js` file using Notepad.
3. Add the following statement on a line by itself somewhere in the file:

   ```
   user_pref("javascript.classic.error_alerts", true);
   ```

4. Save and close the `prefs.js` file.

NOTE If you leave Netscape Navigator running when you modify the `prefs.js` file, your changes will be overridden when Netscape is later closed.

Displaying the JavaScript Console

If you prefer, you can configure Netscape Navigator to automatically open the JavaScript Console instead of the pop-up error dialog boxes every time there is an error using the following procedure:

1. Close all active Netscape Navigator sessions.
2. Open the `prefs.js` file using Notepad.
3. Add the following statement on a line by itself somewhere in the file:

   ```
   user_pref("javascript.console.open_on_error", true);
   ```

4. Save and close the file.

Working with Advanced Debugging Tools

Netscape and Microsoft both offer advanced script debugging tools that provide a host of powerful debugging capabilities. Netscape's debugger is called the Netscape JavaScript Debugger; Microsoft's debugger is called the Microsoft Script Debugger.

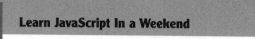

Both are tightly integrated with each company's browser, and both provide the same basic set of capabilities.

As of the writing of this book, you can find the Microsoft Script Debugger at http://msdn.microsoft.com/scripting/default.htm?/scripting/vbscript/default.htm. The Netscape JavaScript Debugger is available at http://developer.netscape.com/tech/javascript/index.html.

Both debuggers allow you to debug scripts as they execute. This means that you can monitor variable and object property values and watch them change as the script executes. Here is a short list of some of the other features provided by both these debuggers:

- **Breakpoints:** Allow you to interrupt script execution at any given point. Breakpoints are markers that tell the debugger when to pause script execution. When paused, you can use each debugger command console to execute commands that run functions and object methods or to view variable and property values. There is no limit to the number of breakpoints you can set. When the script runs, it stops at each breakpoint and waits for you to click on the Run button before continuing.

- **Interrupts:** Allow you to stop script execution at any time. The script pauses as soon as the currently executing statement completes.

- **Step-by-step execution:** Allows you to control how the script executes after resuming from a breakpoint or interrupt. For example, you can choose to run through the rest of the script normally or to step through the script a line at a time, pausing after each line is processed.

- **Call stacks:** Displays windows that show you what components the script is currently executing so that you can determine the order in which things are logically executing.

There is not enough time to discuss either of these debugging tools in great detail, so I will try to focus on some key points that will give you an understanding of how each debugger works.

Netscape JavaScript Debugger

The Netscape JavaScript Debugger is a Java applet that runs inside the Netscape Navigator browser. Unfortunately, it works only with Netscape Navigator versions 4.02 or later.

When you first install the debugger, you will see several dialog boxes requesting various privileges. You must grant approval for each request. After the installation is complete,

you will be presented with the main JavaScript Debugger HTML page and are advised to bookmark the page and use the bookmark to load the Netscape JavaScript Debugger in the future (see Figure 6.16).

You also can start the Netscape JavaScript Debugger by loading `jsdebugger.html` on the computer where you installed it. It is located in the Netscape directory.

To work with the debugger, start Netscape Navigator and click on the Netscape JavaScript Debugger Start Page bookmark. The debugger will begin monitoring all scripts that you load from this point. Open an HTML page that contains the script you want to debug in Netscape. Click on the Open button on the debugger's toolbar. A list of open HTML pages is displayed. Select the entry that represents the HTML page that contains your script. The script appears in the debugger's top frame as shown in Figure 6.17. The debugger will then track the activity of this script.

As Figure 6.17 shows, the Netscape JavaScript Debugger is divided into three panes. The upper pane is the Source View pane and displays the contents of your script. The lower-left pane is the Call Stack, which displays the current execution point in the script. The lower-right pane contains the Console. The Console is divided into two parts: The upper part displays information monitored by the Watch utility and the results of any expression you choose to evaluate. You can evaluate expressions when the script is not executing by typing them into the command line in the lower portion of the Console pane.

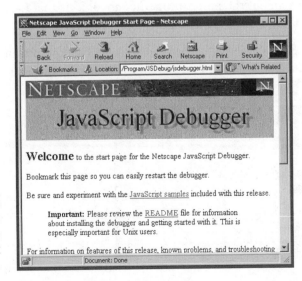

Figure 6.16

The initial startup screen for the Netscape JavaScript debugger.

Figure 6.17

The Netscape
JavaScript
Debugger is a
powerful
debugging tool that
you can download
from Netscape.

The Source View pane displays information about script components using different colors in the left margin of the pane. For example, a red dot identifies any breakpoints that have been set, a bark-colored arrow shows the currently executing line, yellow lines identify script code, and orange bars identify functions.

The Netscape JavaScript Debugger includes other tools, including the Inspector shown in Figure 6.18. The Inspector allows you to interrogate the current status of any object and its properties. If any of the object properties are objects that have their own properties, you can drill down and view those as well.

The Netscape JavaScript Debugger allows you to set breakpoints and interrupts that will pause execution so that you can view an object's status and use the Command pane

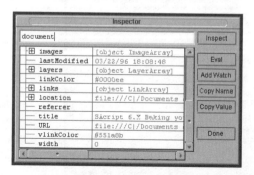

Figure 6.18

The Netscape
JavaScript
Debugger's
Inspector provides
you with a detailed
view of any object's
state while the
script is running.

to execute expressions and interrogate variable values. You can also set *watches*, which are expressions that the debugger continually evaluates each time the debugger is activated. In addition, you can click on the Intrpt button on the toolbar, and the debugger will pause execution as soon as the current statement is processed. The debugger also stops when it reaches a breakpoint you have set or when it encounters an error.

Netscape supports two types of breakpoints:

○ **Unconditional:** Halts the interpreter as soon as a breakpoint is encountered.

○ **Conditional:** Instructs the interpreter to evaluate a condition when the breakpoint is encountered and to halt execution only if the result is `true`.

The debugger provides an assortment of options for resuming execution that are located on the debugger's toolbar as shown in Figure 6.17:

○ **The Run icon:** Click to resume execution with the next statement.

○ **The Into icon:** Allows you to execute statements one at a time within a function or to execute a single statement if you are not in a function.

○ **The Over icon**: Allows you to execute at once all the statements within a function to execute a single statement if you are not in a function.

○ **The Out icon**: Allows you to finish executing any remaining statements within a function before execution is again halted.

Microsoft Script Debugger

The Microsoft Script Debugger requires Internet Explorer 4 or later. It can be used to debug ActiveX, VBScript, and JavaScript. You can start the Microsoft Script Debugger by starting Internet Explorer, choosing View, Script Debugger, and then clicking on Open. After the debugger is installed, any errors that occur within your scripts automatically prompt Internet Explorer to offer to start the debugger as shown in Figure 6.19.

If you want to debug a script, the script must first be executing. Figure 6.20 shows the debugger's Running Documents window that allows you to select a script to debug from a list of active Internet Explorer windows.

After you select the script you want to debug, the script appears in the main debugger window as shown in Figure 6.21. A nice feature provided by this debugger is the color-coded text, which makes your scripts much easier to read. Like the Netscape JavaScript Debugger, the left margin in the Microsoft Script Debugger is used to identify specific information. For

Figure 6.19

After you install the
Microsoft Script
Debugger, JavaScript
error messages
display a prompt
with the option of
automatically
launching the
debugger.

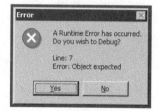

Figure 6.20

The Microsoft Script
Debugger keeps
track of all open
Internet Explorer
browser windows
and allows you to
debug any of them.

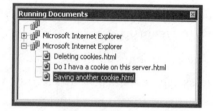

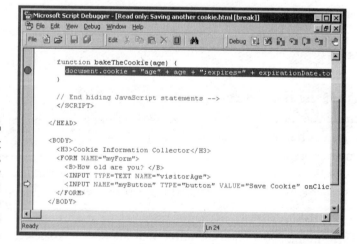

Figure 6.21

The Microsoft Script
Debugger provides
a color-coded view
of your script and
allows you to
control its
execution.

example, a red dot indicates a breakpoint, and a yellow arrow shows the current execution
point. Also like the Netscape JavaScript Debugger, the icons on the Microsoft Script Debugger
toolbar provide features that control the following aspects of script execution:

✪ Run

- ✪ Stop Debugging
- ✪ Break at Next Statement
- ✪ Step Into
- ✪ Step Over
- ✪ Step Out
- ✪ Toggle Breakpoint
- ✪ Clear All Breakpoints
- ✪ Running Documents
- ✪ Call Stack
- ✪ Command Window

The Call Stack, shown in Figure 6.22, displays a list of currently active functions and event handlers to help you follow script execution. This Call Stack is very similar to the Netscape JavaScript Debugger Call Stack.

The Command Window, shown in Figure 6.23, allows you to execute commands, to interrogate variable and property values, and to run object methods and subroutines.

All in all, the Microsoft Script Debugger provides debugging capabilities for Microsoft Internet Explorer that are equivalent to those provided by the Netscape JavaScript Debugger for Netscape Navigator. However, the Microsoft Script Debugger has the advantage of being capable of debugging more than just JavaScript; if you support more than one scripting language, it might be the better tool for you.

Figure 6.22

The Microsoft Script Debugger's Call Stack dialog box lets you view a list of all active functions and event handlers while your script is being debugged.

Figure 6.23

The Microsoft
Script Debugger's
Command Window
allows you to view
variable and
property contents
and to execute
methods while your
script is paused.

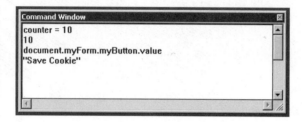

```
Command Window
counter = 10
10
document.myForm.myButton.value
"Save Cookie"
```

What's Next?

Congratulations! You have finished all the JavaScript lessons in this book. You should feel proud of yourself. Learning a new programming language is a significant accomplishment. Of course, your learning is not over—in fact, it has only just begun. As with most things in life, you really learn by doing. In this case, you learn by writing your own JavaScripts. As you go along, you will encounter problems and then learn to fix them. As you tackle more and more difficult projects, your expertise with JavaScript will continue to increase. With HTML, JavaScript, and the power and freedom offered by the Internet, you now have all the fundamental tools you need to truly express yourself in today's electronic society.

But before you run off to conquer the world, this book offers one last session for this evening that I think you will want to review. Tonight I will show you an example of a Web site that leverages the power of JavaScript to build an online bookstore. This example shows you how just a little JavaScript can make a big difference on any Web site. So, why don't you go get a bite to eat, and I will see you back here in a little while.

Putting It All Together

- Overview of the On-line Bookmall Web site
- Crafting the index page
- The featured book
- Navigating the Bookmall
- Finishing the Bookmall
- Collecting Visitor Registration
- Receiving Customer Email

Welcome to the final session of the weekend. Tonight you will wrap up this book by taking a look at a fictional Web site that has been enhanced using JavaScript. The idea behind this site is that a book vendor (me) has joined several on-line bookstores' associate programs. These *associate programs* pay a percentage of every sale that is made as a result of somebody entering a bookstore's Web site through my site, which is appropriately called Jerry's On-line Bookmall.

This all works because each on-line bookstore provides a specifically formatted link that, when clicked, allows any traffic originating form Jerry's On-line Bookmall to be tracked. Because people may have a preferred on-line bookstore at which they like to shop, you might decide against joining just one major on-line bookstore's associate program.

You can learn more about each on-line bookstore's associate program by visiting its Web site, where you can read all about the rules of the program and instantly apply them. As you might suppose, bookstores are not the only businesses on the Internet that provide opportunities through associate programs. With just a little surfing, you can find dozens of other opportunities. What is important about tonight's session is not whether you decide to build your own on-line business or are just in this for fun. What's important is that you are here to learn; the fictitious Jerry's On-line Bookmall is just a conduit for tonight's demonstration.

You have already learned a lot about JavaScript in this book. The focus of this final session is on applying much of what you have learned, so I won't waste your time by going over every line of code in excruciating detail and explaining things you have already seen before. Instead, I will lay out the basic structure of the Web site, list its code, and talk at a relatively high level about where and how JavaScript was used.

Because of the limited space available in this last session, the Web site won't be 100 percent complete, but it will serve as an example and a template from which you can begin your own JavaScript experience.

Here's an overview of what is covered in this session:

- Designing a new Web site
- Welcoming returning visitors to your site
- Using frames to organize your site
- Collecting user information and comments

Overview of the On-line Bookmall Web Site

Jerry's On-line Bookmall is a relatively small Web site comprised of a handful of Web pages, as shown in Figure 7.1. The site starts off with a typical index page from which other pages in the site are linked.

In addition to a welcome message and standard HTML links, the index page contains JavaScript statements that add the following functionality:

- Cookie logic for the collection and display of visitor names
- Code to open a new window and display a featured book selection

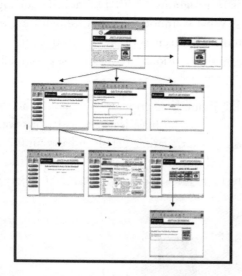

Figure 7.1

Like any Web site, Jerry's On-line Bookmall is based on a series of pages all linked together in an organized fashion.

- A rotating advertisement banner that promotes other fictitious sites belonging to Jerry
- A browser detection example

The next page in this Web site that uses JavaScript is the navigation frame in the actual bookstore section of the Web site. Here, mouse event handlers are embedded in HTML links that provide a flawless and stunning visual presentation of six target options, including a welcome page, links to four major on-line bookstores, and a Jerry's Picks page.

The Jerry's Picks page demonstrates the use of mouse events to post and clear messages on the browser window's status bar. These messages provide additional information about the book over which the visitor hovers the mouse pointer.

The Web site's registration page demonstrates the use of JavaScript to perform several tasks:

- Form validation
- Display of message dialog boxes
- Display of a cycling message on the browser's status bar
- Use of cookie logic to retrieve stored information and automatically fill in form information

As you will see, a small collection of carefully placed JavaScripts can make a big impact on any Web site. As you work your way through this sample Web site, I will point out other ideas for ways to use JavaScript to further enhance the Web site. Without further delay, let's get to it!

Crafting the Index Page

The HTML and JavaScript statements that make up the index page of Jerry's On-line Bookmall are listed here. As you can see, the list of elements is fairly lengthy compared to the other examples you have seen throughout this book. It begins by defining all the variables and functions used on the page in the head section:

- `expiration_date`: A variable used to build the expiration date for the site's cookie.
- `MyBannerArray[]`: An array loaded with three graphic images that will be used to display a rotating banner advertisement.

- **CycleBanner()**: A function that continuously loops through the `MyBannerArray[]` to display the page's banner advertisement.
- **BakeTheCookie()**: A function that, when called, creates and stores a cookie containing the visitor's name on the visitor's computer.
- **CookieCheck()**: A function that, when called, checks to see whether there is a cookie stored on the visitor's computer. If a cookie is not found, the function asks the visitor for his or her name and then calls the `BakeTheCookie()` function.
- **OpenNewWindow()**: A function that, when called, opens a new browser window and loads the Web page that presents the Web site's featured book of the month.
- **BrowserCheck()**: A function that, when called, checks to see whether the visitor is using either Netscape Navigator version 4 or Internet Explorer version 4.

The page's <BODY> tag has been modified so that the first thing that happens is that the `CycleBanner()` function is executed using `onLoad="CycleBanner()"`. The page itself is arranged using a series of tables that organize and display the information presented. In the middle of the body section, the `BrowserCheck()` and `CookieCheck()` functions are called. Next, the link for the featured book has been modified to call the `OpenNewWindow()` function as shown here:

```
<A HREF="javascript:OpenNewWindow()"><IMG HEIGHT="170" SRC="htmlbook.jpg"
   ALT="Learn HTML In a Weekend" WIDTH="126"></A>
```

The last table on the page provides a simple navigation menu that is used throughout the Web site.

Here is the JavaScript that sets up and defines the index page of Jerry's On-line Bookmall:

```
<HTML>
  <HEAD>
    <TITLE>Script 7.1 - Jerry's On-line Bookmall Index Page</TITLE>
    <SCRIPT LANGUAGE="JavaScript" TYPE="Text/JavaScript">
    <!-- Start hiding JavaScript statements
```

```javascript
 //Define an array that will be used to
//manage banner advertisements
 MyBannerArray = new Array(3);
 MyBannerArray[0]="banner0.jpg";
 MyBannerArray[1]="banner1.jpg";
 MyBannerArray[2]="banner2.jpg";
 current_banner=0;
 no_of_banners=MyBannerArray.length;
 function CycleBanner() {
     if (current_banner==no_of_banners) {
        current_banner=0;
     }
     document.myBanner.src=MyBannerArray[current_banner];
     current_banner++;
     setTimeout("CycleBanner()", 5*1000);
 }

 //Declare a variable used to set the cookie expiration date
 ExpirationDate = new Date;
 ExpirationDate.setMonth(ExpirationDate.getMonth() + 3);

 //Define a function that will store a
 //cookie on the visitor's computer
 function BakeTheCookie(name) {
    document.cookie = "name=" + name + ";expires=" +
    Expiration_date.toGMTString();
 }

 //Define a function to check for the cookie
 //and use it in the welcome message if found
```

```javascript
function CookieCheck() {
  visitor_name = "";
  cookie_name = "";
if (document.cookie != "") {
  visitor_name = document.cookie.split("=")[1];
  document.write("<H4>Hello " + visitor_name + ",</H4>");
}
  else {
    input = window.prompt("Welcome to the Bookmall. " +
        "What is your name?","");

    //user click on cancel
    if (input != null) {
      //user left blank and clicked on ok
      if (input != "") {
        BakeTheCookie(input);
        document.write("<H4>Welcome " + input + "," + "</H4>");
      }
      else {
        document.write("<H4>Welcome.</H4>");
      }
    }
    else {
      document.write("<H4>Welcome.</H4>");
    }
  }
}


//Define a function to load a html page Into a new window
function OpenNewWindow() {
```

```
    window.open('script7.2.html', 'window1', 'width=640,height=420');
}


    //Define a function that determines
    //the visitor's browser type and version
    function BrowserCheck() {
      browser_name=navigator.appName;
      browser_ver=parseInt(navigator.appVersion);
      if ((browser_name=="Netscape") ||
          (browser_name=="Microsoft Internet Explorer")) {
        if (browser_name=="Netscape") {
          if (browser_ver!=4) {
            window.alert("This Web site is best viewed " +
                    "with Netscape 4.X or higher!");
          }
        }
        else {
          if (browser_name=="Microsoft Internet Explorer") {
            if (browser_ver!=4) {
              window.alert("This Web site is best viewed with " +
                      "Internet Explorer 4.X or higher!");
            }
          }
        }
      }
      else {
        window.alert("This Web site is best viewed with " +
              Netscape 4.X or Internet Explorer 4.X or higher!");
      }
    }
```

```
        // End hiding JavaScript statements -->
        </SCRIPT>
    </HEAD>
    <BODY onLoad="CycleBanner()">
        <TABLE BORDER="0" WIDTH="590">
            <TR>
                <TD>
                    <CENTER>
                        <P><IMG NAME="myBanner" SRC="banner0.jpg"></P>
                        <IMG BORDER="0" HEIGHT="78" SRC="bstorelogo.jpg"
                                WIDTH="636">
                    </CENTER>
                </TD>
            </TR>
        </TABLE>
        <TABLE BORDER="0" WIDTH="590" STYLE="HEIGHT: 25px; WIDTH: 643px">
            <TR>
                <TD>
                </TD>
            </TR>
        </TABLE>
        <TABLE BORDER="0" WIDTH="590" STYLE="HEIGHT: 254px; WIDTH: 643px">
            <TR>
                <TD>
                    <SCRIPT LANGUAGE="JavaScript" TYPE="Text/JavaScript">
                    <!-- Start hiding JavaScript statements
                        //Execute the function that determines the visitor's
                        //browser type and version
                        BrowserCheck();
                        //Execute the function that looks
```

```
        //for the web site's cookie
        CookieCheck();
    // End hiding JavaScript statements -->
    </SCRIPT>
    <H2 ALIGN="left">
        <FONT COLOR="red">Welcome to Jerry's Bookmall.</FONT>
    </H2>
    <HR>
    <FONT SIZE="5">F</FONT>or your convenience I have assembled
    a collection of the finest bookstores on the World Wide
    Web. Jerry's On-line Bookmall is your one stop shopping
    place for all your reading needs. Whether you are
    interested in fiction, non-fiction, history, literature, or
    computer books, you will find exactly what you are looking
    for here. Don't forget that you can also purchase your
    favorite toys, videos,  and CDs as well. Feel free to
    browse to your heart's content and  thanks for visiting us!
    <HR>
</TD>
<TD>
    <CENTER>
        <H3>Featured Book!</H3>
        <A HREF="javascript:OpenNewWindow()">
        <IMG HEIGHT="170" SRC="htmlbook.jpg"
                ALT="Learn HTML In a Weekend"
                WIDTH="126"></A>
        <BR>
    <B>Learn HTML In a Weekend</B>
    </CENTER>
</TD>
```

```
    </TR>
  </TABLE>
  <TABLE BORDER="0" STYLE="HEIGHT: 25px; WIDTH: 643px" WIDTH="590">
    <TR>
      <TD>
        <CENTER>
          <BR>
          [ <A>Main Menu</A> ]
          [ <A HREF="script7.3.html">Bookstore</A> ]
          [ <A HREF="script7.11.html">Register</A> ]
          [ <A HREF="script7.12.html">email Us</A> ]
        </CENTER>
      </TD>
    </TR>
  </TABLE>
  </BODY>
</HTML>
```

When someone visits Jerry's On-line Bookmall for the first time, or when he or she visits for the first time in over 90 days—that is, after the expiration date for the site's cookie has expired as set by expiration_date.setMonth(expiration_date. getMonth() + 3)—the CheckCookie() function displays the prompt shown in Figure 7.2, asking the visitor to type his or her name. The BakeTheCookie() function then stores the cookie on the visitor's computer.

The visitor's name, if supplied, is then displayed under the page's graphic logo in the form of "Welcome *xxxxxxx*," as shown in Figure 7.3. The next time the visitor returns to the Web site, he or she will be greeted by the message "Hello *xxxxxxx*," unless the cookie has expired. If the user chose not to provide a name, whether by clicking on Cancel or by simply not providing his or her name, the message will simply read "Welcome," and the visitor will be prompted for his or her name again the next time he or she visits the Web site.

Figure 7.2

The `document`
object's
`prompt()`
method provides
the perfect tool for
interactively
collecting small
pieces of inform-
ation from visitors.

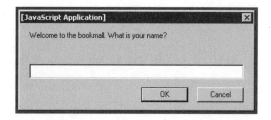

Figure 7.3

Because of its role
as home page, a
site's index page is
often one of the
more lengthy and
complex pages
involving heavy use
of JavaScript.

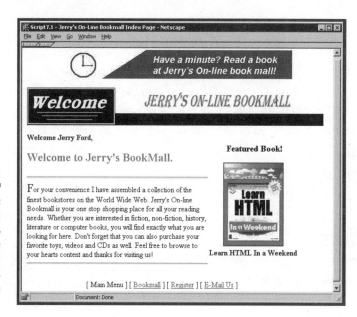

The Featured Book

When a visitor clicks on the link for the featured book, a new window measuring 640
pixels wide by 420 pixels high opens, and the Web page for the site's featured book is
loaded into it. This page contains only HTML, although you might want to add a little
JavaScript that uses mouse events to display more detailed information about the book
by opening a new window. You might also want to display a message that explains what
the rating system is when the visitor moves the pointer over the graphic rating. This
could be done using the ALT attribute of the <IMG> tag or by using JavaScript to open

a new window or by enabling the status bar and posting messages to it. The HTML statements that make up this page are listed here:

```
<HTML>
  <HEAD>
    <TITLE>Script 7.2 - This month's featured book</TITLE>
  </HEAD>
  <BODY>
    <CENTER>
      <H2 ALIGN="left">
        <IMG BORDER="0" HEIGHT="78" SRC="bstorelogo.jpg" WIDTH="636">
      </H2>
    </CENTER>
    <H2 ALIGN="center">
      <FONT COLOR="#ff0000">This month's featured book:</FONT>
    </H2>
    <P ALIGN="center">
        <IMG BORDER="0" HEIGHT="209" SRC="htmlbook.jpg"
            ALT="Learn HTML In a Weekend" WIDTH="165"></P>
      <CENTER>
      Learn HTML In a Weekend is your ultimate
      source for HTML programming.
      <B>Rating:</B>
        <IMG ALT="" BORDER="0" HEIGHT="15" SRC="star.gif" WIDTH="14">
        <IMG ALT="" BORDER="0" HEIGHT="15" SRC="star.gif" WIDTH="14">
        <IMG ALT="" BORDER="0" HEIGHT="15" SRC="star.gif" WIDTH="14">
        <IMG ALT="" BORDER="0" HEIGHT="15" SRC="star.gif" WIDTH="14">
        <IMG ALT="" BORDER="0" HEIGHT="15" SRC="star.gif" WIDTH="14">
      </CENTER>
  </BODY>
</HTML>
```

Figure 7.4 shows what the featured book page looks like when loaded.

Script 7.2 - This month's featured book - Netscape

Figure 7.4

Opening a new window is an effective presentation tool for placing extra emphasis on a specific page.

Navigating the Bookmall

The actual bookmall opens when the visitor clicks on the Bookmall link at the bottom of the index page. The bookmall is actually a simple HTML page that defines two frames as shown here. The left frame loads a navigation page from which the visitor selects an option; the right frame holds the contents of the page specified by the selected link.

```
<HTML>

  <HEAD>

    <TITLE>Script 7.3 - Bookmall frame's page</TITLE>

  </HEAD>

  <FRAMESET COLS="175,*">

    <FRAME SRC="script7.4.html" NAME="left"

            SCROLLING="no" FRAMEBORDER="1" NORESIZE>

    <FRAME SRC="script7.5.html" NAME="right2"

            SCROLLING="auto" FRAMEBORDER="1" NORESIZE>

  </FRAMESET>

</FRAMESET>

</HTML>
```

The contents of the navigation page are listed next. JavaScript statements have been added to the head section to define and preload all the graphic images used to create the rollover effects for the page. The rest of the page is contained in the body section and is comprised of six HTML links. The first link reloads a welcome page. The next four links load the URLs for various on-line bookstores. I also modified the tags to include the onMouseOver and onMouseOut events that drive the rollover effects.

NOTE This is the point where you would cut and paste the special HTML links that each on-line bookstore provides you when you join its associates program. Of course, you would have to make a modification to each link to load it in the frame on the right (that is, you have to add the attribute TARGET="right2").

```
<HTML>
  <HEAD>
    <TITLE>Script 7.4 - Navigation/Rollover page</TITLE>
    <SCRIPT LANGUAGE="JavaScript" TYPE="Text/JavaScript">
    <!-- Start hiding JavaScript statements
            amazon1             =new Image;
            amazon2             =new Image;
            bn1                 =new Image;
            bn2                 =new Image;
            borders1            =new Image;
            borders2            =new Image;
            a1books1            =new Image;
            a1books2            =new Image;
            bookstore1          =new Image;
            bookstore2          =new Image;
            featured1           =new Image;
            featured2           =new Image;
            amazon1.src         ="amazon1.jpg";
            amazon2.src         ="amazon2.jpg";
            bn1.src             ="bn1.jpg";
```

```
            bn2.src                ="bn2.jpg";

            borders1.src           ="borders1.jpg";

            borders2.src           ="borders2.jpg";

            a1books1.src           ="a1books1.jpg";

            a1books2.src           ="a1books2.jpg";

            bookstore1.src         ="bookstore1.jpg";

            bookstore2.src         ="bookstore2.jpg";

            featured1.src          ="featured1.jpg";

            featured2.src          ="featured2.jpg";

       // End hiding JavaScript statements -->

       </SCRIPT>

   </HEAD>

   <BODY>

      <P><IMG SRC="book.jpg" WIDTH="154" HEIGHT="74" BORDER="0"></P>

      <A HREF="script7.5.html" TARGET="right2"

        onMouseover="document.mybutton1.src=bookstore2.src"

        onMouseout="document.mybutton1.src=bookstore1.src">

      <IMG SRC="bookstore1.jpg" BORDER="0" NAME="mybutton1"></A><P>

      <A HREF="http://www.amazon.com" TARGET="right2"

        onMouseover="document.mybutton2.src=amazon2.src"

        onMouseout="document.mybutton2.src=amazon1.src">

      <IMG SRC="amazon1.jpg" BORDER="0" NAME="mybutton2"></A><P>

      <A HREF="http://www.bn.com" TARGET="right2"

        onMouseover="document.mybutton3.src=bn2.src"

        onMouseout="document.mybutton3.src=bn1.src">

      <IMG SRC="bn1.jpg" BORDER="0" NAME="mybutton3"></A><P>

      <A HREF="http://www.borders.com" TARGET="right2"

        onMouseover="document.mybutton4.src=borders2.src"

        onMouseout="document.mybutton4.src=borders1.src">

      <IMG SRC="borders1.jpg" BORDER="0" NAME="mybutton4"></A><P>

      <A HREF="http://www.a1books.com" TARGET="right2"
```

```
        onMouseover="document.mybutton5.src=a1books2.src"
        onMouseout="document.mybutton5.src=a1books1.src">
    <IMG SRC="a1books1.jpg" BORDER="0" NAME="mybutton5"></A><P>
    <A HREF="script7.6.html" TARGET="right2"
        onMouseover="document.mybutton6.src=featured2.src"
        onMouseout="document.mybutton6.src=featured1.src">
    <IMG SRC="featured1.jpg" BORDER="0" NAME="mybutton6"></A>
  </BODY>
</HTML>
```

Figure 7.5 shows what the navigation page looks like when it is opened by the browser without the use of frames. The graphic image of the book is not a link; its only purpose is cosmetic. Each of the remaining links represents a different menu selection that will be loaded into the right frame (when the frames are enabled). Each button is green with gold lettering, but when the pointer passes over one of the buttons, it changes to a golden background with green lettering.

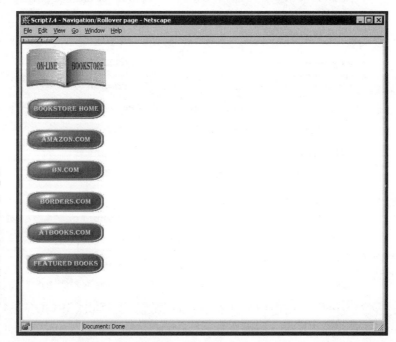

Figure 7.5

When this page is loaded into a frame as a navigation page, it is really just a regular Web page except that its links contain additional attributes that load URLs into a second frame.

The following listing shows the Web page that is initially loaded into the right frame when the bookmall is loaded. As you can see, it is a simple HTML page that displays basic welcome information. This page provides a lot of opportunities for JavaScript. For example, you could again address the visitor by name, run a plug-in to play an audio greeting message, post messages on the status bar, or add some animated effects such as a book that opens and closes.

```html
<HTML>
  <HEAD>
    <TITLE>Script 7.5- Bookstore welcome page</TITLE>
  </HEAD>
  <BODY>
    <TABLE BORDER="0" WIDTH="590">
      <TR>
        <TD>
          <CENTER>
            <IMG SRC="bstorelogo.jpg" BORDER="0" HEIGHT="78"
                   WIDTH="636">
            <P><H2>Hello and welcome to Jerry's On-line Bookmall!</H2>
            </P>
            <P>Feel free to shop some of the finest on-line
                 bookstores on the Web.
            </P>
            <P><FONT COLOR="red">Thanks for stopping by!</FONT></P>
          </CENTER>
        </TD>
      </TR>
    </TABLE>
  </BODY>
</HTML>
```

Figure 7.6 shows what the welcome page looks like when it is opened by the browser outside of any frames.

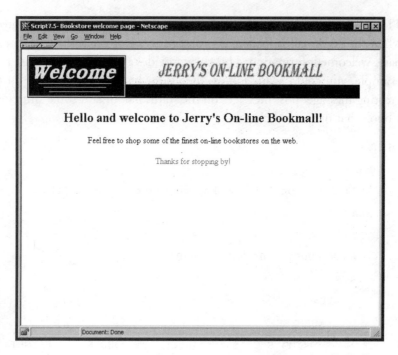

Figure 7.6

Not every page
requires JavaScript.

Figure 7.7 shows what the bookmall looks like when visitors come to shop. As you can see, the combination of frames, rollover graphics, and simple HTML present an elegantly simple yet functional interface.

When the visitor is ready to go shopping, he or she simply clicks on one of the buttons representing an on-line bookstore. Figure 7.8 displays what happens if the user clicks on the amazon.com button. As you can see, the amazon.com Web site is loaded into the right frame, and the visitor can begin shopping. Because the visitor enters the Amazon site using the special links on your navigation Web page, you are credited with a portion of every sale this visitor makes. Best of all, the visitor never really leaves your Web site. This makes it easy for him or her to jump between other bookstores or to load other pages where you may have added valuable content. This technique also makes small Web sites seem much bigger than they actually are. By adding rollover links to other on-line businesses, you can easily expand the Web site to take advantage of a diverse set of business opportunities.

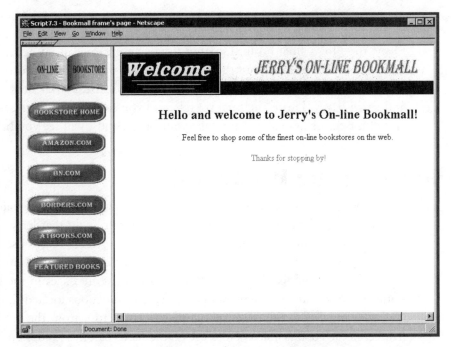

Figure 7.7

When combined, frames, HTML, and JavaScript create one of the most powerful organization and presentation tools available to any Web page designer.

Figure 7.8

Frame technology makes it possible to load URLs from other Web sites into one of your frames so that your visitors can continue to explore the Internet without ever leaving your Web site.

Take a Break

Okay, time for a final break. Go ahead, you have earned it. When you return, I will finish the review of the rest of the pages that make up the framed portion of the on-line bookmall. Then you will wrap up by taking a look at the Web site's registration form and email pages. This is the final stretch, and you should be able to see the light at the end of the tunnel. Go ahead and take your break, and I will see you back in a little bit.

Finishing the Bookmall

The Jerry's Picks page is the last option on the navigation menu. It is loaded into the right frame of the bookmall and presents a selection of four books that Jerry has singled out as his personal recommended picks. A single HTML <TABLE> tag is used to organize the display of the book images. An onMouseOver and an onMouseOut event handler has been embedded into each book's link to display descriptive messages in the browser window status bar. These mouse events call two JavaScript functions located in the head section. The PostMsg() function writes the message passed to it from the onMouseOver event handler in each book's link as a message on the status bar; the ClearMsg() function clears the message from the status bar when the mouse pointer moves away from the link.

```
<HTML>
  <HEAD>
    <TITLE>Script7.6 - Jerry's picks page</TITLE>
      <SCRIPT LANGUAGE="JavaScript" TYPE="Text/JavaScript">
      <!-- Start hiding JavaScript statements
        //Define a function that writes the message
        //onto the browser's statusbar
        function PostMsg(msg) {
          window.status = msg;
        }
        //Define a function that clears the message off of
        //the browser's status bar
        function ClearMsg() {
          window.status="";
```

```
        }
      // End hiding JavaScript statements -->
    </SCRIPT>
</HEAD>
<BODY>
  <TABLE BORDER="0" WIDTH="590">
    <TR>
      <TD>
        <CENTER>
          <H2 ALIGN="left">
            <IMG BORDER="0" HEIGHT="78" SRC="bstorelogo.jpg"
               WIDTH="636">
          </H2>
          <BR>
          <H1> Jerry's picks of the month!</H1>
    <A HREF="script7.7.html"
      onMouseOver="PostMsg('Electrify Your Web Site In a Weekend');
      return true;" onMouseOut="ClearMsg();">
    <IMG SRC="electrify.jpg" BORDER="0"
      ALT="Electrify Your Web Site In a Weekend"></A>
    <A HREF="script7.8.html"
      onMouseOver="PostMsg('Learn Microsoft Windows Me
      Millenium Edition In a Weekend'); return true;"
      onMouseOut="ClearMsg();">
    <IMG SRC="me.jpg" BORDER="0" ALT="Learn Microsoft Windows
      Me Millenium Edition In a Weekend"></A>
    <A HREF="script7.9.html"
      onMouseOver="PostMsg('Learn Windows 98 In a Weekend');
      return true;" onMouseOut="ClearMsg();">
    <IMG SRC="w98.jpg" BORDER="0"
```

```
      ALT="Learn Windows 98 In a Weekend"></A>
  <A HREF="script7.10.html"
    onMouseOver="PostMsg('Learn HTML on the MAC In a weekend');
    return true;" onMouseOut="ClearMsg();">
  <IMG SRC="mac.jpg" BORDER="0"
    ALT="Learn HTML on the MAC In a weekend"></A>
      </CENTER>
    </TD>
  </TR>
  </TABLE>
  </BODY>
</HTML>
```

Figure 7.9 shows how the Jerry's Picks page appears in the bookmall. Notice that the status bar is displaying a message for the *Electrify Your Web Site In a Weekend* book because the mouse pointer is currently positioned over that book's graphic. Each book's image is actually a link that opens a new page into the right frame. Optionally, you might prefer to borrow some of the JavaScript logic in the index page to display each book's linked page in new window outside the frame rather than inside it.

The next four pages show the contents of the Web page associated with each of the four books. These pages contain only HTML and are organized using a single table. The code for the first of these pages is shown here. This page represents the *Electrify Your Web Site In a Weekend* book.

```
<HTML>
  <HEAD>
    <TITLE>Script 7.7 - Book pick number 1</TITLE>
  </HEAD>
<BODY>
  <H2 ALIGN="left"><IMG BORDER="0" HEIGHT="78" SRC="bstorelogo.jpg"
    WIDTH="636"></H2></CENTER>
  <BR>
```

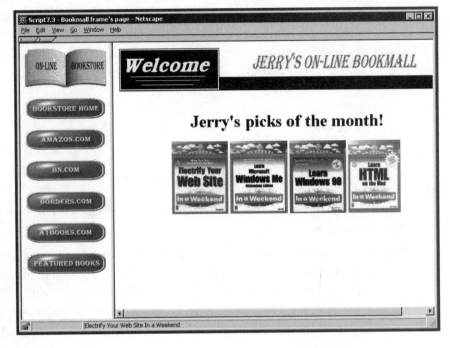

Figure 7.9

The Jerry's Picks
page provides
descriptive
information about
each book using
the browser's
status bar.

```
<TABLE BORDER="3" WIDTH="590" STYLE="HEIGHT: 254px; WIDTH: 633px">
  <TR>
    <TD>
      <H2 ALIGN="left">
          <FONT COLOR="red">Electrify Your Web Site
            In a Weekend</FONT></H2>
      <P ALIGN="left">Learn everything that you
            need to know to start building your own
            super-charged Web site!</P>
    </TD>
    <TD>
      <H3 ALIGN="center">Featured Book!</H3>
      <P ALIGN="center">
```

```
<IMG ALT="" BORDER="0" HEIGHT="133" SRC="electrify.jpg"
     WIDTH="108">
  </P>
  </TD>
  </TR>
  </TABLE>
  </BODY>
</HTML>
```

Figure 7.10 shows what the preceding example looks like when loaded directly into a browser window.

The visitor can select individual books to view more detailed information. This next page represents the *Learn Microsoft Windows ME In a Weekend* book. Its structure is the same as the previous example in that it relies only on the use of HTML. After all, just because JavaScript is powerful and can do many things doesn't mean it has to be used on every page. Like any other tool, it is better used in some places and not in others.

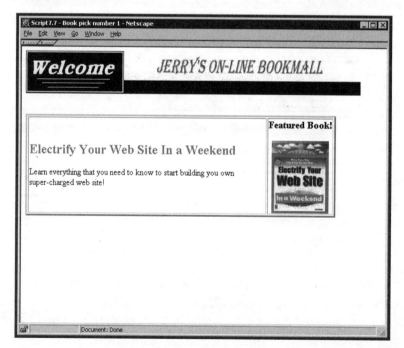

Figure 7.10

Opening an individual book's page.

```
<HTML>
  <HEAD>
    <TITLE>Script 7.8 - Book pick number 2</TITLE>
  </HEAD>
  <BODY>
    <H2 ALIGN="left">
        <IMG BORDER="0" HEIGHT="78" SRC="bstorelogo.jpg" WIDTH="636">
    </H2>
    <BR>
    <TABLE BORDER="3" WIDTH="590" STYLE="HEIGHT: 254px; WIDTH: 633px">
      <TR>
        <TD>
          <H2 ALIGN="left">
          <FONT COLOR="red">Learn Microsoft Windows ME Millenium
            Edition In a Weekend</FONT></H2>
          <P ALIGN="left">Learn everything that you need to know
                about this exciting Microsoft operating system.</P>
        </TD>
        <TD>
          <H3 ALIGN="center">Featured Book!</H3>
          <P ALIGN="center">
          <IMG ALT="" BORDER="0" HEIGHT="133" SRC="me.jpg"
                WIDTH="108">
          </P>
        </TD>
      </TR>
    </TABLE>
  </BODY>
</HTML>
```

Figure 7.11 shows how the preceding page looks when selected by visitors of Jerry's On-line Bookmall.

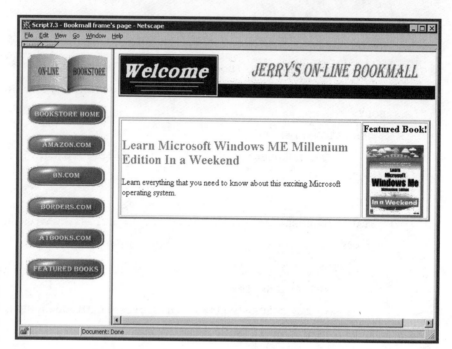

Figure 7.11

Looking at one of
Jerry's picks as it is
seen by visitors to
the bookmall.

The next two scripts show the HTML contents for the pages that represent the last two
of Jerry's picks. These pages are structured similarly to the previous two examples and
are provided here for consistency. The first script is for the *Learn Windows 98 In a
Weekend* book:

```
<HTML>

  <HEAD>

    <TITLE>Script 7.9 - Book pick number 3</TITLE>

  </HEAD>

  <BODY>

    <H2 ALIGN="left">

        <IMG BORDER="0" HEIGHT="78" SRC="bstorelogo.jpg"

            WIDTH="636"></H2>

    <BR>

    <TABLE BORDER="3" WIDTH="590" STYLE="HEIGHT: 254px; WIDTH: 633px">
```

```
        <TR>
          <TD>
            <H2 ALIGN="left">
            <FONT COLOR="red">Learn Windows 98 In a Weekend</FONT>
            </H2>
            <P ALIGN="left">Learn everything that you need to know
                    about this exciting Microsoft operating system.</P>
          </TD>
          <TD>
            <H3 ALIGN="center">Featured Book!</H3>
            <P ALIGN="center">
            <IMG ALT="" BORDER="0" HEIGHT="133" SRC="w98.jpg"
                    WIDTH="108"></P>
          </TD>
        </TR>
      </TABLE>
    </BODY>
</HTML>
```

The next Web page displays the HTML statements that display the description for the
Learn HTML on the Mac In a Weekend book:

```
<HTML>
  <HEAD>
    <TITLE>Script 7.10- Book pick number 4</TITLE>
  </HEAD>
  <BODY>
    <H2 ALIGN="left">
      <IMG BORDER="0" HEIGHT="78" SRC="bstorelogo.jpg"
          WIDTH="636">
    </H2></CENTER>
```

```
<BR>
<TABLE BORDER="3" WIDTH="590" STYLE="HEIGHT: 254px; WIDTH: 633px">
  <TR>
    <TD>
      <H2 ALIGN="left">
      <FONT COLOR="red">Learn HTML on the MAC In a Weekend</FONT>
      </H2>
      <P ALIGN="left">Learn everything that you need to know
            to begin creating exciting Web sites using your Mac.</P>
    </TD>
    <TD>
      <H3 ALIGN="center">Featured Book!</H3>
      <P ALIGN="center">
      <IMG ALT="" BORDER="0" HEIGHT="133" SRC="mac.jpg"
          WIDTH="108">
      </P>
    </TD>
  </TR>
</TABLE>
</BODY>
</HTML>
```

Collecting Visitor Registration

The listing that follows shows the HTML and JavaScript statements that make up the bookmall's registration page. As you can see, this is another fairly long example. It starts by defining all the variables and functions used on the page in the head section. These include the following:

○ msg: A message that is to be displayed in the browser window's status bar.

○ i: A variable used as a counter in the CycleMsg() function.

- CycleMsg(): A function that continuously cycles a scrolling message on the browser's status bar.
- ValidateOrder(): A function that validates the form's name and address entries.
- CookieCheck(): A function that checks to see whether the visitor's computer contains the Web site's cookie; if it does, the function sets the user_name variable equal to the value stored in the cookie.

```
<HTML>
  <HEAD>
    <TITLE>Script 7.11 - Registration page</TITLE>
    <SCRIPT LANGUAGE="JavaScript" TYPE="Text/JavaScript">
    <!-- Start hiding JavaScript statements
       //Define the message that will be
       //displayed on the browser's statusbar
       msg = "                         Thank you for taking the time to " +
             "register with Jerry's On-line Bookmall............... " +
             "                         ";
       i = 0;
       //Define a function that displays a message on the statusbar
       //using a wrap around affect
       function CycleMsg() {
         window.status = msg.substring(i, msg.length) +
               msg.substring(0, i);
         i++;
         if (i > msg.length) {
           i = 0;
         }
         window.setTimeout("CycleMsg()",200);
       }
       //Define a function that verifies that various
```

```
    //form elements have been properly filled out
    function ValidateOrder() {
       if (document.myForm.visitor_name.value.length < 1) {
          window.alert("Missing name! Please correct");
          return;
       }

       if (document.myForm.address.value.length < 1) {
          window.alert("Missing Address! Please correct");
          return;
       }

       window.alert("Validation complete. Please submit " +
                "when ready!");
    }

    //Define a function that extracts the visitor's
    //name from the web site's cookie
    function CookieCheck() {
     visitor_name = "";
     cookie_name = "";
     if (document.cookie != "") {
      user_name = document.cookie.split("=")[1];
     }
      else {
        user_name = "empty";
      }
    }
  // End hiding JavaScript statements -->
  </SCRIPT>
</HEAD>
<BODY onLoad="CycleMsg()">
  <CENTER>
```

```
<H2 ALIGN="left">
<IMG BORDER="0" HEIGHT="78" SRC="bstorelogo.jpg"
    WIDTH="636"></H2>
</CENTER>
<DIV ALIGN="left">
  <H4>
  <FONT COLOR="blue">Please complete the following
      registration form</FONT></H4>
</DIV>
<FORM NAME="myForm" ACTION="mailto:jlf04@yahoo.com"
          ENCTYPE="text/plain">
  <P><B>Name:</B>
  <INPUT NAME="visitor_name" SIZE="15" MAXLENGTH="20" ></P>
  <P><B>Mailing Address:</B>
  <INPUT NAME="address" SIZE="30" MAXLENGTH="50" ></P>
  <P><B>What is you overall opinion of this Web site?</B>
    High:
   <INPUT NAME="radio_option1" TYPE="radio"
         VALUE="high" CHECKED>
   Average:
   <INPUT NAME="radio_option1" TYPE="radio" VALUE="average">
   Low:
   <INPUT NAME="radio_option1" TYPE="radio" VALUE="low"><BR></P>
  <P><B>Additional Comments: (Optional) </B>
  <TEXTAREA COLS="40" NAME="myTextarea" ROWS="4" ></TEXTAREA>
  </P>

  <P><B>How did you learn about this Web site?:</B>
  <SELECT NAME="myList">
    <OPTION SELECTED VALUE="wom">Word of mouth
```

```
            <OPTION VALUE="banner">Banner Advertizement
            <OPTION VALUE="search">Internet Search Engine
            <OPTION VALUE="other">Other</OPTION>
        </SELECT></P>
        <P>
        <FONT COLOR="blue">Please validate before submitting
            your registration!</FONT></P>
        <INPUT TYPE="reset" VALUE="Reset Form">
        <INPUT TYPE="submit" VALUE="Submit Order"
                onClick="window.alert('Thanks For Registering!')">
        <INPUT onclick="ValidateOrder()" TYPE="button"
                VALUE="Validate Order?">

    </FORM>
<SCRIPT LANGUAGE="JavaScript" TYPE="Text/JavaScript">
<!-- Start hiding JavaScript statements
    CookieCheck();
    if (user_name != "empty") {
        document.myForm.visitor_name.value = user_name;
    }
// End hiding JavaScript statements -->
</SCRIPT>
<TABLE BORDER="0" WIDTH="590">
    <TR>
        <TD>
            <CENTER>
                [ <A HREF="script7.1.html">Main Menu</A> ]
                [ <A HREF="script7.3.html">Bookstore</A> ]
                [ <A>Register</A> ]
                [ <A HREF="script7.12.html">email Us</A> ]
```

```
        </CENTER>
      </TD>
    </TR>
  </TABLE>
 </BODY>
</HTML>
```

The page's `<BODY>` tag has been modified so that the first thing that happens is that the `CycleMsg()` function is executed. The `<FORM>` tag then is defined so that the contents of the form will be sent by email when the user clicks on the form's Submit button:

```
<FORM NAME="myForm" ACTION="mailto:jlf04@yahoo.com"

          ENCTYPE="text/plain">
```

Next, individual form elements are defined. The `onClick` event handler is added to the form's Submit button to display an alert dialog box thanking the visitor for taking the time to register. A Validate button has also been defined; when clicked, it calls the `ValidateOrder()` function. Finally, a few JavaScript statements that execute the `CookieCheck()` function, which sets the value of the `user_name` variable, are added to the bottom of the page. An `if` statement checks to see whether this variable contains the visitor's name; if it does, the `if` statement automatically fills in the form's Name field:

```
document.myForm.visitor_name.value = user_name
```

 TIP

By expanding your use of cookies to collect the visitor's address on the index page, you can save the visitor the trouble of filling in the Mailing Address field as well. Optionally, you can modify the form using the `onChange` event handler on the Mailing Address field to store an address cookie. The idea here is to get information from your visitors only once and to reuse that data wherever possible to save your visitors time and effort.

Figure 7.12 shows how the registration form looks when the user first loads it. As you can see in this example, the user's name is automatically added to the Name field.

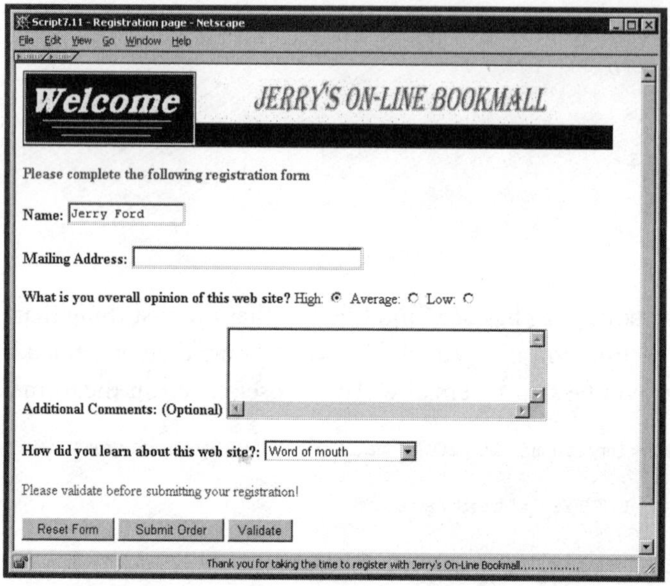

Figure 7.12

JavaScript can be used to validate form contents and even help fill in required information.

Figure 7.13 shows the alert dialog box that appears when the user tries to validate an incomplete form.

> **NOTE** In this example, only the user's name and address are required for the form to be complete. Everything else is optional.

Figure 7.14 shows an example of the alert message that is displayed when the user submits the form using a Netscape browser.

Figure 7.13

A good validation procedure not only detects an error in the way the form is filled out, but also clearly explains the problem to the visitor.

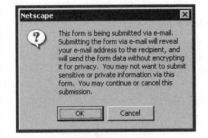
Figure 7.15 shows the message that appears when the browser gets ready to submit the contents of the form by email. As you can see, Netscape posts a warning message and gives the visitor a chance to terminate the submission. Internet Explorer displays a similar message. There is no way you can avoid this message from the browser.

Receiving Customer Email

The final Web page in Jerry's On-line Bookmall is a simple HTML page that contains a link that, when clicked, opens the visitor's email client and places the specified email address in the address field. Although this page contains no JavaScript, I am listing it here to give you a complete view of all the pages in this Web site.

```
<HTML>

  <HEAD>

    <TITLE>Script7.12 - email page</TITLE>

  </HEAD>
```

```
<BODY>
  <TABLE BORDER="0" WIDTH="590">
    <TR>
      <TD>
        <IMG BORDER="0" HEIGHT="78" SRC="bstorelogo.jpg" WIDTH="636">
          <CENTER>
            <BR>
            <BR>
            <BR>
            <BR>
<H3>If you have any suggestions or comments we would
  appreciate hearing from you.</H3>
            <P><B>Please email us at:</B>
            <A HREF="mailto:jlf04@yahoo.com">jlf04@yahoo.com</P>
            <BR>
            <BR>
            <BR>
            <BR>
            <BR>
            <BR>
            <BR>
            [ <A HREF="script7.1.html">Main Menu</A> ]
            [ <A HREF="script7.3.html">Bookstore</A> ]
            [ <A HREF="script7.11.html">Register</A> ]
            [ <A>email Us</A> ]
          </CENTER>
        </TD>
      </TR>
    </TABLE>
  </BODY>
</HTML>
```

Figure 7.16 shows what the email page looks like when loaded.

Figure 7.16

Every good Web site provides a way for visitors to communicate with the site owner; email provides the easiest solution to the communication dilemma.

What's Next?

Congratulations! Reading this book may not have been as fun as a weekend vacation in the mountains or at the beach, but I hope that you found it rewarding. Now you are ready to begin creating your own exciting adventure on the Internet where—with a little imagination, hard work, and JavaScript—you can build world-class Web pages.

Don't let this book be the end of your JavaScript education. Instead, start writing your own scripts right away and spend some time surfing the Internet looking at the thousands of free scripts that are available. With a little more effort, you can find new ideas and ways of expanding both your knowledge of JavaScript and your imagination.

What's on the CD

The CD that accompanies this book contains a 30-day trial version of HomeSite 4.5.1. HomeSite is an HTML and scripting editor that features a WYSIWYG interface and tons of features, such as HTML and JavaScript wizards. You will also find a special Links Page that provides dozens of links to Web sites where additional information on JavaScript and related topics can be found.

All of the sample code and sample files used in this book are included on the CD. In addition, you will find five bonus appendixes:

- ✿ Appendix A, "A Brief JavaScript Object Reference"
- ✿ Appendix B "A Summary of JavaScript Events"
- ✿ Appendix C "JavaScript Reserved Words"
- ✿ Appendix D "Using HomeSite 4.5"
- ✿ Appendix E "A Basic HTML Overview"

Running the CD with Windows 95/98/2000/NT

To make the CD user-friendly and take less of your disk space, no installation is required to view the CD. This means that the only files transferred to your hard disk are the ones you choose to copy or install. You can run the CD on any operating system that can view graphical HTML pages; however, not all the programs can be installed on all operating systems.

If autoplay is turned on, the HTML interface will automatically load into your default browser.

If autoplay is turned off, access the CD by following these steps:

1. Insert the CD into the CD-ROM drive and close the tray.

2. Go to My Computer or Windows Explorer and double-click the CD-ROM drive.

3. Find and open the start_here.html file (this works with most HTML browsers).

NOTE The first window you see contains the Prima License Agreement. Take a moment to read the agreement, and if you agree, click the I Agree button to accept the license and proceed to the user interface. If you do not agree to the terms of the license, click the I Disagree button. The CD will not load.

Running the CD with Macintosh OS 7.0 or Later

To make the CD user-friendly and take less of your disk space, no installation is required to view the CD. This means that the only files transferred to your hard disk are the ones you choose to copy or install. You can run the CD on any operating system that can view graphical HTML pages; however, not all the programs can be installed on all operating systems.

If autoplay is turned off, access the CD by following these steps:

1. Insert the CD into the CD-ROM drive and close the tray.

2. Double-click on the icon that represents your CD-ROM.

3. Find and open the start_here.html file (this works with most HTML browsers).

NOTE The first window you see contains the Prima License Agreement. Take a moment to read the agreement, and if you agree, click the I Agree button to accept the license and proceed to the user interface. If you do not agree to the terms of the license, click the I Disagree button. The CD will not load.

The Prima User Interface

The opening screen of the Prima user interface contains a two-panel window. The left panel contains a directory of the programs on the disc. The right panel displays a description of the entry selected in the left panel.

Using the Left Panel

If you want to view a sample HTML file, click /Book Files. A drop-down menu appears listing sample files. Next, click the topic you want to access. To view the programs on the CD, click /Programs and select the program you want.

Using the Right Panel

The right panel describes the entry you choose in the left panel. The information provided tells you about your selection, such as the functionality of an installable program. To download a particular file, position the mouse over the file icon, click and hold the mouse, and drag the file to a folder in an open Windows Explorer window.

Resizing and Closing the User Interface

To resize the window, position the mouse over any edge or corner, click and hold the mouse, drag the edge or corner to a new position, and release the mouse when the size is acceptable.

To close and exit the user interface, select File, Exit.

GLOSSARY

A

abort. An event that occurs when the user aborts the loading of a page and that triggers the `onAbort` event handler.

ActiveX. A proprietary Microsoft technology for embedding Windows components into Web pages.

alert() method. A document object method that can be called to display an alert dialog box for the user. This dialog box displays a text message and waits for the user to click on the OK button before returning control to the calling statement.

anchor object. Represents a location in a Web page that is the target of a link.

Applet. A small program written in Java that executes on the client computer.

applet object. An object created by the HTML `<APPLET>` tag that provides access to that applet.

area object. A type of link object that provides access to an area in an imagemap.

Argument. A piece of data passed to a function as input.

Array. A logical collection of related data that is indexed and can be programmatically manipulated.

Array object. An object that allows you to work with arrays in your JavaScript.

B

blur. An event detected by the browser when an object looses focus because a different object has received the focus. The `blur` event triggers the `onBlur` event handler.

Boolean. A variable that can store either a `true` or `false` value.

Boolean object. An object that treats a Boolean value as an object.

Break. A JavaScript statement you can use to terminate the processing of a loop.

Browser. A software application that displays Web pages and that may provide a JavaScript environment.

button object. A representation of a button on a form that has its own methods and properties and that is subject to various events.

C

CamelBack. A type of programming notation that uses a combination of uppercase and lowercase letters to create descriptive names.

case. A JavaScript statement that is used in conjunction with the `switch` statement to test for a particular condition.

change. An event detected by the browser when the user changes an object (such as the contents of a form's text field) and that triggers the `onChange` event handler.

CGI (Common Gateway Interface). An interface or communications specification used in creating Web server-based applications using languages such as Perl.

checkbox object. A representation of a check box on a form. The object has its own methods and properties and is subject to various events.

Check points. A debugging technique that displays the value of variables during the processing of a script so that the variables can be checked when the script is tested. Check points also can be used to verify the logical flow of your scripts.

click. An event detected by the browser when the user clicks the mouse button while

the pointer is placed over an object. This event triggers the `onClick` event handler.

Cookie. A small piece of information stored on client computers that contains information collected when users visit Web sites.

Comments. Statements added to Web pages and scripts that are ignored by the browser but which provide valuable information to anyone editing or reading the page or script.

Compiling. The process of converting a program to machine code before it can be executed.

Concatenation. The process of combining two or more strings into a single string.

confirm() method. A document object method that can be called to display a confirmation dialog box for the user. This dialog box displays a text message and waits for the user to click on the OK or Cancel button before returning control to the calling statement.

continue. A JavaScript statement that allows you to skip the remaining statements in a loop and to continue on with the loop's next iteration.

D

Date object. An object that allows your script to access and manipulate time and date information.

dblClick. An event detected by the browser when the user double-clicks the mouse button while the pointer is placed over an object. This event triggers the `onDblClick` event handler.

Debug. The process of testing and fixing errors in programs and scripts.

Dense array. An array that is populated with data at the time of its creation.

document object. An object that provides access to the document that is currently loaded into a browser window and whose properties and methods provide access to viewing and changing the page content.

do...while. A type of loop that executes as long as a given condition remains `true`.

E

Element. An individual entry in an array that may be referenced by a name or an index number.

else. The counterpart to the `if` statement that provides an alternative action when the `if` condition proves `false`.

Error. An event detected by the browser when there is an error with a window, frame, or image. This event triggers the `onError` event handler.

Event. The occurrence of a predefined action such as a mouse click on a object in a Web page.

event object. An object that provides access to properties that describe an event.

Event handler. A JavaScript construct that automatically executes when a given event occurs. For example, the `onClick` event handler executes when the `Click` event occurs for an object.

Expression. A statement that evaluates the value of variables and constants.

F

fileUpload object. An object that represents the file upload HTML element.

focus. An event detected by the browser when the user selects an object (such as a form text field). This event triggers the `onFocus` event handler.

for. A JavaScript statement that repeats a series of statements until a condition proves `false`.

for...in. A loop that iterates repeatedly through a specified object's list of properties.

form object. An object created by the HTML `<FORM>` tag that provides access to all the elements on a form.

frame object. An object created by the HTML `<FRAME>` tag that allows JavaScript to reference frames.

Function. A collection of JavaScript statements that perform a specific action and that can be referenced and called repeatedly from different locations in the Web page.

function object. A JavaScript statement that is compiled as a function.

G

GIF. A format for saving graphic images. GIF files are typically larger than JPEG files and provide slightly lower image quality, but take less time to load.

Global variable. A variable whose scope is such that its value is available throughout the Web page.

H

hidden object. A text-based object that is not displayed on a form but that can be programmatically accessed.

history object. An array containing information about all the URLs that have been loaded into the browser window.

HomeSite. A program editor that supports both HTML and JavaScript languages. HomeSite includes such advanced features as color coding, integrated browser support, visual layout, code templates, and wizards.

HREF. A hypertext reference used to specify a URL.

Hypertext Markup Language (HTML). A programming language used to deliver text and graphic information over the Internet.

I

if. A conditional statement that tests whether a condition is `true` of `false`.

image object. An object created by the HTML `<IMG>` tag that provides access to image attributes.

Internet Explorer. A popular Internet browser developed by Microsoft that supports JScript, VBScript, ActiveX, and other advanced features.

Interpreted language. A language used to develop programs or scripts that are not compiled in advanced before execution. Instead, each statement in an interpreted language script is processed as it is read.

J

Java. An object-oriented language descended from C and C++. A variation of Java allows small programs known as applets to be added to Web pages.

JavaScript. A programming language developed by Netscape that supports the development of client-side scripts that execute inside of Internet browsers.

JavaScript Console. A Netscape Navigator debugging utility that receives JavaScript error messages and allows you to test JavaScript commands and expressions.

JPEG. A format for saving high-quality graphic images. JPEG files are typically smaller than GIF files and provide superior image quality, but take slightly longer to load.

Jscript. Microsoft's version of JavaScript. The only Internet browser that currently supports Jscript is Internet Explorer.

K

keyDown. An event detected by the browser when the user presses a keyboard key. This event triggers the `onKeyDown` event handler.

keyPress. An event detected by the browser when the user presses and releases a keyboard

key. This event triggers the onKeyPress event handler.

keyUp. An event detected by the browser when the user releases a keyboard key. This event triggers the onKeyUp event handler.

L

Label. A JavaScript statement that allows you to associate a label with a JavaScript statement so that it can be referenced from other parts of a script.

layer object. An object that represents an HTML layer.

link object. An object that represents an HTML hypertext link.

LiveAudio plug-in. A plug-in that provides the Netscape Navigator browser with the capability of playing audio files. This plug-in is included by default with Netscape Navigator.

LiveScript. A scripting language introduced in Netscape Navigator version 2.0 and later renamed JavaScript.

load. An event that occurs when the browser finishes loading a Web page. This event triggers the onLoad event handler.

Load-time errors. Errors that occur when loading Web pages in a browser that typically involve basic syntax issues.

Local variable. A variable whose scope is such that its value is limited to the function in which it is declared.

location object. An object that provides access to the window object's location property.

Logic errors. Errors that occur as a result of human error and that produce unexpected results.

Loop. The processing of repeating a set of instructions indefinitely.

Lynx. A text-based, non graphical Internet browser noted for its speed and exceptional performance.

M

Math object. An object that provides access to various mathematical functions and constants.

Method. A function associated with an object.

Microsoft Script Debugger. A debugging tool compatible with Internet Explorer that can be used to debug ActiveX, VBScript, and JavaScript.

mimeType object. A predefined JavaScript object that provides access to a specific browser-supported MIME type.

mouseDown. An event detected by the browser when the user presses a mouse button over an object. This event triggers the object's onMouseDown event handler.

mouseMove. An event detected by the browser when the user moves the mouse. This event triggers the object's onMouseMove event handler.

mouseOut. An event detected by the browser when the user moves the mouse off an object. This event triggers the object's `onMouseOut` event handler.

mouseOver. An event detected by the browser when the user moves the mouse over an object. This event triggers the object's `onMouseOver` event handler.

mouseUp. An event detected by the browser when the user releases a mouse button over an object. This event triggers the object's `onMouseUp` event handler.

N

Netscape JavaScript Debugger. A debugging tool that runs in the form of a Java applet inside the Netscape browser. It works with Netscape browser versions 4.02 or above.

Netscape Navigator. A popular Internet browser that supports JavaScript, plug-ins, and other advanced features.

navigator object. An object that provides access to the information about the version of Netscape Navigator supported by the browser.

new. A JavaScript keyword that supports the declaration of new JavaScript objects.

Number object. A predefined object that allows numbers to be represented as objects.

null. An empty value.

O

Object. A programming construct that contains its own properties and methods.

Object object. A root object from which all objects are based.

Object-based language. A programming language providing some but not all of the features of an object-oriented programming language.

onAbort. An event handler that is triggered when the browser detects the `abort` event, indicating that the user has aborted the loading of the Web page.

onBlur. An event handler that is triggered when the browser detects the `blur` event, indicating that an object has lost focus.

onChange. An event handler that is triggered when the browser detects the `change` event, indicating that an object (such as form text field) has been changed.

onClick. An event handler that is triggered when the browser detects the `click` event, indicating that a user has clicked the mouse while the pointer is over an object.

onDblClick. An event handler that is triggered when the browser detects the `dblClick` event, indicating that a user has double-clicked the mouse while the pointer is over an object.

onError. An event handler that is triggered when the browser detects the `error` event, indicating that an error has occurred with a window, frame, or image.

onFocus. An event handler that is triggered when the browser detects the `focus` event, indicating that an object has been selected or has received focus.

onKeyDown. An event handler that is triggered when the browser detects the keyDown event, indicating that the user has pressed a keyboard key.

onKeyPress. An event handler that is triggered when the browser detects the keyPress event, indicating that a user has pressed a keyboard key.

onKeyUp. An event handler that is triggered when the browser detects the keyUp event, indicating that a user has released a pressed keyboard key.

onLoad. An event handler that is triggered when the browser detects the load event, indicating that a Web page has been completely loaded by the browser.

onMouseDown. An event handler that is triggered by the mouseDown event, indicating that the user has pressed a mouse button over an object.

onMouseMove. An event handler that is triggered by the mouseMove event, indicating that the user has moved the mouse.

onMouseOut. An event handler that is triggered by the mouseOut event, indicating that the user has moved the pointer off an object.

onMouseOver. An event handler that is triggered by the mouseOver event, indicating that the user has moved the pointer over an object.

onMouseUp. An event handler that is triggered by the mouseUp event, indicating that the user has released a mouse button over an object.

onReset. An event handler that is triggered when the browser detects the reset event, indicating that the user has clicked on a form's Reset button.

onResize. An event handler that is triggered when the browser detects the resize event, indicating that the user has changed the dimensions of a browser window.

onSelect. An event handler that is triggered when the browser detects the select event, indicating that the user has selected an object such as a form's text field.

onSubmit. An event handler that is triggered when the browser detects the submit event, indicating that the user has clicked on a form's Submit button.

onUnload. An event handler that is triggered when the browser detects the unLoad event, indicating that a Web page has been closed by the browser.

Opera. A new Internet browser that supports JavaScript, plug-ins, and other advanced features.

option object. An object created by the HTML <OPTION> tag that provides access to the list of options in a select list.

P

password object. An object created by the HTML <INPUT> tag's TYPE="password" option that represents a form's password field.

Perl. A programming language often used in conjunction with CGI to deliver server-based Web content.

Plug-ins. Add-on modules that can be installed to add or extend the capabilities of the Netscape browser.

plug-in object. An object whose properties represent all the browser's plug-ins.

Program. A collection of stored programming statements that constitute a script or application.

prompt() method. A `document` object method that can be called to display a prompt dialog box for the user. This dialog box displays a text message and allows the user to type a response before clicking on either the OK or Cancel button and returning control to the calling statement.

Property. A variable associated with an object.

R

RAD (Rapid Application Development). A specialized programming tool or suite of tools designed to support the rapid creation of programs and applications.

radio object. A representation of a radio button on a form. This object has its own methods and properties and is subject to various events. Radio buttons are created in groups; only one option in a group can be selected at a time.

reset. An event detected by the browser when the user clicks on a form's Reset button. This event triggers the `onReset` event handler.

reset object. A specialized type of button object that has its own methods and properties and is subject to various events. The `reset` object is used to clear the contents of a form and to restore the form's default values.

resize. An event detected by the browser when the user changes the dimensions of a browser window. This event triggers the `onResize` event handler.

Rollover. A graphical effect that swaps between two images as the pointer selects or passes over a graphic image. A rollover is used to simulate a selection or identify the focus of a selected graphic image.

Runtime error. An error that occurs when a script attempts to do something that is against the rules, such as referencing an undefined function or variable.

S

Scope. The portion of a Web page in which a variable can be accessed, either locally or globally.

screen object. An object that contains information about the current screen display.

Script. A group of program statements embedded inside a Web page and interpreted by the browser as a separate language.

select. An event detected by the browser when the user selects an object such as a form text field. This event triggers the `onSelect` event handler.

select object. An object created by the HTML `<SELECT>` tag that provides access to a form's select list.

Statement. A line of code in a Web page or JavaScript.

Status bar. The area located at the bottom of Internet browsers that is used to display text-based messages.

String. A group of text characters such as `"Hello world!"`

String object. An object that references the value of a string and that provides methods for working with the string.

style object. An object that describes the style used by HTML elements and whose properties provide access to specific style attributes.

submit. An event detected by the browser when the user clicks on a form's Submit button, causing the form's contents to be sent to a Web server or emailed to a designated email address. This event triggers the `onSubmit` event handler.

submit object. A specialized type of button object on a form that has its own methods and properties and that is subject to various events. The `submit` object is used to submit form data to a Web server for processing or to email form contents.

switch. A JavaScript statement that allows you to test for multiple conditions using a series of `case` statements.

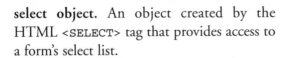

Table. An HTML construct that allows page content to be organized and presented within predefined tables.

text object. A representation of a single-line text field on a form that has its own methods and properties and that is subject to various events.

textarea object. A representation of a multi-line textbox on a form that has its own methods and properties and that is subject to various events.

U

unLoad. An event that occurs when the browser closes a Web page. This event triggers the `onUnload` event handler.

URL (Universal Resource Locator). An address used to identify a site on the World Wide Web.

V

Validation. The process of verifying that the data typed into a form conforms to required specifications.

var. A keyword used to explicitly declare a variable.

Variable. A programming construct that contains a value and that can be accessed by its name.

VBScript. A scripting language developed by Microsoft as an alternative to JavaScript. VBScript is derived from the Visual Basic programming language. The only Internet browser that currently supports VBScript is Internet Explorer.

Visual JavaScript. A professional developer's tool for building large cross-platform applications. It includes a WYSIWYG HTML editor and supports visual JavaScript development. In addition, you can use this tool to cut and paste prebuilt HTML, Java, and JavaScript components into JavaScript applications.

W

while. A loop that iterates until a condition proves `false`.

window object. An object that represents a browser window or frame and whose methods can be used to control the window or frame.

WWW. The World Wide Web.

WYSIWYG. What you see is what you get.

INDEX

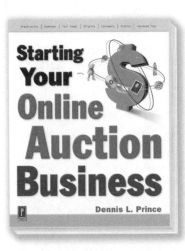
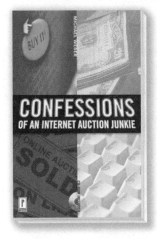